T0328303

SUSTAINABLE INVESTING

SUSTAINABLE INVESTING

Socio-Economic Impacts of Exchange-Traded Funds

ADAM MARSZK

Faculty of Management and Economics,
Gdańsk University of Technology (Fahrenheit Universities),
Gdańsk, Poland

EWA LECHMAN

Faculty of Management and Economics,
Gdańsk University of Technology (Fahrenheit Universities),
Gdańsk, Poland

ACADEMIC PRESS

An imprint of Elsevier

ELSEVIER

Academic Press is an imprint of Elsevier
125 London Wall, London EC2Y 5AS, United Kingdom
525 B Street, Suite 1650, San Diego, CA 92101, United States
50 Hampshire Street, 5th Floor, Cambridge, MA 02139, United States
The Boulevard, Langford Lane, Kidlington, Oxford OX5 1GB, United Kingdom

ISBN: 978-0-12-823871-4

For information on all Academic Press publications visit our
website at https://www.elsevier.com/books-and-journals

Publisher: Joseph P. Hayton
Acquisitions Editor: Kathryn Eryilmaz
Editorial Project Manager: Aleksandra Packowska
Production Project Manager: Omer Mukthar
Cover Designer: Matthew Limbert

Typeset by TNQ Technologies

Working together
to grow libraries in
developing countries

www.elsevier.com • www.bookaid.org

Contents

Foreword

The issue of sustainable development can be regarded as one of the most broadly and intensively discussed in contemporary academic literature. The growing interest in the topic of sustainable development has been spurred by a large number of public and private initiatives, above all the ones agreed on and promoted at the global or regional level. Some of the key examples include the Millennium Development Goals, followed by the more recent Sustainable Development Goals (SDGs), in both cases established on the United Nations (UN) level, through its member states. Other important sustainability-related decisions, in particular with the focus on environmental problems, are the consequences of the international climate summits, including the most influential Paris Agreement of 2015; the most recent summit was held in Glasgow in late 2021. In the European region, the fundamental initiatives are the EU Action Plan Financing Sustainable Growth and the European Green Deal. Many sectors of the economy are also affected by the implementation of the EU Taxonomy regulations. Apart from the public policy developments, there have been multiple initiatives aimed specifically at the private sector or resulting, in many elements linked to the aforementioned. Significant examples include the UN Global Compact or UN Guiding Principles on Business and Human Rights as well as sustainability reporting standards setting and implementation movements, with noticeable integration and unification trend.

The completion of the sustainable development aims requires the coordination of the financial system with the sustainability requirements. As mentioned in the Paris Agreement, financial flows should be adapted to the objective of a temperature increase of a maximum of 1.5 or 2°C at the end of the century. Unfortunately, this is by far not the case.

The increasing prominence of "sustainable investing" is one of the trends substantially shaping the financial systems in the developed economies, influenced by both public policy (e.g., governmental actions aimed at the completion of the SDGs) and private (e.g., pressure from investors) factors. Sustainable investing, also known as ESG (environmental, social, and corporate governance) investing, can most generally be understood as the investment approach that takes into consideration sustainability-related factors. There are many possible implementations of the sustainable investing ideas in practice—this part of the financial sector has become increasingly complex in line with the growth in the popularity of sustainability-related financial products and services. Complexity is a factor of profit for banks active in this field (see Chesney et al. (2022) "Interest rates, bounded rationality, and complexity: demand and supply of retail financial products").

The development of sustainable investing has raised some doubts concerning its various aspects. Probably, the most significant and, at the same time, most controversial issue concerns the actual contribution of sustainable investing to the process of sustainable development at large (for instance, considered in the context of the SDGs or aims of the EU-level policies). These concerns have led to the frequent utilization of terms such as "greenwashing" or "sustainable washing," previously applied mostly in the context of consumer goods and services, used to emphasize the ambiguous sustainability compliance of the investments and indicate that their ESG declarations are mostly elements of the marketing strategy, adopted to respond to the changing preferences of the investors. So-called "sustainable investments" activities remain controversial, and the high dynamics of the entire sustainable finance sector makes any reliable assessments even more difficult to formulate.

Prof. Marc Chesney, Chair of the Center for Sustainable Finance, University of Zurich.

Acknowledgments

This book could not have been prepared without the support and helpful criticism from a large number of people. We are deeply indebted and would like to thank all of them. We are especially thankful to Professor Paul Dembinski for his support during Adam's stay at the University of Fribourg and for many extremely valuable ideas concerning our research. We appreciate the help of all people from Switzerland, including the current and former employees of the University of Fribourg: Dr. Fred von Gunten, Andrew Mungall, Professor Dušan Isakov and his team, other members of the Faculty of Management, Economics and Social Sciences, and the employees of the Environmental Sciences and Humanities Institute (UniFR_ESH Institute).

Our book benefited greatly from the participation in various meetings and seminars, in particular, Association pour Renouveler la Recherche et l'Enseignement en Economie et Finance (AREF; many thanks to Dr. Virgile Perret), Observatoire de la Finance, and the seminars of the Chair of Economics (earlier Chair of Economic Sciences) at Gdańsk University of Technology. Our colleagues were a great source of ideas, encouragement, and inspiration. We also thank the support personnel of Refinitiv for help in data acquisition and processing, and the editorial team of Elsevier for their contribution to the preparation of the final manuscript.

Last but not least, we are very grateful to Professor Mark Chesney from the University of Zurich for the foreword.

The research presented in this book has been conducted as part of Bekker's project, no. PPN/BEK/2020/1/00089/U/00001, financed by the Polish National Agency for Academic Exchange. Moreover, it is a result of the project financed by the National Science Centre of Poland (project no. 2020/37/B/HS4/00717).

As always, responsibility for any errors in the book remains our own.

CHAPTER 1

Introduction

There is an urgent need to mobilize (...) financial resources for sustainable development. At the same time, the sustainable finance market is growing rapidly, with investors increasingly focusing on corporate environmental, social and governance (ESG) factors (......). Exchange traded funds that track ESG criteria (ESG ETFs), although still small in size, have the potential to grow into a mass market investment vehicle for sustainable development.
United Nations Conference on Trade and Development (2020), p. 1.

1.1 Context

Despite the necessary global approach to addressing the challenges of sustainable development and despite the worldwide initiatives, in many aspects, the sustainability-focused actions remain highly region specific. Taking into account the attitudes of the private entities, the substantial attention directed toward sustainability and related issues is limited mostly (with some notable exceptions) to the corporate sectors and financial systems of the most advanced economies while the low developed and emerging countries still lag behind—this is particularly noticeable in the field of sustainable finance, including sustainable investing. Europe, in particular the EU member states and some other highly developed European economies (e.g., Switzerland), are undeniably among the global leaders in these fields.

Conducting any study in the area of sustainable development is hindered by some substantial methodological problems, starting with the exact definitions of the issues to be examined. In particular, despite the burgeoning academic and nonacademic literature that focuses on multiple dimensions of the sustainability and sustainable development, there are still many ambiguities concerning these fundamental concepts, necessary to be defined to facilitate robust analysis, leading to reliable conclusions that can be used both in academic studies and implemented in practice. One of the most basic problematic issues is the explanation of the "sustainable development," with many definitions and interpretations (Mebratu, 1998;

Sustainable Investing
ISBN 978-0-12-823871-4
https://doi.org/10.1016/B978-0-12-823871-4.00005-2

Mensah, 2019), leading to insufficient theoretical framework (Jabareen, 2008). Among many definitions of sustainable development (and, accordingly, sustainability), one of the most influential and still broadly used is the explanation of the concept included in the so-called Brundtland Report (named after the chairman of the commission) published by the UN World Commission on Environment and Development in which it was defined as development satisfying the needs of the present society without negatively affecting the ability of future generations to satisfy their needs (World Commission on Environment and Development, 1987). More specifically, the report emphasized the importance of the integrity of natural systems and the fundamental role of human development, with the equitable distribution of resources within and across generations (Wuelser et al., 2020). To some degree, the use of the sustainable development concept in academia and practice has become more consistent due to the development of the UN-level goals such as Millennium Development Goals (Tomislav, 2018). To make the issue even more complicated, as Cuevas Fernández (2019) emphasized, it is necessary to distinguish "strong" from "weak" sustainability (and, consequently, also sustainable development), the former understood as considering the social, economic, and environmental dimension of sustainability as linked but to a high degree separate, whereas in the latter economic dimension is a part of the social dimension of sustainability (and social dimensions is an element of environmental).

The growing awareness of the necessary harmonization of the financial systems with the targets of sustainable development has led to the development of the highly heterogonous sector of sustainable finance (Migliorelli, 2021; Schoenmaker & Schramade, 2019) that consists of, among others, the rapidly expanding segment of sustainable investing. The more distant roots of sustainable investing can be traced back to various types of religious and faith-based organizations albeit the contemporary form has undeniably been shaped by the establishment and increasingly broader adoption of the UN-supported Principles for Responsible Investment (PRI) by the global leading institutional investors, especially asset management companies. The role of the institutional investors for the global economy has become central for some economies since approximately the 1970s in what is perceived as fiduciary capitalism (Hawley & Williams, 1997). For this crucial group of entities in the financial system, PRI guidelines have become the globally leading set of principles applied in the sustainable investing processes. More recently, a noticeable self-regulation trend among the world's largest asset management companies has resulted in multiple initiatives, with climate-related actions as the prevalent issue addressed. Nonetheless, it should again be stressed that the vast majority of financial corporations taking part in these programs are the ones from the advanced economies, with their investment focus on the assets from the most developed countries. These differences are extremely well pictured by the shares of the sustainable investing in the total assets under management in various regions—even though, due to considerable problems with data availability and consistency, the detailed comparisons are difficult, in the developed economies these assets currently constitute an undeniably important part of the investment industry whereas in the rest of the world their position is negligible.

The diversity of the sustainable investing industry is observable in terms of both the types of financial products available and investment strategies employed (examples include negative exclusions, positive screening, or various types of active ownership engagement). In the former perspective, as emphasized in the opening quote (extracted from the UNCTAD's report), one of the important categories is exchange-traded funds (ETFs) with a sustainability investing profile.

Rapid development of the global ETFs market is another fundamental process in the contemporary financial system, in the last years taking place concurrently to the increasing importance of sustainable investing. ETFs have emerged as a new category of investment funds in the early 1990s in the North American financial markets yet globally their presence can be identified as starting from the early 21st century, with the most significant growth of the sector during the last 10 or 15 years. ETFs, due to the favorable attributes for their users, have become an important segment of the investment funds industries, as evidenced not only by the growth of their total net assets but also by their shares in the total assets of the investment funds, in many cases growing in line with the decreasing share of the more established category—mutual funds. However, there are still many countries with no ETFs present in the local financial systems or with the availability of ETFs limited to a few funds (from the perspective of investors this barrier is diminished by the opportunity to invest in the foreign-listed ETFs). The group of ETFs offered on various markets continues to expand not only in terms of the assets but also with regard to their exposure, with sustainable investing (ESG) funds among the most recent types of ETFs yet, at the same time, receiving the most attention from the investing audience, especially in Europe (Le Sourd & Safaee, 2021).

Over the last years, one of the rapidly growing parts of the sustainable investing sector was ESG investment funds, in particular ESG ETFs. Their predominantly passive nature, with the most frequent investment aim of tracking certain (usually equity) ESG index, has raised some doubts concerning their actual role in the sustainable development. Linked controversies focus on the selection of the indexes tracked by the sustainable investing ETFs and their compliance with the sustainability aspects, especially when compared to the conventional (non-ESG) indexes. ESG ETFs, despite their rapid growth, remain a relatively understudied topic, in particular in the context of their socio-economic and environmental impact, with most studies concentrating on their financial performance or similar attributes.

1.2 Aims and scopes

The aims of this book are strongly shaped by the unresolved problems concerning in particular the multifaceted interactions between ETFs markets, sustainable investing, and sustainable development, as outlined in the book's background. We focus in particular on the ETFs with the sustainability-related exposure and discuss them in the context of sustainable development, the perspective that was rarely adopted in the previous publications in the field of ETF studies. In the geographical terms, our book concentrates on the ETFs and sustainability issues in the European region due to its globally leading position with regard to the development of the ESG ETFs, also in comparison to the world's largest financial system and the most developed ETFs market, that is, in the United States. Europe was selected also due to a large number of significant policies and private initiatives concerning sustainability (including sustainable finance), established at both regional (mostly in the EU) and country levels.

The main aim of the book is to contribute to the present state of knowledge through the investigation of various dimensions of the development of the European markets for the sustainable investing ETFs. Our book covers both theoretical (as well as methodological) and empirical issues.

In the predominantly theoretical-methodological sections of the book, we intend to provide the reader with the necessary background for the subsequent empirical part; therefore, we present the overview of the most recent and relevant issues in the areas of ETFs and sustainable investing, discussing the conclusions drawn from the in-depth review of the literature.

Furthermore, we discuss the highly complex methodological challenges associated with the sustainable investing.

The empirical part of the book may be regarded as its main contribution as it consists of the pioneering analysis of the sustainable investing ETFs markets in Europe, addressing the issues that were absent from or only partially covered in the previous publications. More detailed empirical targets include the following:

1. Assessment of the sustainable investing ETFs markets development in Europe both at the regional and country levels;
2. Examination of the macrolevel consequences of the European sustainable investing ETFs markets development for the financial sectors, socio-economic systems, and environment;
3. Assessment of the contribution of the sustainable investing ETFs in Europe in the perspective of sustainable development, in particular with regard to the sustainable development goals.

As it was already mentioned, the book revolves around the topic of the ESG ETFs in Europe. More specifically, our empirical study covers all such funds primarily listed on the European stock exchanges and the time period of the examination is 2006—20 in most parts of the analysis (in some aspects extended up to 2021, i.e., the most recent data available). In the country-level analysis, we consider above all the following European economies: France, Germany, Italy, Switzerland, and the United Kingdom; the other countries are briefly outlined due to some methodological limitations such as difficulties in assigning ETFs to a particular country as well as insufficient data. Additionally, to present the global perspective and compare the European ESG ETFs to their counterparts in the other regions, in some sections, we consider also the evidence for the markets such as the United States, Canada, or the ones in the Asia—Pacific region. Nevertheless, due to the scarcity of data (in most cases caused by the lack or negligible size of the local ETFs markets), majority of the study covers exclusively the European ETFs industries. Our analysis is based predominantly on the values of assets as representing the development levels of the ETFs markets.

Our book can be considered a part of the "science for sustainability" trend, as called for the UN in the context of the Sustainable Development Goals, for example in the 2019 report entitled "The future is now—science for achieving sustainable development." In the case of the research in economic sciences, as noted by Wuelser et al. (2020), it mostly covers studies about the ways to promote distributional justice and internalize environmental costs. However, our study focuses rather on the general idea of science contributing to explaining the challenges of sustainability and suggesting solutions, the field that is still suffering from concerns with regard to its basic assumptions (Nagatsu et al., 2020). The report by Wuelser et al. (2020) listed the issue of the role of finance as one of the key unresolved questions with regard to the relationship between finance and economics versus sustainability. More specifically, the exact question concerns the potential of the banking and financial system to support the transition of the real economy to higher sustainability (Lagoarde-Segot & Paranque, 2018; Ziolo et al., 2021). In line with this approach, we devote substantial attention in our analysis to the effects of the European ESG ETFs in terms of sustainability of the European countries, considering financial, socio-economic, and environmental aspects.

The aims and the scope of the book were also strongly influenced by the topics of the research projects that we conduct at Gdansk University of Technology and University of Fribourg—due to the obtained financial support, we were able to gain access to the necessary databases and consult our results with both academics and practitioners in the field, especially the representatives of one of the globally leading sustainable investing sectors, that is, in Switzerland. It should be stressed that our books cover only the selected issues related to the sustainable investing ETFs and the projects will be continued, resulting in further publications, addressing the issues such as the empirical analysis of the determinants of the development of these funds or their microlevel effects (e.g., for the companies whose securities constitute their portfolios).

1.3 Book's structure and contents

The book consists of six parts, structured in line with its aims and scope. Chapter 1 is Introduction. Consecutive Chapters 2 and 3 provide the conceptual background for the subsequent analysis. Chapters 4 and 5 are predominantly empirical and they cover the results of our study focused on the sustainable investing ETFs markets. Chapters 2—5 are followed by case studies. Chapter 6 concludes the book by presenting the main findings from the previous chapters accompanied by the practical implications and recommendations. The last substantive part of the book is the Methodological annex.

Chapter 1 introduces the background and the context of our discussion, together with a brief overview of each chapter.

Chapter 2 outlines the carefully chosen issues concerning ETFs, discussing them in the extensive context of the markets for these funds. The first presented issue is the overview of the main attributes of ETFs as well as their classifications. Moreover, the mechanisms of the primary and secondary ETFs markets are covered. The second issue is the comparison of the main types of contemporary investment funds: ETFs and mutual funds, intended at showing the relative strengths and weaknesses of these two categories, indicating also the innovative attributes of ETFs. The next issue covered is the discussion of the effects of the development of ETFs markets, explaining the multifaceted linkages between ETFs and other parts of the economy, with the additional discussion of the relationship between FinTech and ETFs.

Chapter 3 concentrates on the main features of sustainable investing, with a particular focus on the investment funds aimed at ESG-compliant investing, including sustainable investing ETFs. The discussion starts with an outline of the definitions of the sustainable investing concept and its historical background. It is followed by the presentation of the key categories and approaches to categorize sustainable investing financial products and services. The next part of the chapter focuses on the sustainable investing environment, in particular the sustainable development policies, considered both at a global and European level, with the description of the most recent initiatives as of the book's preparation. Furthermore, we show different sustainable investing tools, examining the main attributes of various solutions. In the next part of the chapter, we discuss the complicated yet extremely important issue of the methodologies utilized to identify and categorize sustainable investing financial services and products.

Chapter 4 discusses sustainable investing ETFs primarily listed in the European countries, showing them from the perspective of the European and global sustainable investing sectors, in particular, the markets for the ESG investment funds (i.e., mutual funds and ETFs). In the first two parts of the chapter, we present the global as well as European sustainable investing industry, that is, their sizes, structures, and main trends. In the third part, the European sustainable investment funds markets are presented. In the core segments of the chapter, we present the results of the analysis of the European ETFs market, followed by a similar analysis at the country level. The analysis covers the issues such as the sizes of the ETFs markets, their structures, and key trends. Furthermore, the development of these markets is examined using the diffusion models.

Chapter 5 comprises the results of the study concerning the effects of the development of the European sustainable investing ETFs markets, in the socio-economic and environmental contexts, presented in the perspective of the sustainable development policies. The first part of the chapter introduces some methodological issues and presents the data sources, time period, and sample of the analysis, followed by the assessment of the European ETFs' sustainability; finally, it shows the results of the empirical study of the relationships between the development of the European markets and financial, economic, and social indicators. In the second section, these empirical results are interpreted, in the context of the theoretical concepts and previous studies. We examine the consequences of the development of the ESG ETFs markets for the financial and socio-economic systems as well as the environment, emphasizing the elements of the strongest and weakest influence. The third part of the chapter covers a different perspective as it assesses the effects for the funds' providers, drawing conclusions from the literature review. The fourth section puts the preceding conclusions in the broad context of the sustainable development policies, studying the possible contribution of ESG ETFs to the achievement of the sustainability targets.

Chapter 6 presents the main conclusions of the preceding chapters, in particular the ones formulated based on the empirical study. They are followed by a discussion of their importance in the practical context, showing the key recommendations as well as directions for future studies.

The book is accompanied by the Methodological annex that presents the main research methods utilized in the empirical part of the book, including the diffusion and panel regression models used in the analysis of the development of the ESG ETFs markets and its consequences.

Apart from the core content of the main chapters (2—5), they include, as the final section, the case studies of some among the key sustainable investing ETFs markets in Europe: Switzerland, Germany, United Kingdom, France, and Sweden (the last one described in the context of the Scandinavian markets); Chapter 4 includes two case studies as it is the main part of the book with regard to the analysis of the development processes of the ESG ETFs. Each case study covers the issues such as sustainable investing in a particular country, local sustainable investment funds, and ETFs, to show the possible positive and negative factors of the development of the latter.

Our book was prepared to correspond to the needs and expectations of various target groups of readers. Even though it focuses predominantly on the issues and perspectives that are consistent with the academic studies in the fields of sustainability and sustainable finance, there are also multiple issues that should be of interest for the other types of readers, that is, students, financial professionals, or representatives of the public authorities. In our coverage of the sustainable investing ETFs, we discuss their basic attributes, explaining their market environment and the complicated, multidimensional area of sustainable investing. Moreover, we present the up-to-date state of knowledge with regard to these funds, their environment, regulatory issues, methodologies, and, most importantly, their linkages to the socio-economic systems and the environment, thus providing substantial (yet still inconclusive) arguments in the very intensive and at times controversial debate concerning the actual level of their sustainability.

Fribourg/Gdańsk, May 26, 2022.

References

Cuevas Fernández, B. (2019). Banking, ethics and sustainability: The need for a self-critical look at corporate social responsibilities strategies. In P. H. Dembinski, J. Kamerling, & V. Perret (Eds.), *Changing frontiers of ethics in finance. Ethics & trust in finance global prize awards 2012—2017* (pp. 359—370).

Hawley, J., & Williams, A. (1997). The emergence of fiduciary capitalism. *Corporate Governance: An International Review, 5*(4), 206—213.

Jabareen, Y. (2008). A new conceptual framework for sustainable development. *Environment, Development and Sustainability, 10*(2), 179—192.

Lagoarde-Segot, T., & Paranque, B. (2018). Finance and sustainability: From ideology to utopia. *International Review of Financial Analysis, 55*, 80—92.

Le Sourd, V., & Safaee, S. (2021). The European ETF market: Growth, trends, and impact on underlying instruments. *The Journal of Portfolio Management, 47*(7), 95—111.

Mebratu, D. (1998). Sustainability and sustainable development: Historical and conceptual review. *Environmental Impact Assessment Review, 18*(6), 493—520.

Mensah, J. (2019). Sustainable development: Meaning, history, principles, pillars, and implications for human action: Literature review. *Cogent Social Sciences, 5*(1).

Migliorelli, M. (2021). What do we mean by sustainable finance? Assessing existing frameworks and policy risks. *Sustainability, 13*(2).

Nagatsu, M., Davis, T., DesRoches, C. T., Koskinen, I., MacLeod, M., Stojanovic, M., & Thorén, H. (2020). Philosophy of science for sustainability science. *Sustainability Science, 15*(6), 1807—1817.

Schoenmaker, D., & Schramade, W. (2019). *Principles of sustainable finance.* Oxford University Press.

Tomislav, K. (2018). The concept of sustainable development: From its beginning to the contemporary issues. *Zagreb International Review of Economics & Business, 21*(1), 67—94.

United Nations Conference on Trade and Development. (2020). Leveraging the Potential of ESG ETFs for Sustainable Development.

World Commission on Environment and Development. (1987). *Our common future.* United Nations.

Wuelser, G., Chesney, M., Mayer, H., Niggli, U., Pohl, C., Sahakian, M., Stauffacher, M., Zinsstag, J., & Edwards, P. (2020). Priority themes for Swiss sustainability research. *Swiss Academies Reports, 15*(5), 1–56.

Ziolo, M., Bak, I., & Cheba, K. (2021). The role of sustainable finance in achieving Sustainable Development Goals: Does it work? *Technological and Economic Development of Economy, 27*(1), 45–70.

CHAPTER 2

Exchange-traded funds: background and concepts

2.1 Definition, mechanisms, and classification of ETFs

To be able to conduct a meaningful study of exchange-traded funds (ETFs) (including the sustainable investing category), it is first necessary to refer to some of their broadly accepted and used definitions—we will thus be able to clearly establish the key subject of our analysis. After the brief overview of the basic clarifications of ETFs, we discuss the basic aspects of the primary and secondary ETFs markets. Furthermore, we show the major classifications of these investment funds, proving their substantial diversity.

Despite the undeniable popularity of ETFs among various classes of retail and institutional investors as well as the widespread use of the label "ETF" in the names of the instruments offered by financial institutions, there are some (albeit rather minor) differences in their definitions and explanations provided in the publications related to this topic. We attempt to focus on their common elements to be able to clearly identify the fundamental features of ETFs.

According to one of the most frequently cited authors who cover the topic of ETFs in his studies, A.N. Madhavan, ETFs should be regarded as investment vehicles with two key attributes—their aim is tracking the financial performance of selected indexes and their shares[1] are traded intraday and seek to track the performance of some particular indexes (Madhavan, 2016). The first part of the aforementioned definition is similar in kind to the explanation provided by one of the leading global associations of the regulated funds—Investment Company Institute (ICI). In the ICI's 2021 fact book, ETFs were defined as investment companies whose shares are characterized by two attributes: they are traded intraday on stock

---

[1] Throughout the book, we also use the term "units of ETFs," as the synonym to "shares of ETFs."

Sustainable Investing
ISBN 978-0-12-823871-4
https://doi.org/10.1016/B978-0-12-823871-4.00004-0

exchanges and their prices are determined in the course of the market transactions (Investment Company Fact Book (ICI, 2021)). The definition by ICI indicates another important aspect of ETFs, which is the continuous pricing of their shares, resulting from the transaction conducted on stock exchanges or other trading venues for financial instruments. Another publication in which a similar definition was applied is one of the milestone books concerning ETFs, by Gastineau (2010)—ETFs were defined as the financial products whose main attribute is that they can be traded throughout the day and the value of their shares is kept close to the value of the underlying assets (the latter, as explained in the subsequent part of the chapter, is possible due to activity of arbitrageurs). The trading feature of ETFs is also emphasized in the definition by R.A. Ferri who stated that shares of ETFs can be traded in a manner similar to individual stocks (Ferri, 2009).

Apart from the books or reports of financial organizations, the conceptualizations of ETFs were also presented in a vast number of articles in journals addressing the topic of ETFs. For example, M. Lettau and A.N. Madhavan compared ETFs to index mutual funds by stating that their core feature is aiming to mirror the performance of a particular index (Lettau & Madhavan, 2018). In one of the earliest and most frequently referred to articles about ETFs, A. Agapova stated that they are a category of financial innovations that offers a claim on various underlying indexes (like index mutual funds but with substantially different organizational structures) (Agapova, 2011). The same elements as presented in the academic publications can be found in explanations provided by the financial institutions, including the ones being key actors on the ETFs markets (such as Deutsche Bank or BlackRock).

One important element of the definitions presented in the preceding paragraphs can be questioned as it does not fully correspond to the current state of the global ETFs market that has become much more diversified in the last 2 decades in comparison to its initial form. In their initial and still most basic and common form ETFs were, as implied by, for example, definition by A.N. Madhavan, passive investment products with exposure to stock market indexes (usually blue chip or broad market ones). Nonetheless, despite the prevalence of such ETFs on a global scale, the intensive competition between ETF providers and also the demand from their users have led to the launch and spread of ETFs that are neither passive (i.e., linked to some benchmark) nor based on the prices of equities (Charupat & Miu, 2013). Classification of ETFs will be presented in the later part of the chapter. To sum up, our overview of various explanations of the ETF concept indicates the following common features of these funds: their shares are listed and can be traded through stock exchanges or other trading systems, the shares of ETFs are valued frequently in the course of the market transactions, trading mechanisms of shares of ETFs are comparable to those of the equities of listed companies, and (in their basic form) the aim of ETFs is to track (offer exposure) to (stock market) indexes. Legal structure of ETFs is to a high extent dependent on their domicile and listing location; therefore, it will be omitted in the current general overview (the main subject of our study are European ETFs—their legal aspects were addressed in the overview of the European market presented in Marszk and Lechman (2019a)).

Gaining insight into the advantages and disadvantages of ETFs in comparison to other investment funds and examination of the relationships between ETFs markets and their environment requires taking into consideration the mechanisms of ETFs that distinguish them from more established types of similar investment solutions. In many dimensions that can be considered innovative, thus showing that ETFs constitute a part of the innovative financial solutions category. Using the label "financial innovations" to describe all kinds of ETFs may raise some doubts due to their relatively long history in some developed financial systems (first ETFs were launched in Canada and the United States in the late 1980s and early 1990s (Abner, 2016; Elton et al., 2002; Foucher & Gray, 2014; Gastineau, 2010; Hill, 2016)); most other major ETFs markets were started at the end of 20th and beginning of 21st century—this includes the key European or Asia–Pacific markets (Gastineau, 2010; Hill et al., 2015). Nonetheless, it should be remembered that ETFs are still absent from the majority of investment industries in the world, in particular in the least developed or emerging countries (with some exceptions yet the number of such countries is rather low). Moreover, designating ETFs as financial innovations is to some degree substantiated by the high dynamics of the global ETFs industry—the category of ETFs continues to expand not only in terms of the assets under management or number of funds but also with regard to the diversity of the funds available to customers, among them, particularly important from the perspective of this book, sustainable investing ETFs which are one of the most recent innovations in the ETFs industry, attracting undeniably rapidly growing attention in the investing community.

In the book, we frequently refer to the term "development of ETFs market," considering, for example, its level or dynamics, thus it requires some explanation before further discussion. With the development of the ETFs market, we understand the strengthening of the position of ETFs in a certain financial system, either on a standalone basis or in relative terms (compared to the other similar financial instruments, products, etc.). We do not adopt a single approach to its measurement in order not to limit the scope of the analysis—we understand the process of the development of the ETFs market as its growth in the following dimensions (considered separately or jointly): assets under management of ETFs (the primary approach), the number of ETFs or the turnover of their shares. From a geographical perspective, we analyze the development on a regional or country level. In the possible case of conflicting trends in the aforementioned dimensions, the changes in the assets are regarded as the major indicator, as they represent the fundamental aspect of the investment funds' activity.

ETFs market consists of two fundamental parts: primary and secondary market (Bhojraj et al., 2020); to some extent, this structure resembles the division of the markets for listed securities such as stocks or bonds (there are, though, some differences as explained later—in the basic form the mechanisms of ETFs were influenced by the operations on the commodities market). In our discussion in the subsequent paragraphs, we omit the technical and legal details that are of lesser importance in the context of the book's topic. Moreover, we discuss exclusively the basic model of ETFs markets—other structures (including other roles of the core participants) are also possible.

Primary ETFs market, as its name indicates, is the segment in which the initial operations in the shares of ETFs take place (Alexander & Peterson, 2020; Aquilina et al., 2020; Box et al., 2019). Key participants of the primary market are, first, ETF providers (sponsors), that is, the managing companies most strongly associated with the fund by investors (such as the global leader BlackRock) and, second, authorized participants (APs) (Bhattacharya & O'Hara, 2020). ETF providers are responsible for the preliminary activities. The first core step in the functioning of the ETF is the initial public offering (IPO) of its shares. The shares issued during the IPO are purchased by the APs with the aim of further distribution on the secondary market. Throughout the course of the fund's functioning next shares can be created, depending on the demand from APs (influenced indirectly by the demand from the participants of the secondary ETFs market). However, in contrast with, for example, equity markets, the reverse transactions are also quite common, that is, the redemption of the shares of ETFs. Overall, the primary ETFs market can be regarded as the segment in which the creation and redemption of the shares of funds take place (Liebi, 2020).

Despite the apparent similarities between the primary equity and ETFs markets, there are some important differences due to the attributes that are almost unique for the ETFs' shares creation and redemption. In the basic model of ETFs, the APs willing to purchase (i.e., create) or sell (i.e., redeem) the shares of ETFs do not exchange them for cash but rather for "creation (redemption) units," being multiples of "creation (redemption) baskets"[2] (Calamia et al., 2019). Creation baskets are portfolios of assets (usually securities) whose exact composition is determined by the fund's provider and subject to frequent (even daily) changes—nonetheless, it usually corresponds closely to the composition of the fund's benchmark (as in the vast majority ETFs are passive funds this may simply be the tracked index, e.g., stock market one). Apart from the application in the creation and redemption mechanism, creation baskets are also used for the calculation of the net asset value (NAV) of the ETF's shares that plays some important roles, for instance, in the light of the arbitrage transactions (described later). The other term used in this paragraph, that is creation (redemption) unit, is linked to the everyday aspects of the creation and redemption mechanism—due to, for example, costs of the transactions and time burdens it would be impractical to swap a small amount of the creation (redemption) baskets for shares; therefore, the transactions cover some multiples of the shares and the most frequent industry standard is 50,000.

The process of the creation and redemption of ETF's shares is called "in-kind" because it includes the swap of one type of assets (shares of ETFs) for the other type (assets included in the creation (redemption) baskets). In some cases, cash is used as a supplementary method of payment (Ferri, 2009; Wiandt & McClatchy, 2002). Creation of ETF's shares consists of the exchange of the creation basket delivered by the AP for the shares of ETFs; reversely, redemption is the swap of shares of ETFs delivered by the AP for the redemption basket. Such a mechanism is substantially different from the one employed by the main competing investment products—mutual funds for which the fund providers are responsible for the creation and redemption that involves simply an exchange of money for fund's units rather than an in-kind mechanism. In-kind process is unique for ETFs

---

[2] Creation and redemption baskets (and, consequently, also units) are usually identical albeit sometimes small differences can be noticed. We use thus both terms interchangeably.

within the investment funds sector and can be regarded as one of the key innovative attributes—it is linked to some important effects concerning, among others, taxation or tracking performance in the case of the passive funds (see the discussion concerning arbitrage later). Historically, the application of such a structure of the primary market stems from the design of the pioneering ETFs, with their creators aiming to adopt some commodities trading mechanisms (for more details see Gastineau (2010)).

Secondary ETFs market to a higher degree (than in case of the primary market) resembles its equity counterpart. Using the most basic explanation, it is the segment in which the shares of ETFs are purchased and sold by their end users (either retail or institutional investors) (Alexander & Peterson, 2020; Duffy et al., 2021). The opposite side of transactions may involve other end users of ETFs or other participants of the ETFs markets such as APs (as well as other entities who act as market makers). What is important, the evidence for the most developed ETFs market shows that the latter group plays the key role as the opposite party of the operations due to almost unlimited access to the shares of ETFs on the primary market (Antoniewicz & Heinrichs, 2014; Ben-David et al., 2017; Pagano et al., 2019). Secondary market transactions take place on stock exchanges or other trading venues, including the over-the-counter facilities as well as in dark pools (in the case of retail investors usually on the stock exchanges and similar venues) (Jurich, 2021). Market participants have access to a broad range of possible operations in the shares of ETFs, comparably to other listed securities (for instance, utilizing short sales or derivatives based on the shares of ETFs). The demand and supply in the secondary ETFs market (and indirectly also the situation on the markets for the assets underlying ETFs) determine the prices of their shares; another crucial factor are arbitrage activities outlined in the subsequent paragraph. Results of the study by Antoniewicz and Heinrichs (2014) clearly demonstrated that the volume of transactions on the secondary ETFs markets is substantially higher than on the primary segment and therefore it can be perceived as the key part for the majority of ETFs users.

An important element that links primary and secondary markets is the arbitrage operations. They are linked to in-kind transactions and can be perceived as one of the fundamental mechanisms that distinguish ETFs from mutual funds. Taking into account the fact that the vast majority of ETFs are passive funds, their investors focus mostly on their tracking performance (the ability to obtain financial results of the shares as close as possible to their benchmarks). This parameter can be assessed using various metrics, above all tracking error or, less frequently, tracking difference (Charupat & Miu, 2013; Madhavan, 2016). From the investor's perspective, the desired choice with regard to a certain benchmark is the fund with the lowest tracking error. Consequently, the funds with relatively lower tracking error can be expected to attract relatively more inflows from the investors (thus this constitutes an important parameter affecting the development of the markets for certain funds)[3]; for more detailed discussion concerning tracking performance with regard to ETFs, see Marszk and Lechman (2019a). In-kind mechanism is strongly linked to arbitrage actions of APs that contribute to maintaining the low tracking error (in comparison to competing investment choices). These actions are based on the differences between the prices of the shares on the secondary ETFs market and the NAV of these shares, the latter being linked to the prices for the underlying assets (i.e., the ones covered by the benchmark) (Ben-David et al., 2017). In case of deviations between these values exceeding the inherent costs, APs can conduct profitable operations including purchase or share of the shares of ETFs or the assets included in the creation (redemption) baskets on the secondary markets (depending on the type of mispricing) and swapping them on the primary markets. They can thus receive the incorrectly valued assets which can be profitably sold on the relevant markets. In the scale of the whole ETFs market, such operations contribute to the lowering of the tracking error (difference). It should be added that transactions with similar effects (yet without accessing the primary market) may also be conducted by the secondary market participants, observing the deviations between share's price and its NAV, expecting the discrepancies to diminish over time.

The growth of the global ETFs market has been followed and, at the same time, driven by (establishing the cause-and-effect relationship is impossible) the increasing diversity of this category of financial products. Initially, exclusively ETFs with the exposure to the stock market indexes had been available (i.e., passive equity funds); however, soon the range of possible investment strategies expanded and currently ETFs offer investment strategies linked to all major asset classes and do not only necessarily simply track the return indexes (currently semipassive or even active funds can be accessed on some markets). Consequently, due to their substantial variety, multiple approaches to the classification and categorization of ETFs

---

[3] Obviously, the other important aspect is the cost—we compare the costs of ETFs versus mutual funds in the subsequent section.

can be adapted, utilizing different criteria. We list the key types of ETFs in Table 2.1, supplemented (if necessary) by a brief overview. The list of categories and particular types of ETFs is by no means exhaustive—we decided to include the major classifications from the perspective of both further study and their significance in the ETFs industry.

Classifications in Table 2.1 do not include one distinction that is mostly related to the mechanisms of ETFs and the method of providing the exposure declared by the fund's provider: physical versus synthetic ETFs. Even though this classification may seem mostly technical and irrelevant in the broader context, it can have substantial consequences for the possible impact of ETFs (see the relevant discussion in the further part of this chapter).

Physical ETFs are the funds that employ the base in-kind mechanism of the creation and redemption process, as shown in the preceding paragraphs. The managing company purchases and holds either the portfolio of the assets exactly the same as in its benchmark (the case of full replication) or some selection of the assets covered by the benchmark (the case of sampling) (Nikbakht et al., 2016); the latter method is utilized above all when the assets that constitute the benchmark are relatively illiquid and/or the number of constituents is relatively high and the full replication is impossible or too expensive (Hill et al., 2015).

In contrast with physical ETFs, synthetic funds operate using radically different internal processes with regard to the creation and redemption of the shares and provision of the desired exposure declared by the fund (Broby & Spence, 2020; Koshoev, 2018; Mateus & Rahmani, 2017; Meinhardt et al., 2015). Instead of purchasing the full or sampled basket of the securities within the tracked benchmark, providers of synthetic ETFs achieve the desired exposure by entering derivatives contract, in the vast majority of total return swaps, in which they act as the party which receives the cash flows corresponding to the return on the index tracked by the fund. Consequently, no in-kind creation and redemption take place in the case of synthetic funds—shares of ETFs are exchanged for cash.

Synthetic ETFs constitute the minority of ETFs available globally yet they are noticeable in Europe, which may be considered as the key region of these funds (albeit on a regional scale they are also less widespread than their physical counterparts). The most frequent benefit of synthetic ETFs in relation to physical ones declared by their providers is lower tracking error (i.e., higher tracking efficiency). However, the empirical evidence provides mixed results to support this claim (Broby & Spence, 2020; Chu & Xu, 2021; Maurer & Williams, 2015; Meinhardt et al., 2015).

Table 2.1 Main classifications of ETFs.

Criterion of classification	Categories of ETFs	Additional information
Exposure to asset class	Equity	ETFs with exposure to equities, most frequently having stock market indexes as their benchmarks. They are the oldest and the most frequent type of ETFs worldwide (substantial share of investors associates ETFs exclusively with this category). Initially, their benchmarks had been almost exclusively blue-chip and broad stock market indexes but over time the range of equity ETFs has expanded and covers a substantial number of diversified equity-linked benchmarks.
	Fixed income	Funds with exposure to debt securities, in most cases bonds (therefore the other frequently used name of this category is "bond ETFs"). Their creation and management are hindered by the insufficient number of the indexes to serve as benchmarks for the funds (due to, primarily, low liquidity of the secondary markets for the constituents). Another, linked problematic issue is the determination of the NAV due to limited market-based pricing of the tracked instruments.
	Commodity	ETFs with exposure to various types of commodities, mostly precious metals (above all gold). They should not be mistaken with exchange-traded commodities (ETCs) that are debt securities with commodity exposure rather than category of ETFs; the same applies to exchange-traded notes (ETNs).
	Other	Consists of several subcategories: real estate, currency, volatility, money-market, mixed, and other (with negligible share in the global market).
Relation to benchmark	Passive	The most basic, oldest, and most popular category of ETFs—funds aiming to replicate the performance of the mandated benchmarks, minimizing the tracking error.

Continued

Table 2.1 Main classifications of ETFs.—cont'd

Criterion of classification	Categories of ETFs	Additional information
	Semipassive	Also known as "semiactive," "smart beta," "factor" or "enhanced indexing." They combine the features of the passive funds (tracking certain benchmarks) with the attributes characteristic for the active funds; managers change the weights of the constituents of the portfolio through selection of at least one factor (thus one of the names) affecting the rates of return.
	Active	Active ETFs do not trace the benchmark—they attempt to outperform it. Some active ETFs cover nonquantifiable themes and utilize machine-learning algorithms rather than human-based management. Such ETFs comprise a negligible segment of the global ETFs market.
Other	ESG	For a detailed discussion, see Chapter 3.
	Geared	This category covers leveraged (with returns as some multiple of the benchmark, usually 2× or 3×), inverse (with returns inversed in relation to the benchmark), and inverse-leveraged (combination of the two former groups) ETFs.

Source: Own elaboration based on Abner, D. (2016). *The ETF Handbook. How to value and trade exchange-traded funds* (2nd ed.). John Wiley & Sons; Amenc, N., Goltz, F., & Le Sourd, V. (2017). *The EDHEC European ETF and smart beta Survey*. EDHEC-Risk Institute; Cameron, R. (2015). *ETFs Exchange Traded Funds: Everything to know about trading exchanges traded funds*. Amazon, UK; Hill, J.M., Nadig, D., & Hougan, M. (2015). *A comprehensive guide to exchange-traded funds (ETFs)*. CFA Institute Research Foundation; Kumar R. (2021). Active vs. smart beta etfs: Two sides of active management. *The Journal of Index Investing, 11*(4-1), 25−40; Lee, J. (2019). New Revolution in Fund Management: ETF/Index Design by Machines. *Global Economic Review, 48*(3), 261−272; Lettau, M., & Madhavan, A. (2018). Exchange-traded funds 101 for Economists. *Journal of Economic Perspectives, 32*(1), 135−154; Madhavan, A.N. (2016). *Exchange-traded funds and the new dynamics of investing*. Oxford University Press, Mateus, C., Mateus, I. B., & Soggiu, M. (2020). Do smart beta ETFs deliver persistent performance? *Journal of Asset Management, 21*(5), 413−427, Meziani, A.S. (2016). *Exchange-traded funds: Investment practices and Tactical approaches*. Palgrave Macmillan; Nikbakht, F., Pareti, K., & Spieler A.C. (2016). Exchange-Traded Funds. In H.K. Baker, G. Filbeck, & H. Kiymaz, (Eds.), *Mutual Funds and Exchange-Traded Funds: Building Blocks to Wealth* (pp. 153−168). Oxford University Press.

Moreover, synthetic structures are in some cases the only one possible (or the least expensive) to attain the desired exposure—this applies to, for example, the funds with return modified in relation to their benchmarks such as leveraged or inverse ETFs for which it would be impossible to generate the required returns without derivatives; it applies to some currencies or commodities as well. Finally, rarely the combinations of physical and synthetic structures are utilized.

2.2 ETFs versus mutual funds: comparison

Growing prominence of ETFs in the global financial system (evidenced by, e.g., an increasingly larger number of their applications) has led to the rising importance of the issue of their advantages and disadvantages in comparison to the other types of financial instruments and products. Due to their historical background and position in the financial system as well as the aims of this book, in which we regard ETFs as a category of investment funds, in the current section, we compare ETFs to mutual funds. Other possible approaches, not presented here, may include comparisons of ETFs to closed-end funds or certain types of derivatives (for a detailed overview see, among others, Marszk et al. (2019)).

From the historical perspective, ETFs emerged as an alternative to index funds—they had been launched as an attempt to mitigate some of the disadvantages of this category of mutual funds (see our discussion concerning differences between ETFs and mutual funds in the remainder of this section). The rising prominence of both index funds and ETFs can be linked to the milestones in the academic discussion yet having deep practical implications in the financial community, concerning the benefits of passive investing, dubbed even "passive revolution" (Braun, 2016); these arguments stemmed from, among others, concepts such as Markowitz's modern portfolio theory (Markowitz, 1952, 1959), Capital Asset Pricing Model (CAPM) (Lintner, 1965, 1969; Mossin, 1966; Sharpe, 1964), or capital markets efficiency hypotheses (Fama, 1965, 1970). This discussion was initiated in the United States in the 1970s and 1980s and resulted from seeking an alternative to the conventional investing method, which later became known as "active" investing—the alternative constituting the possibility to receive the financial performance of certain indexes (Ellis, 1975; Ferri, 2009; Malkiel, 2016; Samuelson, 1974). First attempt to adopt this approach had been index mutual funds—pioneering fund was launched in the mid-1970s (Bogle, 2016). In the further time period, the launch of the next rather short-lived investment solutions, resulted in the development of the ETFs concept, in the form known today on the brink of the 1980s (minor attempts) and 1990s (introduction of some funds still in existence today).

It should be emphasized that because of their common focus on mirroring the performance of certain benchmarks (as passive investment products; at least in the case of most prevalent ETFs) ETFs and index funds can be considered to belong to the same part of the investment industry in terms of the investment strategies offered (Agapova, 2011). Consequently, the discussion in this section includes in fact comparison between ETFs and index funds; nevertheless, with some stipulations, it may also be applied to other types of mutual funds (important justification is the broadening range of ETFs, even with active strategies). Most generally, both ETFs and mutual funds constitute categories of investment funds (which includes also, e.g., closed-end funds, not discussed here). Other more specific similarities between ETFs and mutual funds stem from the aforementioned core resemblance (Hill et al., 2015): investing entails paying various fees (including the management fees collected by the provider), providers are financial institutions (they are frequently parts of the large financial multinational corporations) and they designate financial professionals to manage the funds (it is assumed that they are managed consistently with the fund's mandate), and, last but not least, in line with the basic concept of investment funds, through investing into the units of investment funds their users become owners of the proportional interest in the combined assets.

We conduct our discussion by presenting the most apparent and fundamental differences between ETFs and mutual funds,[4] perceived from the perspective of both investor and the macrolevel effects (both levels are described jointly).

One of the most fundamental and, at the same, most noticeable differences is that units (shares) of ETFs have the legal form of equity securities (listed and traded through publicly or privately accessible trading facilities) in contrast with no such structure in case units of mutual funds.

The abovementioned dissimilarity has some profound consequences, above all concerning the distribution channels of the units of the presented investment funds. Units of ETFs can be bought and sold using the channels

---

[4] The discussion in the remainder of this section is based on several publications in the field, above all following:

Abner (2016), Agapova (2011), Aquilina et al. (2020), Baker et al. (2016), Baker et al. (2020), Bello (2012), Box et al. (2020), Cameron (2015), Chang et al. (2018), Crigger (2017), Diltz and Rakowski (2018), Elton et al. (2019), Farinella and Kubicki (2018), Ferri (2009), Gastineau (2010), Hill et al. (2015), Lettau and Madhavan (2018), Madhavan (2016), Nikbakht et al. (2016), Sherrill and Upton (2018), Stankevičienė and Petronienė (2019), Todorov (2021), Wiandt and McClatchy (2002).

typical for securities such as with the intermediation of the stock brokers—using the terminology introduced in the previous section these transactions are conducted on the secondary ETFs market. On the contrary, despite various distribution channels of the units of mutual funds (such as bank branches or wealth management advisors), they cannot be purchased or sold on the trading venues comparable to shares of ETFs. The discrepancy in terms of the distribution mechanism can generally be perceived as the source of the relative benefit of ETFs. The minimum required entry commitment in the case of ETFs is usually limited to the purchase of one share of the fund; the same requirement applies to the decrease or closing of the investment position (both types of transactions are conducted through the brokerage accounts or similar channels). It results in high accessibility of ETFs, even for investors with a limited supply of capital. In opposition, in the case of mutual funds, the minimum values of the investment can be set by the providers at levels hindering their usage by such investors. Furthermore, the fact that shares of ETFs are available on the stock exchanges or other securities trading systems gives the investors access to various transactions that can be utilized such as short selling or selling on margin; the other related advantage is (in some cases) possibility to employ derivatives based on ETF shares such as options (the market for these financial instruments has been developing substantially in some countries, for instance, China (Dong et al., 2021; Wang et al., 2018)). There are no such possibilities with regard to the units of mutual funds that may be regarded as their relative weakness in comparison to the more recent category of investment funds.

However, it needs to be added that in some cases the aforesaid apparent advantage of ETFs (i.e., shares of ETFs as publicly listed securities) may be actually its weakness. This statement applies to less sophisticated investors, in particular the ones in the countries with the less developed capital markets and infrequent securities investing among the households. Mutual funds have a more established position in the financial system and are broadly recognized among the investors. Nonetheless, in line with the rising prominence of ETFs, this difference may diminish.

Finally, the listing of shares of ETFs provides their users with one more relative advantage (albeit not equally important for all users, depending on the adopted investment strategy and horizon)—the transactions in the shares of ETFs may be conducted much more frequently and with lesser time delays (consistently with the organization of the trading venue) as contrasted with the units of mutual funds that usually can be sold and redeemed once a day and the settlement process can include substantial time delays.

All attributes of ETFs mentioned in the preceding paragraphs can be associated with a larger and more diversified range of investment strategies available for their users (for instance, allowing for acting promptly on the most recent developments in the financial-economic system). Using ETFs with foreign exposure or funds listed abroad (in a manner similar to foreign-listed equities) can provide their investors with the access to the financial markets other than the domestic one; despite the highly diversified offer of mutual funds in terms of their exposure, utilizing the funds provided by foreign financial institutions is on average more complicated and expensive than in case of ETFs (even though the employment of foreign-listed ETFs is also usually more expensive than domestically listed ones; however, the full picture has become more complicated with the onset of various Fin-Tech based investment services—the discussion in the further part of this chapter).

Another difference linked to the listing and trading location of the shares of ETFs and the lack of such attributes concerning mutual funds is observed with regard to the pricing of their units. In the case of the units of the mutual funds, their NAV is published (usually once a day) by the fund's provider (even though technically the pricing process may be actually conducted by different entity)—this value is binding in case of creation and redemption of the units (i.e., in the transaction between their users and providers). On the contrary, the pricing of the units of ETFs takes place twofold: on the primary market in a manner similar to mutual funds (the price used in the operation between providers and APs) and, which constitutes a substantial difference, on the secondary market in the course of transactions in the shares of ETFs, which means that this price results from the interaction of demand and supply. What is important, the latter price is updated much more frequently, in line with the particular trading location's rules—therefore, the investors gain access to continuously updated key parameters of the fund's units. Due to, among others, the arbitrage mechanisms, the discrepancies between the prices of the ETFs' shares in the two segments should be negligible.

The next difference, to some extent already mentioned in the preceding discussion, is linked to the legal form of the units of both types of invest-ment funds is the structure of their markets. As we discussed in the pre-ceding section, the duality of the ETFs market (divided into primary and secondary) is among their distinctive features, with important associated effects. No primary market for mutual funds corresponding to the ETFs primary segment exists—market for mutual funds is much simpler and one-segmented. This difference between the two types of investment funds can have significant consequences with regard to, among others, the impact of ETFs on the markets for the underlying securities or financial systems at large due to the complicated effects linked to the interplay between primary and secondary ETFs market.

Some further among the most basic differences between ETFs and mutual funds are related to the dissimilarities in the creation and redemption mechanism of their shares. The internal process of the creation and redemption of the units of ETFs (presented in the previous section) differs substantially from the mechanism utilized by the mutual funds for which they occur directly between providers and investors (or with the intermediation of other entities such as financial advisors), and involve the exchange of cash for the fund's units. Even though this structure to some extent may be compared to the practices utilized by the synthetic ETFs, it should be remembered that even in this case the transactions are not conducted directly between investors and fund's providers. Regardless of the type of ETF, in their general design, the entities separate from providers (known as APs) are responsible for the creation and redemption of their shares; the lack of direct relationship between investors and providers (sponsors) of ETFs is noticeable even in case of ETFs markets on which due to legal and organizational reasons the role of APs (or other comparable participants of the ETFs markets) differs from the base model (established on the US market).

Due to the fact that in our discussion we focus on the passive funds (consistently with their domination on the ETFs market), it is necessary to consider the consequences of the abovementioned differences for the tracking errors and the costs of the funds. One of the most important (yet not observed in all cases) effects of the arbitrage operations conducted by the participants of the ETFs market is a more efficient tracking mechanism in the case of ETFs rather than mutual funds which can be evidenced by the lower tracking error (as well as tracking differences). The correct functioning of the arbitrage mechanism is also related to the trading and pricing relative advantages of ETFs. Still, it should be noted that the comparison of this attribute should be made on the fund by fund basis (Zawadzki, 2020); the same comment applies to the cost feature discussed later.

ETFs had initially been developed and launched as low–cost substitutes for the more established types of investment funds. Therefore, their lower costs (as we concentrate on the passive funds, it is in fact the tracking cost) are frequently indicated as the key strengths of ETFs in relation to mutual funds. However, the exact comparison of the costs of ETFs versus mutual funds is hindered by their different structure (in our discussion, we omit taxes due to their highly country-specific nature). Total costs of ETFs include above all management fees and trading costs. The latter element is absent in the case of mutual funds. Despite the apparent advantage of mutual funds, the consideration of the total costs suggests the cost advantage of ETFs because of their lower overhead expenses such as marketing or distribution costs. Moreover, the other source of potentially lower costs is the duality of ETFs markets and to some extent their independent functioning (i.e., transactions on one segment are not necessarily linked to the transactions on the other). Another source of lower management costs of ETFs is the in-kind mechanism of the primary market and the favorable cost treatment in case of investors entering or leaving the fund. Nonetheless, despite the aforesaid relative benefit of ETFs being frequently mentioned in various publications (in particular reports published by or in cooperation with their providers, to some extent serving as advertising materials), the results of empirical analyses are less clear-cut (for more details see, e.g., Baker et al. (2020), Chen et al. (2018), Elton et al. (2019) or Madhavan (2016)).

Yet another advantage of ETFs when juxtaposed with mutual funds is the higher transparency of the portfolios managed by the more recent category of investment funds—such information is disclosed frequently on a daily basis (yet in some rare cases less frequently) in contrast with once a month or quarter for mutual funds. Higher transparency plays a relatively more important role for the nonpassive ETFs (passive ETFs are required to replicate the index that can be easily checked) and can contribute to the correct functioning of the arbitrage processes and facilitate the more informed decision making by their users.

Regardless of the preceding discussion which, in most cases, was linked with the identification of the variety of comparable advantages of ETFs, there are some aspects for which mutual funds have relative strength over the more recent category of investment funds, including lower recognition and awareness of the features of ETFs among investors, more diversified product range of mutual funds (in particular in the segments of nonpassive and/or nonequity funds), empirical evidence indicating more beneficial application of mutual funds by investors with a lower preference for highly liquid funds, and, last but not least, regulations concerning some institutional investors prohibiting or limiting the employment of instruments such as ETFs (the importance of the last aspect, though, has been diminishing in the last years).

To finalize our comparative discussion of mutual funds and ETFs it is necessary to present briefly the results of the empirical studies in which the issue of the substitution between the two types of investment funds was verified based on the market data, thus showing whether in fact the relative benefits of ETFs have resulted in them gaining position in the investment industry at the expense of mutual funds. We focus exclusively on the selected academic publications but it should be added that this issue was also undertaken in various reports by financial companies or organizations.

Park et al. (2014) studied the Korean markets for index mutual funds and ETFs, focusing on their cash flows—the results of their analysis provide no significant evidence for the switching between ETFs and mutual funds, implying rather that they can be perceived as complementary financial products, used due to varying attributes. Similar conclusions were reached by Guedj and Huang (2009) who showed that the two types of investment funds correspond to users with different liquidity preferences. Hull (2016) studied the US market and analyzed the position of ETFs versus other categories of investment funds over 1993—2014, using data on flow of funds and values of financial assets—the key conclusion is the sustained strengthening of the position of ETFs. In a rather unusual approach, Sherrill and Upton (2018) juxtaposed the active segment of both ETFs and mutual funds markets. The results of their study confirm the limited substitution between ETFs and mutual funds in the subcategory of funds with equity and mixed exposure, indicating the preference for ETFs for taxation and, to a lesser extent, liquidity benefits. In our previous works, among others, Marszk (2017), Marszk et al. (2017), Marszk and Lechman (2018), we provided evidence for the occurrence of switching of investors from mutual into ETFs on a number of markets, including Japan, South Korea, Mexico, and the United States.

2.3 Effects of the development of ETFs markets

The study of sustainable investing ETFs presented in this book consists, among others, of the examination of the consequences of the spread of sustainable investing ETFs. Therefore, it seems necessary to address these issues first in general perspective, that is, with regard to ETFs markets at large (discussion of the relevant relationships concerning sustainable investing is covered in Chapter 5, accompanied by the results of the empirical study).

In the initial stages of the global ETFs market development, the issue of their possible impact had been almost neglected due to the small assets and limited availability of these funds. The possible consequences had been limited to the narrow group of their users and financial institutions participating in the primary and secondary markets. However, in line with the strengthening position of ETFs in the financial systems (beginning with the North American ones, later also in the other regions), their potential effects could no longer be neglected. In the remainder of this section, we outline some among the most fundamental effects of the development of ETFs markets. We focus on the broader consequences rather than the immediate effects for the tracked (underlying) assets or the investors in shares of ETFs—there is a rich literature on these topics and the conclusions reached in the empirical studies in the field are far from clear-cut (they are highly fund- or investor-specific).

We start our overview with the consequences of the spread of ETFs for the investment industry. These effects cannot be considered separately from the general consequences of the rising popularity of passive investing. As the low costs of the offered investment strategies are perceived as one of the main benefits of the passive in relation to active investing, the providers of passive funds face pressure to improve their cost attributes through, for example, benefits from the economies scale by accumulating increasingly more assets. One of the key results of this trend is the increased concentration of the stock ownership (i.e., share of the aggregate equity market held by the largest investors (Ben-David et al., 2017)). This change may have some adverse consequences such as growing volatility of the securities held in the portfolios of these funds linked to nonfundamental events inflicted by certain changes in the largest investment companies (e.g., financial distress of the fund unrelated to the conditions of certain market). In another dimension, the innovative attributes of ETFs (such as higher accessibility or lower costs), as well as their increasing diversity, can be perceived as factors contributing to attracting new groups of investors or growing activity of the already present ones, thus boosting the overall development of the investment industry (Lettau & Madhavan, 2018). However, the actual occurrence of this impact seems limited and region-specific as shown by Thomadakis (2018)—on the European ETFs markets the share of retail users remains negligible, in contrast, in the United States the shares of retail and institutional investors are comparable.

The issue of the consequences of the competition between ETFs and mutual funds for the investment industry at large was to some extent addressed by Braun (2016) who discussed, for example, political economy of the ETFs market, focusing on their relatively lower costs in comparison to the conventional mutual funds. The study considered also the competition among funds to offer and advertise the lowest costs possible ("ETF price war"). The reactions of the more established mutual funds to mitigate the comparative advantage of ETFs included both innovatory measures—the launch and development of smart beta funds (as an attempt to follow the growing popularity of index investing but, at the same time, utilize to some extent active investing typical for the traditional funds) and fraudulent actions— "closet indexing," that is, collecting high fees from investors for declared active strategies that are in fact mostly passive. As Braun (2016) concluded, the rising popularity of ETFs is bound to negatively affect both profitability and salaries of managers in the investment industry over time.

Apart from the effects for the investment funds and asset management industry, the crucial consequences of the development of ETFs markets have prevalently been assessed with regard to their impact on the financial systems, in particular the financial markets (for a detailed up-to-date overview, see Liebi (2020)). One of the fundamental and most frequently studied issues is the impact of ETFs on the liquidity of the financial markets. Some authors claim that ETFs influence negatively the liquidity of the tracked assets by various mechanisms such as increased market segmentation (Piccotti, 2018). Nevertheless, the results of a number of studies prove that ETFs boost the liquidity of the tracked securities (see, for example, Madhavan and Sobczyk (2016)). Holden and Nam (2019) studied the corporate bonds ETFs and found that the high liquidity of the markets for these funds diffuses to the markets for the underlying assets through the arbitrage mechanism. In another perspective, Agarwal et al. (2017) examined the arbitrage processes of ETFs and showed that this link leads to higher liquidity comovement of the assets and thus constitutes an additional, nondiversifiable type of risk. ETFs may also influence the informational efficiency (price informativeness) of the individual securities by affecting their supply and number of informed traders (Israeli et al., 2017). Moreover, Bhojraj et al. (2020) showed that ETFs with the exposure to particular sectors improve the transfer of information related to announcements of earnings between companies. Overall, Liebi (2020) concluded that based on the empirical evidence the influence of ETFs on the price discovery (market efficiency) is controversial.

Issue that requires particular attention due to the increasing prominence of ETFs in the financial systems is their possible impact on systemic risk (Bhattacharya & O'Hara, 2020). One of the key potential threats posed by ETFs to the financial system is the possibility of shock propagation (shock transmission) from the ETFs market to the markets for underlying assets. Various aspects of the possible shock propagation linked to ETFs were verified in a number of empirical studies—most of them focused on the issue of volatility (Krause & Tse, 2013). The most famous example of possible shock propagation inflicted by ETFs is the "Flash Crash" that took place on the US equity market on May 6, 2010. However, results of the studies about the real reasons and course of the crash, conducted in its aftermath, present mixed conclusions, some of them being partially contradictory, including Abner (2016), Madhavan (2016), Ben-David et al. (2017). Similar discussion was conducted with regard to the next similar event, in 2015 (Abner, 2016; Madhavan, 2016).

Possible negative channel of transmission between ETFs and markets for the associated assets is through the actions of APs, in particular in case of relatively illiquid markets for the underlying assets—in case of disruptions these entities may limit their activity on the primary ETFs markets thus threatening the fundamental mechanisms of creation/redemption and arbitrage (Pan & Zeng, 2017). Another possible transmission process is through the inclusion of shares of ETFs in the portfolios of the other investment funds and regarding them as substitutes to cash holdings (Bhattacharya & O'Hara, 2020). In a complex study of the impact of the increasing role of passive investing (taking into account both passive mutual funds and ETFs) Anadu et al. (2020) demonstrated that the effects with regard to financial stability are multidimensional. The risks associated with increased market volatility and market concentration seem amplified yet the redemption and liquidity risks are moderated by the expansion of the passive funds. What is important, as Dannhauser (2017) concluded, the increased concentration can be observed with regard not only to the most frequent equity funds but also fixed-income funds—the share of retail owners of the tracked bonds declined but the share of institutional ones increased.

Another type of shock transmission risk concerns the internationally cross-listed ETFs, that is, funds whose shares are listed on trading facilities in multiple countries. Apart from the possible positive effects for the local economy linked to the associated increased financial openness, negative consequences may involve the propagation of disruptions between various markets. The exact mechanism can include, for example, the transactions which cover the creation and redemption of the shares of ETFs and take place on various markets, sometimes with substantially varying infrastructural and regulatory environments.

Our presentation of the classifications of ETFs was accompanied by an overview of some specific types of these funds. In particular two categories are frequently mentioned in the context of the possible negative impact of ETFs for their users (or in case of magnified disruptions for the entire ETFs market or financial system): synthetic and geared funds. Synthetic ETFs can expose investors to some types of risks that are less substantial in physical funds (yet frequently also present) such as collateral or counterparty risk (Blocher & Whaley, 2016; Liebi, 2020). Bhattacharya and O'Hara (2020), in their detailed discussion of the ETFs' impact on financial stability, showed that geared ETFs may increase financial markets' stress levels even outside the episodes of serious disruptions. Geared ETFs could magnify the current trends in volatility due to the end-of-the-day rebalancing of their positions required to uphold the mandated exposure. Furthermore, according to Pessina and Whaley (2021), failure is the inherit attribute of geared funds and they cannot be perceived as effective tools for investment management. Similar stipulations have been formulated with regard to yet another type of ETFs—volatility funds (Bhansali & Harris, 2018).

The full assessment of the impact of ETFs on the financial markets and, at large, systems (including the potential effects for the financial stability) remains to some degree hindered by the scope of turnover on the off-exchanges trading venues that is substantial in some regions, for example, in Europe (c. 70% (Thomadakis, 2018)). However, the reporting requirements may increase in the future in line with the regulatory developments.

2.4 ETFs and FinTech

In the previous section, we focused on various possible effects of the ETFs market development; in other words, we discussed the environment of the ETFs industry. There is, though, one issue that requires additional scrutiny because of its high importance from the contemporary financial system's perspective—the role of the new technologies in the financial sector, in particular various services labeled together as "FinTech." In the current section, we discuss the meaning of the FinTech sector for the ETFs markets, starting with a more general discussion of the role of new technologies in the introduction and spread of ETFs through the macroeconomic and financial effects of information and communication technologies (ICT).

Introduction and adoption of ICT in certain economy and society, including the participants and infrastructure of the financial system, lead to deep changes that can significantly affect the ETFs market in a local and international perspective. Some of the most significant transformations inflicted by the diffusion of ICT in the macro dimensions include (Asongu & Moulin, 2016; Banaji et al., 2018; Castells et al., 2009; Chien et al., 2020; Miller & Skinner, 2015; Shapiro & Varian, 1998):

— facilitating unrestricted flows of information and knowledge which lead to the rise of new products and services as well as emergence of new industries and business models;
— rise of the economies of networks, boosting economic activities in previously marginalized and peripheral areas;
— transformation of the financial markets' infrastructure, with the milestones such as adoption of electronic systems, allowing for unprecedented rapid dissemination of financial data and information, reducing the information asymmetries and time delays, as well as decreased physical distance barriers;
— improved possibilities of financial data application (i.e., collection and analysis of data) with the aim of preparing and providing financial products adopted to the clients' needs in terms of time, price, and attributes;
— adoption of the technology-based systems for improved risk management processes of financial institutions, for example, in the banks, as well as, in a broader scale, improved consumer protection and antimoney laundering mechanisms.

The effects of the ICT adoption for the development of the ETFs market can be discussed by diving them into the ones with key importance for the demand versus supply side. Consequently, on the demand side following linkages between ICT and ETFs can be noticed (EY, 2017; Lettau & Madhavan, 2018; Thomadakis, 2018):

— reduction of trading costs and improved pricing mechanisms by adoption of the ICT-based trading systems and resulting higher digitalization of turnover;
— reduction of distribution costs (and thus associated fees for investors) by using digital distribution channels;
— ability of funds providers to offer other types of exposure than to the core equity market indexes (e.g., by providing semipassive or sustainable investing ETFs) through more efficient data management services based on new technologies.

Supply-side effects are linked above all to the infrastructure of the ETFs markets and operations of the market participants other than end users of the shares of these funds. They include (Blitz & Huij, 2012; Lettau & Madhavan, 2018; Marszk & Lechman, 2019b; Thomadakis, 2018):

— before the advent of the new technologies the serious barrier to launch and management of index funds was the necessity to manage portfolios with hundreds or thousands of elements that resulted to be unfavorable in terms of costs in comparison top active funds—substantial reductions in the costs of computing technologies and electronic data delivery systems allowed overcoming this barrier;

— utilization of ICT-based systems both in particular ETF-related financial institutions and as the part of the financial markets' infrastructure facilitates the low-cost transfer of assets during operations on the primary ETFs markets and, consequently, also affects the arbitrage mechanism;

— in the case of the ETFs with shares traded on multiple exchanges, in particular in more than country, ICT allows for more efficient centralization of settlement procedures, including the procedures of issuance and posttrade processing, thus lowering the funds' transaction costs and increasing provision of liquidity on exchanges.

As the preceding outline clearly showed, the functioning of the ETFs market can be hypothesized to be strongly affected by the new technologies, in particular ICT. The discussion in the previous paragraphs covered the general influence of the new technologies on the ETFs market. The area in which these interactions are clearly visible is the FinTech sector.

There are various explanations of the "FinTech" concept, with slight differences in terms of the covered products and services. The definition that will be used in our discussion was suggested by Ancri (2016) who explained FinTech as the sector of the economy that includes the companies using technology (our addition: by assumption—ICT and related) to transform the financial systems and deliver various financial products and services. Dorfleitner et al. (2017) divided the FinTech into following categories:

— households and corporate financing (e.g., crowdfunding, online factoring);

— transfer and settlement of payment (e.g., mobile payments, cryptocurrencies);

— asset management (e.g., robo advising, social trading);

— other (e.g., insurance, regulatory).

Below we show some selected key applications of ETFs in the FinTech sector. However, it should be added that some broad trends in the FinTech sector such as increased applications of machine learning and AI solutions for the investment industry may generally be associated with the growing use of ETFs by FinTech companies (Baek et al., 2020).

Probably, the most explicit cases of the ETFs utilization by the FinTech companies are in robo advisory platforms. Robo advice is an online system utilizing various algorithms in the provision of a rather heterogenous group of investment services: portfolio monitoring, portfolio rebalancing, port-folio optimization, model-based portfolio solutions (Agarwal & Chua, 2020; Ji, 2017; Madhavan, 2016; Phoon & Koh, 2018; Shanmuganathan, 2020). What is important, robo advisory services are strongly linked to the ETFs markets due to the predominantly passive nature of the investing strategies implemented through the built-in algorithms of robo advisors, with limited necessary portfolio management, for example, rebalancing (Chen et al., 2018; Faloon & Scherer, 2017; Lee, 2017). Additional important issue is that the conceptual background of most robo advisory services is strongly grounded in the theoretical concepts (e.g., modern portfolio theory or efficient market hypotheses) that led to the rise of passive investing; to some extent, the mechanisms of robo advisors are also aimed at mitigating the typical behavioral biases of investors or generating tax savings (Bhatia et al., 2020; Sironi, 2016). Consequently, shares of ETFs are the core types of financial instruments utilized by robo advisors (Ahn et al., 2020), with the exception of countries with no or highly underde-veloped ETFs markets. The base reason is the ability to obtain low-cost diversification (Singhvi, 2021). Some linkages between ETFs and robo advisors are rather surprising—as Bach (2021) observed, robo advisory services can boost the development of the Sharia-compliant funds, and, in a broader perspective, Sharia-compliant financial markets.

It should be emphasized that in our discussion we focus mostly on the robo advisors aimed at retail investors, rather than business-to-business services—such approach is linked to explicit possible effects for ETFs markets development. Potentially, one of the most important consequences of the growth of the robo advisory services for the development of the ETFs markets is the mitigation of one of its key weaknesses (especially in some regions such as Europe) mentioned in the previous section, that is, the limited participation of the retail investors on the ETFs markets. Through the utilization of robo advisory accounts, retail investors may gain easier and cheaper access to the shares of ETFs (Thomadakis, 2018). Moreover, due to their digital-based attributes robo advisors may attract new types of investors, with no previous experience in the investment funds market or reluctance toward using traditional financial services such as young people, thus increasing the levels of their financial inclusion in some spheres (Tan, 2020). However, the possible threat to such a positive relationship is constituted by the increasingly complicated product range of automated advice, which may defer the less sophisticated investors. Last but not least, another link between robo advisors and ETFs is that the providers of ETFs have already recognized the development opportunities posed by robo advisors and have entered the partnerships with or even acquired them, regarding these platforms as increasingly important distribution channels for the managed funds (EY, 2017).

Even though robo advisory services are the key type of FinTech applications linked to ETFs, there are also some other, albeit less obvious, examples of such relationship between the new technologies and the presented category of investment funds: turnkey asset management programs (TAMPs) and social trading.

TAMPs can be explained as the third-party fee-account platforms for the financial advisors that include a broad range of services such as the development of investment strategies, the implementation and monitoring of such strategies (and thus also the clients' accounts), back-office support (e.g., record-keeping) and communication with their clients (and in some cases also other entities such as custodians and brokers) (Crigger, 2017, pp. 12–15; Kim et al., 2019). TAMPs are linked to the ETFs markets due to the fact that shares of ETFs are among key types of the financial assets utilized in the TAMPs' accounts; moreover, they are frequently the core elements of the model portfolios that can be accessed through these programs.

Social trading can be defined as a combination of social networks and investing services—in one of the first and most frequently cited publications on this topic Wohlgemuth et al. (2016) described it as an online community used by investors to copy the investments of other trusted investors in an automatic, simultaneous and unconditional method. In other words, social trading means that investors follow the decisions shared by the so-called signal providers (Oehler et al., 2016). It should be added that social trading communities involve also discussions concerning investment strategies and opportunities (Gemayel & Preda, 2018; Lee & Ma, 2018). Furthermore, the transactions may be executed by the platform rather than by the user using outside tools (Dorfleitner & Scheckenbach, 2022; Oehler et al., 2016; Wohlgemuth, 2016). Shares of ETFs are among the key investment products offered by the leading social trading platforms (Czaja & Röder, 2020; Röder & Walter, 2019)—consequently, the growth of the social trading FinTech services may be considered as potential contribution to the development of the ETFs markets. This effect may be magnified by high trading activity of some groups of users of social trading platforms as shown by Pelster and Breitmayer (2019). The potential impact of social trading, not only on the ETFs markets but also for financial markets at large should not be disregarded as evidenced by the increasing size of the platforms such as eToro (Reith et al., 2020) or the 2021 events on the US equity markets linked to the Robinhood platform (Ferré, 2021).

In spite of the preceding discussion of the impact of FinTech on ETFs, the relationship is not exclusively one-sided as the ETFs may also contribute to the growth of FinTech sector. This includes some rather straightforward influences such as the feedback loop between the development of robo advisors and ETFs markets—growth of this type of FinTech services boosts demand for the shares of ETFs but, at the same time, the availability of the ETFs preconditions the functioning of robo advisors and boosts their relative advantages such as low costs. Similar observation, albeit to a lesser extent, may be noted with regard to other ETF-related FinTech services, for example, social trading.

However, there are also some less obvious interlinkages. One of the key attributes of the contemporary ETFs markets is their continuously increasing diversity. Among the most recent types of ETFs there are funds whose financial performance is tied to the returns on equities of various companies from the FinTech sector. Their diversity reflects the heterogeneity of the FinTech sector as this category of ETFs includes the funds with the exposure to themes including digital payments, digital wallets, peer-to-peer payments and financing, fundraising, payment processing, FinTech software, AI, big data solutions, data processing, etc. These ETFs may be either passive (e.g., tracking certain indexes covering the equities of FinTech-related companies) or nonpassive funds (even active FinTech ETFs are available despite the general obscurity of the active ETFs segment). It should be noted, though, that despite the repeated attempts, resulting, e.g., from the pressure from some sectors of the investment industry, the launch of ETFs with direct exposure to bitcoin or other digital currencies has for many years been unsuccessful due to lack of regulatory approval. Most such attempts have been undertaken in the United States yet US financial regulatory bodies, in particular Securities and Exchange

Commission have been highly reluctant to approve the launch of "bitcoin ETFs." However, in October 2021, first ETF with exposure to the bitcoin market through the bitcoin futures (fund called "ProShares Bitcoin Strategy ETF") began trading on the New York Stock Exchange (La Monica, 2021). The most immediate effect of this fund's launch was the strong upsurge of the bitcoin's prices—nonetheless, the medium- or long-term effects on the bitcoin market (as well as the other cryptocurrencies) remain to be seen. One of the expected effects is the broadening of the group of investors on the cryptocurrency markets through the inclusion of the ones already active on the ETFs market (or, more generally, on financial markets through brokerage accounts) and previously unwilling to access the markets for cryptocurrencies (La Monica, 2021). It is still too early to predict the future of this nascent segment of ETFs market. From the investor's perspective, one of the possible methods to overcome the very low number of lack of cryptocurrency ETFs on their local markets is by accessing equity ETFs with exposure to stocks of companies that in some way have ties to the digital currencies or, more generally, blockchain applications.

2.5 Sustainable investing ETFs in the European countries: case study (I)—Switzerland

As we show in Chapter 4, there are substantial between-country differences in the European ETFs markets in terms of their sustainable investing category, with some countries being among the global leaders in this aspect. In this section, we provide an overview of the Swiss sustainable investing ETFs market which undeniably is in the aforementioned group. First, we provide an insight into sustainable investing in Switzerland: the size of this part of the investment industry, its structure, and regulatory environment. Next, we shortly cover the issue of the sustainable segment of the Swiss investment funds markets. Finally, in the last part of the case study, Swiss sustainable investing ETFs are presented (their discussion continues in Chapter 4 in which we examine all European markets for these funds). It should be emphasized that the Swiss sustainable investing market at large is probably the easiest to examine on a global scale due to multiple in-depth reports and exhaustive data sources.

Strong position of Switzerland in the sustainable investing segment of the global investment industry is clearly evidenced by the assets managed and their rapid development. Fig. 2.1. shows the evolution of the value of

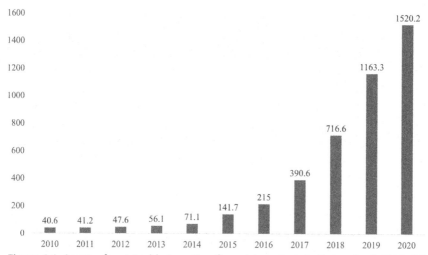

Figure 2.1 Assets of sustainable investing financial products in Switzerland: 2010—20 (CHF billion). *(Source: Own elaboration based on Swiss Sustainable Finance (2021). Swiss Sustainable Investment Market Study 2021.)*

these assets over the last several years—as it can clearly be seen the process of their growth has been unidirectional (no year-to-year declines were noted). As of 2020, the assets reached the record-high level of over 1.5 trillion CHF; 2019 was the first year with their value exceeding the symbolic level of 1 trillion CHF. The rate of growth was the highest in the subperiod 2015—19 when sustainable investing in Switzerland seems to have entered the rapid development phase (up to 2014 the growth rates had been much more moderate—sustainable investing remained still on the margin of the investment industry).

Fig. 2.2 presents the most recent (i.e., as of 2020) structure of the Swiss sustainable investing industry. Taking into consideration the structure of these assets, the most prominent category are investment funds with the sustainable investing exposure (including ETFs), followed by internally managed sustainable investing assets, and (as the rather minor category) mandates. The structure has thus changed quite substantially over the last few years as the category of investment funds used to be the second- or even (e.g., in 2014—15) the third-largest. Nonetheless, investment funds have demonstrated the highest rates of growth in terms of assets over the last few years. More detailed information about the current structure of the Swiss sustainable investing industry can be obtained from the report by Swiss Sustainable Finance (2021). The results of the conducted analysis

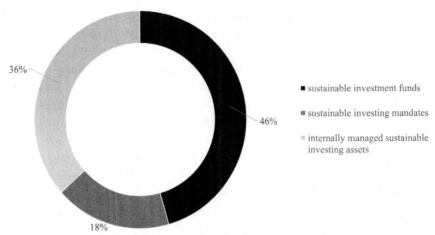

36%

46%

18%

- sustainable investment funds
- sustainable investing mandates
- internally managed sustainable investing assets

Figure 2.2 Structure of the assets of sustainable investing financial products in Switzerland in 2020. *(Source: Own elaboration based on Swiss Sustainable Finance (2021). Swiss Sustainable Investment Market Study 2021.)*

show that in 2020 the leading asset class was equity, followed by sustainable investment strategies with exposure to corporate bonds (both categories jointly accounted for c. 60% of total assets); equity became the largest category in 2019, previously, for example, real estate was the leading group (Swiss Sustainable Finance, 2020). In terms of the specific sustainable investing topics, the climate change ranked first as the engagement strategy and coal as exclusion criterion, respectively. This should be not regarded as surprising as the studies prove that Switzerland is among the global leaders in terms of the sensitivity of the government and citizens toward the issues of climate change (Dopierała et al., 2020).

An interesting and valuable exercise would be a comparison of the size of the various Swiss sustainable investing segments to the value of the global industry. However, due to a lack of consistent data, such comparisons are substantially hindered. Still, some insights can be gained through the examination of the indicators provided by the aforementioned report by the Swiss Sustainable Finance and the global report published by the Global Sustainable Investment Alliance (2021) that utilize to a large extent consistent approaches to the identification of sustainable investments. According to the global data for the beginning of 2020, sustainable investing financial products gathered c. 35 trillion USD of assets (this value does not include the minor financial markets from an international perspective), and in Europe, the respective value was at c. 12 trillion USD (again, this value covers exclusively the major markets). It unequivocally proves that the Swiss sustainable investing sector, with approximately 1.5 trillion USD of assets, can be considered as one of the global leaders in this industry, in particular taking into consideration the size of the Swiss economy. Similar conclusions can be found in the academic literature—for example, Camilleri (2020) stated that Switzerland (together with the Netherlands) is the European leader in terms of impact investing (a category of sustainable investing); such statements can also be found in, for example, Meyer and Hess (2018), Uzsoki (2020). The report by SwissBanking, that is, Swiss Bankers Association, demonstrates the leading position in terms of sustainable finance at large, including banking sector (Swiss Banking, 2020). It also means a substantial push forward as the white paper concerning Swiss sustainable finance published in 2016 showed its underdevelopment, apart from some specialized parts of the financial system (Krauss et al., 2016).

Significant development of the Swiss sustainable investment segment of the financial sector can be traced back to the historical developments as well as certain financial and nonfinancial regulatory and self-regulatory aspects.[5] The regulatory environment was substantially developed in the last few years, in particular starting from 2018 (Swiss Sustainable Finance, 2019b), with many proposals suggested by various entities. There are, though, no comprehensive legal acts concerning sustainable investing which is governed by both cantonal- and country-level regulations. The key role in the law setting and regulatory dimension belongs to the Swiss Federal Council (examples of its actions include adoption in December 2020 a set of measures aimed at increasing financial sector's contribution to sustainable development), State Secretariat for International Finance (review of the Swiss law with regard to, e.g., greenwashing issues), the Federal Office for the Environment (assessment of climate compatibility of the Swiss financial institutions),[6] Financial Market Supervisory Authority (imposing requirement of environmental, social and governance (ESG) information for funds

---

[5] The overview of the past and current regulations draws heavily from Swiss Sustainable Finance (2021).

[6] In November 2020 the Federal Office for the Environment published the results of the first climate compatibility tests of the entire Swiss financial market, conducted on a voluntary basis, aimed at creating transparency and boosting the actions of the financial institutions with regard to climate-related investments (Federal Office for the Environment, 2020). Some of the key conclusions of the report are too high investments into the assets linked to the coal and oil extraction (or, more generally, fossil fuels) as well as a lack of full implementation of the declared climate strategies.

that promote sustainability), and Swiss Parliament (various sustainability-regulated proposed regulations such as "Sustainability in the Swiss financial sector" from June 2020 (Der Bundesrat, 2020)). Swiss authorities support various international initiatives, including the ones focusing on the reporting of sustainability issues such as the call of the Federal Council for all companies to adopt voluntarily the Task Force on Climate-related Financial Disclosures (Federal Department of Swiss Sustainable Finance, 2021).[7]

Despite the lack of requirements for Swiss investment companies (e.g., asset managers, investment funds providers) to publish climate-related risk disclosures similar to banks or insurance companies (Federal Office for the Environment, 2021), they may adhere to even more detailed recommendations concerning the integration of sustainability aspects in the offered investment products and services, issued by the Swiss Funds and Asset Management Association and Swiss Sustainable Finance in June 2020; the self-adoption of the recommendations is linked to the expectations of the clients, in particular institutional (Steiner et al., 2021). The aforementioned document covers, apart from the reporting issues at both product and company level, important methodological aspects as it defines various sustainable investing approaches (Swiss Funds & Asset Management Association & Swiss Sustainable Finance, 2020). There are also similar directives issued by the SIX Swiss Exchange for the companies listed on this exchange. The other self-regulation example is the decision of providers to have their funds reviewed by external entities and inclusion in databases such as yourSRI (Center for Social and Sustainable Products, 2018). Furthermore, there are transparency certificates for investment funds issued by the Forum Nachhaltige Geldanlagen (association of financial companies from the German-speaking countries) which also awards prizes for the best funds in this aspect. In our overview, we skip the regional or global initiatives such Sustainable Development Goals (SDGs) or the Paris Agreement as they are covered in Chapter 3.

The development of the sustainable investing segment of the Swiss financial sector has also been supported by the activity of the organizations and associations of financial companies and other entities linked to the financial sector (e.g., NGOs or universities). The objectives of these organizations are to a lower or higher degree focused on the promotion of

---

[7] For more details on the Task Force on Climate-related Financial Disclosures (TCFD), see Section 3.3.

sustainable investing. This group includes a large group of Swiss institutions and initiatives, among them (the list is by no means exhaustive) Swiss Sustainable Finance, Center for Sustainable Finance and Private Wealth, Center for Corporate Responsibility and Sustainability, Center for Financial Networks and Sustainability, Sustainable Finance Geneva, Forum Nachhaltige Geldanlage, Swiss Finance Institute, Association to Renew Research and Education in Economics and Finance. It includes also the joint initiatives such as Building Bridges Summit or Switzerland for Sustainable Finance (Swiss Sustainable Finance, 2019a) or actions of the associations of financial professionals such as CFA Society Switzerland. Some actions are aimed at specific participants of the Swiss financial system, for instance, client advisors within the private wealth management sector (Swiss Sustainable Finance, 2017). Finally, the development of the Swiss sustainable investing industry is related to the activities of the suppliers of ESG data—there are sustainability rating agencies originated in Switzerland, with Asset4 and Inrate as the most prominent examples (Gibson Brandon et al., 2021).

The Swiss sustainable investing ecosystem is not limited to the above-mentioned regulatory and organizational incentives—on another level, it consists of various educational programs linked to the aspects of sustainable finance as well as the research conducted at the leading academic institutions such as University of Fribourg Environmental Sciences and Humanities Institute (UniFR_ESH Institut), launched in 2019. Moreover, the other contributing trend in Switzerland is the emergence and increasing popularity of active stock ownership, with the growing pressure on the company's management to take into account ESG factors in the decision making (Waeger & Mena, 2019). The further process, yet still at rather early stage, is the development of the green category of the Swiss FinTech sector (Puschmann et al., 2020).

An overview of the Swiss sustainable investing industry would be incomplete without even a brief reference to one of the pioneering Swiss financial institutions in this field—Ethos, established in 1997 by D. Biedermann as an investment foundation for the Swiss pension funds, focused on, among others, promoting active ownership exercised by the investment companies (for a detailed history of Ethos and the effects of its actions, see Waeger and Mena (2019)).

However, not all attempts to boost the sustainable investing sector in Switzerland over the last years have been successful—the example is the rejection of the Federal Act on the Reduction of Greenhouse Gas

Emissions (CO_2 Act) in the referendum in June 2021 (Bundeskanzlei, 2021); one of the elements of the act was the change in financial flows to make them more consistent with the climate aims. The other similar example is the rejection (through the cantons' vote) of the "Responsible companies" initiative in the 2020 referendum; the initiative was aimed at, among others, increasing the obligations of companies with regard to ESG standards. Still, despite its rejection, the counter proposal of the Swiss parliament is expected to enter into force in 2022, including elements such as increased ESG reporting requirements (Oser & Marti, 2021).

The decisions of the Swiss providers of the investment funds are also influenced by the EU–level regulations (even though Switzerland is not an EU member state) as evidenced by the contribution of the introduced EU sustainability-linked disclosure regulations (Sustainable Finance Disclosure Regulation) to the share of Swiss funds which apply sustainability approaches—according to the study by the Swiss Sustainable Finance, in 2020 it exceeded for the first time 50% (Swiss Sustainable Finance, 2021). Consequently, sustainable funds constituted in 2020 the majority of investment funds in Switzerland—for comparison, a year earlier they accounted for slightly less than 40%, which shows a substantial growth rate.

As it was already mentioned, investment funds constitute currently the largest and most rapidly growing segment of the sustainable investing industry in Switzerland. Fig. 2.3 presents the development of their assets since

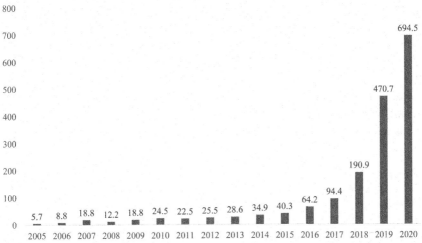

Figure 2.3 Assets of sustainable investing investment funds in Switzerland: 2005–20 (CHF billion). (Source: *Own elaboration based on Swiss Sustainable Finance (2016). Sustainable Investment in Switzerland. Excerpt from the sustainable investment market report 2016. Swiss Sustainable Finance (2021). Swiss sustainable investment market study.)*

2005 (the earliest data available). In 2005, the value of these assets was at merely c. 6 billion CHF and, according to the most recent data for 2020 it reached a value close to 700 billion CHF that representing a more than 100-fold increase over 15 years. Even more strikingly, most of the growth in the assets of sustainable funds can be noted for the period 2015–20, in line with the overall trend in this segment of the Swiss financial system (see Fig. 2.1). Another important conclusion, concerning the early development of the Swiss sustainable investing funds segment, is the lack of unidirectional development observed in the more recent years—in 2008 and 2011 year-to-year declines can be identified (linked to the global financial turmoil in these periods); for comparison, over the next years, no declines took place, even in the light of Covid-19 pandemic in 2020. Thus it may be stated that the sector's growth seems not to be endangered. According to a recent study, the report on the Swiss sustainable investment funds published in November 2021, the growth trend has continued to be strong in 2021, as evidenced by the rapid increases in both the number and assets managed by the funds (Stüttgen & Mattmann, 2021).[8]

In the final part of the section, we focus on the Swiss sustainable investing ETFs. It should be emphasized that, as in the other parts of the book, we follow the classification of ETFs by country based on the location of exchange of fund's primary listing. Therefore, our discussion of the Swiss sustainable investing ETFs takes into account exclusively the funds primary listed on the SIX Swiss Exchange[9]; the inclusion of certain ETFs in the sustainable investing category is based primarily on the classification applied in the Lipper's database (for more detailed methodological discussion concerning this aspect, see Section 3.5 and relevant parts of the subsequent chapters). However, to supplement our discussion within the case study, we also use data on all sustainable investing ETFs listed in Switzerland (regardless whether the SIX Swiss Exchange is their primary listing location or not). It must also be added that data provided in the context of the Swiss ETFs market should not be compared to the previously discussed statistics

---

[8] The report by Stüttgen and Mattmann (2021) provides an in-depth insight into the Swiss sustainable investment funds market, with a detailed analysis of the ESG funds in terms of, for example, exposure. It may be viewed as complementary to our study as we cover above all Swiss sustainable investing ETFs that are not discussed separately in the aforementioned publication.

[9] There are no sustainable investing ETFs primary listed on the second, much smaller Swiss stock exchange BX Swiss; therefore, we omit this exchange in the subsequent discussion.

provided by the Swiss Sustainable Finance—we use the listing location as the classification criteria and the latter was based on the domicile or conducting operations in Switzerland.

According to data as of the end of September 2021, the total net assets of the sustainable investing ETFs primary listed in Switzerland were at approximately 19.41 billion USD, and there were 99 such funds (8 funds were operating in the previous periods yet for various reasons stopped working). The vast majority (c. 70% in terms of assets or their number) were equity funds, the remainder were mostly bond ETFs with exposure to corporate fixed-income securities. Such structure is consistent with the overall sustainable investment assets in Switzerland, as discussed in the preceding paragraphs. The dominant type of sustainable investing ETF in Switzerland is passive funds. The biggest providers are UBS, and (with much weaker position) BlackRock—UBS funds account for c. 90% of all sustainable investing ETFs, regardless of the used measure. Almost all Swiss sustainable investing ETFs were domiciled in Luxembourg or Ireland, with a few funds in France or Switzerland—it is consistent with the situation in most other European ETFs markets, due to legal and tax reasons. The value of the managed assets seems rather small in comparison to the 2020 assets of all Swiss sustainable investment funds—however, the aforementioned methodological differences must be taken into account. Comparison to the size of the other sustainable investing ETFs markets in Europe proves the position of Switzerland as one of the regional leaders in this aspect of the financial system (see the discussion in chapter four).

Table 2.2 presents the leading funds of the Swiss ETFs market in the sustainable investing sector, listed according to the values of their total net assets, in descending order. The assets of the two largest funds exceeded 1 billion USD. Nine out of 10 funds are managed by UBS; the only exception is the single active ETF on the list, managed by JP Morgan Asset Management. Consistently with the overall structure, 9 out of 10 ETFs are equity funds; the ninth place belongs to the single corporate bond ETF. The inception dates of the ETFs show that they are all relatively new (the oldest one was launched in 2015), which corresponds clearly to the quite recent development of this part of the Swiss investment industry. What can be noticed is the similarity of the names of some funds on the list—this is linked to the fact that they are actually different share classes of the same larger funds, hedged to different currencies.

To put the preceding discussion in another perspective, we discuss shortly another indicator. The combined assets of all (almost 400)

Table 2.2 The largest sustainable investing ETFs primary listed in Switzerland (according to the assets under management), September 2021 data.

Name of the fund	Total net assets (bln USD)	Asset class of exposure (Lipper's classification)	Benchmark	Provider	Inception date	Total expense ratio (%)
UBS ETF (LU) MSCI EMU Socially Responsible UCITS ETF (EUR) A-acc	1.30	Equity Eurozone	MSCI EMU SRI Low Carbon Select 5% Issuer Capped Total Return Net	UBS	December 15, 2017	0.23
UBS ETF (IE) MSCI ACWI Socially Responsible UCITS ETF (hedged to USD) A-acc	1.05	Equity Global	MSCI ACWI SRI Low Carbon Select 5% Issuer Capped with Developed Markets 100% hedged to USD Index	UBS	December 20, 2017	0.33
UBS ETF (IE) MSCI ACWI ESG Universal UCITS ETF (hedged to USD) A-acc	0.98	Equity Global	MSCI ACWI ESG Universal Low Carbon Select 5% Issuer Capped with Developed Markets 100% Hedged to USD Index Net	UBS	December 19, 2017	0.33
UBS ETF (IE) MSCI ACWI ESG Universal UCITS ETF (hedged to CHF) A-acc	0.92	Equity Global	MSCI ACWI ESG Universal Low Carbon Select 5% Issuer Capped with Developed Markets 100% Hedged to CHF Index Net	UBS	December 19, 2017	0.33

UBS ETF (IE) S&P 500 ESG UCITS ETF USD A-Acc	0.86	Equity Global	S&P 500 ESG Total Return Net	UBS	April 18, 2019	0.12
UBS ETF (IE) MSCI ACWI ESG Universal UCITS ETF (hedged to EUR) A-acc	0.74	Equity Global	MSCI ACWI ESG Universal Low Carbon Select 5% Issuer Capped with Developed Markets 100% Hedged to EUR Index Net	UBS	December 19, 2017	0.33
UBS ETF (IE) MSCI ACWI Socially Responsible UCITS ETF (hedged to CHF) A-acc	0.42	Equity Global	MSCI ACWI SRI Low Carbon Select 5% Issuer Capped with Developed Markets 100% hedged to CHF Index	UBS	December 20, 2017	0.33
JPMorgan Global Emerging Markets Research Enhanced Index Equity (ESG) UCITS ETF USD (acc)	0.64	Equity Emerging Mkts Global	MSCI Emerging Market Index (Total Return Net) [active fund]	JP Morgan Asset Management	December 6, 2018	0.30
UBS ETF (LU) Bloomberg MSCI US Liquid Corporates Sustainable UCITS ETF (hedged to EUR) A-acc	0.61	Bond USD corporate	Bloomberg MSCI US Liquid Corporates Sustainable Total Return	UBS	September 30, 2015	0.25
UBS ETF (IE) MSCI ACWI Socially Responsible UCITS ETF (hedged to GBP) A-dis	0.55	Equity Global	MSCI ACWI SRI Low Carbon Select 5% Issuer Capped with Developed Markets 100% hedged to GBP Index	UBS	December 20, 2017	0.33

Source: Own elaboration based on Lipper's and justETF databases as well as websites of the funds' providers.

sustainable investing ETFs listed in Switzerland (regardless of their primary listing location) were almost 10 times higher, at c. 146 billion CHF. However, the majority of the largest funds in this approach were funds cross-listed in Switzerland for which this market is just one among many listing locations. For instance, the biggest ETF using this perspective is iShares MSCI USA SRI UCITS ETF USD (Acc), one of the globally largest funds of this category (primary listed in the United Kingdom). The structure in terms of exposure classes or domiciles is similar to the already discussed. However, in terms of the providers, it is much more diversified (UBS is still the leader but not with such an overwhelming advantage over competitors). Comparison of the value of all sustainable investing ETFs listed in Switzerland to the value presented in Fig. 2.3 proves the strong position of ETFs among all investment funds in this class.

It should be emphasized the group of Swiss sustainable investing ETFs undergoes continuing expansion through, for example, the launch of new funds tracking the ESG indexes of the Swiss equity or bond markets, provided by the Six Swiss Exchange (Lord, 2021).

References

Abner, D. (2016). *The ETF handbook. How to value and trade exchange-traded funds* (2nd ed.). John Wiley & Sons.

Agapova, A. (2011). Conventional mutual index funds versus exchange-traded funds. *Journal of Financial Markets, 14,* 323–343.

Agarwal, S., & Chua, Y. H. (2020). FinTech and household finance: A review of the empirical literature. *China Finance Review International, 10*(4), 361–376.

Agarwal, V., Hanouna, P., Moussawi, R., & Stahel, C. (2017). *Do ETFs increase the commonality in liquidity of underlying Stocks.* Fifth Annual Conference on Financial Market Regulation.

Ahn, W., Lee, H. S., Ryou, H., & Oh, K. J. (2020). Asset allocation model for a robo-advisor using the financial market instability index and genetic algorithms. *Sustainability, 12*(3), 849.

Alexander, G. J., & Peterson, M. A. (2020). The pricing of exchange traded funds and the roles of primary and secondary market participants. *Quarterly Journal of Finance, 10*(03).

Amenc, N., Goltz, F., & Le Sourd, V. (2017). *The EDHEC European ETF and Smart beta survey.* EDHEC-Risk Institute.

Anadu, K., Kruttli, M., McCabe, P., & Osambela, E. (2020). The shift from active to passive investing: Risks to financial stability? *Financial Analysts Journal, 76*(4), 23–39.

Ancri, C. (2016). *Fintech innovation: An overview. presentation.* Board of Governors of the Federal Reserve System.

Antoniewicz, R., & Heinrichs, J. (2014). Understanding exchange-traded funds: How ETFs work. *ICI Research Perspective, 20*(5), 1–20.

Aquilina, M., Croxson, K., Valentini, G. G., & Vass, L. (2020). Fixed income ETFs: Primary market participation and resilience of liquidity during periods of stress. *Economics Letters, 193.*

Asongu, S. A., & Moulin, B. (2016). The role of ICT in reducing information asymmetry for financial access. *Research in International Business and Finance, 38*, 202–213.

Bach, P. S. (2021). Robo-advisory: An opportunity for innovation in Sharia-compliant markets. In S. S. Fernández (Ed.), *Islamic Fintech* (pp. 44–51). Routledge.

Baek, S., Lee, K. Y., Uctum, M., & Oh, S. H. (2020). Robo-Advisors: Machine learning in trend-following ETF investments. *Sustainability, 12*(16), 6399.

Baker, H. K., Filbeck, G., & Kiymaz, H. (2016). Mutual funds and related investment vehicles: An overview. In H. K. Baker, G. Filbeck, & H. H. Kiymaz (Eds.), *Mutual funds and exchange-traded funds: Building blocks to wealth* (pp. 3–20). Oxford University Press.

Baker, H. K., Nofsinger, J. R., & Spieler, A. C. (2020). *The Savvy Investor's guide to building wealth through traditional investments.* Emerald Publishing Limited.

Banaji, S., Livingstone, S., Nandi, A., & Stoilova, M. (2018). Instrumentalising the digital: Adolescents' engagement with ICTs in low-and middle-income countries. *Development in Practice, 28*(3), 432–443.

Bello, Z. (2012). The investment performance and tracking errors of small-cap ETFs. *Global Journal of Finance and Banking Issues, 6*(6), 12–20.

Ben-David, I., Franzoni, F. A., & Moussawi, R. (2017). Exchange traded funds. *Annual Review of Financial Economics, 9*, 169–189.

Bhansali, V., & Harris, L. (2018). Everybody's doing it: Short volatility strategies and shadow financial insurers. *Financial Analysts Journal, 74*(2), 12–23.

Bhatia, A., Chandani, A., & Chhateja, J. (2020). Robo advisory and its potential in addressing the behavioral biases of investors—a qualitative study in Indian context. *Journal of Behavioral and Experimental Finance, 25.*

Bhattacharya, A., & O'Hara, M. (2020). *ETFs and systemic risks.* CFA Institute Research Foundation.

Bhojraj, S., Mohanram, P., & Zhang, S. (2020). ETFs and information transfer across firms. *Journal of Accounting and Economics, 70*(2–3).

Blitz, D., & Huij, J. (2012). Evaluating the performance of global emerging markets equity exchange-traded funds. *Emerging Markets Review, 13*, 149–158.

Blocher, J., & Whaley, B. (2016). *Two-sided markets in asset management: Exchange-traded funds and securities lending, 2474904* pp. 1–45). Vanderbilt Owen Graduate School of Management Research Paper.

Bogle, J. C. (2016). The index mutual fund: 40 Years of growth, change, and challenge. *Financial Analysts Journal, 72*(1), 9–13.

Box, T., Davis, R. L., & Fuller, K. P. (2019). ETF competition and market quality. *Financial Management, 48*(3), 873–916.

Box, T., Davis, R., & Fuller, K. (2020). The dynamics of ETF fees. *Financial Analysts Journal, 76*(1), 11–18.

Braun, B. (2016). From performativity to political economy: Index investing, ETFs and asset manager capitalism. *New Political Economy, 21*(3), 257–273.

Broby, D., & Spence, O. (2020). The tracking efficiency of physical and synthetic equity index ETFs. *The Journal of Index Investing, 11*(3), 34–47.

Bundeskanzlei. (2021). *Vorlage Nr. 644 Resultate in den Kantonen.*

Calamia, A., Deville, L., & Riva, F. (2019). Liquidity provision in ETFs markets: The basket and beyond. *Finance, 40*(1), 53–85.

Cameron, R. (2015). *ETFs Exchange Traded Funds: Everything to know about trading exchanges traded funds.* UK: Amazon.

Camilleri, M. A. (2020). The market for socially responsible investing: A review of the developments. *Social Responsibility Journal, 17*(3), 412–428.

Castells, M., Fernandez-Ardevol, M., Qiu, J. L., & Sey, A. (2009). *Mobile communication and society: A global perspective.* MIT Press.

Center for Social and Sustainable Products. (2018). *ESG-Marktbericht Investmentfonds & ETFs — Schweiz*. Ausgabe.

Chang, C.-L., McAleer, M., & Wang, C.-H. (2018). An econometric analysis of ETF and ETF futures in financial and energy markets using generated regressors. *International Journal of Financial Studies, 6*(1).

Charupat, N., & Miu, P. (2013). Recent developments in exchange-traded fund literature: Pricing efficiency, tracking ability, and effects on underlying securities. *Managerial Finance, 39*(5), 427–443.

Chen, L., Liu, K., Wang, Y., & Zhang, H. (2018). A portfolio selection model for robo-advisor. In *2018 5th IEEE international Conference on Cloud Computing and Intelligence Systems (CCIS)* (pp. 693–698). IEEE.

Chien, M. S., Cheng, C. Y., & Kurniawati, M. A. (2020). The non-linear relationship between ICT diffusion and financial development. *Telecommunications Policy, 44*(9).

Chu, P. K. K., & Xu, D. (2021). Tracking errors and their determinants: Evidence from Japan-listed exchange-traded funds. *The Journal of Prediction Markets, 15*(1).

Crigger, L. (September 2017). *How the big three got so big*. ETF Report.

Czaja, D., & Röder, F. (2020). Self-attribution bias and overconfidence among nonprofessional traders. *The Quarterly Review of Economics and Finance, 78*, 186–198.

Dannhauser, C. D. (2017). The impact of innovation: Evidence from corporate bond exchange-traded funds (ETFs). *Journal of Financial Economics, 125*(3), 537–560.

Der Bundesrat. (2020). *Nachhaltigkeit im Finanzsektor Schweiz Eine Auslegeordnung und Positionierung mit Fokus auf Umweltaspekte Bericht des Bundesrates*.

Diltz, J. D., & Rakowski, D. (2018). Mutual fund research: A perspective on how we have arrived at the current state of academic research on mutual funds. *Managerial Finance, 44*(3), 294–302.

Dong, D., Liu, Q., Tao, P., & Ying, Z. (2021). The pricing mechanism between ETF option and spot markets in China. *Journal of Futures Markets, 41*(8), 1286–1300.

Dopierała, Ł., Mosionek-Schweda, M., & Ilczuk, D. (2020). Does the asset allocation policy affect the performance of climate-themed funds? Empirical evidence from the Scandinavian mutual funds market. *Sustainability, 12*(2), 654.

Dorfleitner, G., Hornuf, L., Schmitt, M., & Weber, M. (2017). *FinTech in Germany*. Springer.

Dorfleitner, G., & Scheckenbach, I. (2022). Trading activity on social trading platforms—a behavioral approach. *Journal of Risk Finance, 23*(1), 32–54.

Duffy, J., Rabanal, J. P., & Rud, O. A. (2021). The impact of ETFs in secondary asset markets: Experimental evidence. *Journal of Economic Behavior & Organization, 188*, 674–696.

Ellis, C. D. (1975). The loser's game. *Financial Analysts Journal, 31*(4), 19–26.

Elton, E. J., Gruber, M. J., Comer, G., & Li, K. (2002). Spiders: Where are the bugs? *The Journal of Business, 75*(3), 453–472.

Elton, E. J., Gruber, M. J., & de Souza, A. (2019). Passive mutual funds and ETFs: Performance and comparison. *Journal of Banking & Finance, 106*, 265–275.

EY. (2017). Reshaping around the investor. *Global ETF Research 2017*.

Faloon, M., & Scherer, B. (2017). Individualization of robo-advice. *The Journal of Wealth Management, 20*(1), 30–36.

Fama, E. F. (1965). The behavior of stock-market prices. *The Journal of Business, 38*(1), 34–105.

Fama, E. F. (1970). Efficient capital markets: A review of theory and empirical work. *The Journal of Finance, 25*(2), 383–417.

Farinella, J., & Kubicki, R. (2018). The performance of exchange traded funds and mutual funds. *Journal of Accounting & Finance, 18*(4), 44–55.

Federal Department of Finance. (2021). *Switzerland promotes transparency on climate-related financial risks.*

Federal Office for the Environment. (2020). *Climate benchmarking in the Swiss financial market.*

Federal Office for the Environment. (2021). *Regulatory work on sustainability in the financial market.*

Ferré, I. (2021). *The rise of social trading: How the internet is changing investing.* https://finance.yahoo.com/news/the-rise-of-social-trading-how-the-internet-is-changing-investing-153643100.html (Retrieved 3 November 2021).

Ferri, R. A. (2009). *The ETF book: All you need to know about exchange-traded funds* (Updated ed.). John Wiley & Sons.

Foucher, I., & Gray, K. (December 2014). *Exchange-traded funds: Evolution of benefits, vulnerabilities and risks.* Bank of Canada Financial System Review.

Gastineau, G. L. (2010). *The exchange-traded funds manual* (2nd ed.). John Wiley & Sons.

Gemayel, R., & Preda, A. (2018). Does a scopic regime erode the disposition effect? Evidence from a social trading platform. *Journal of Economic Behavior & Organization, 154,* 175—190.

Gibson Brandon, R., Krueger, P., & Schmidt, P. S. (2021). ESG rating disagreement and stock returns. *Financial Analysts Journal, 77*(4), 104—127.

Global Sustainable Investment Alliance. (2021). *Global sustainable investment review 2021.*

Guedj, I., & Huang, J. (2009). Are ETFs replacing index mutual funds. In *19th Annual conference on financial economics and accounting [working paper].* American Finance Association annual meeting.

Hill, J. M. (2016). The evolution and success of index strategies in ETFs. *Financial Analysts Journal, 72*(5), 8—13.

Hill, J. M., Nadig, D., & Hougan, M. (2015). *A comprehensive guide to exchange-traded funds (ETFs).* CFA Institute Research Foundation.

Holden, C., & Nam, J. (2019). *Market accessibility, corporate bond ETFs, and liquidity.* Kelley School of Business Research Paper.

Hull, I. (2016). The development and spread of financial innovations. *Quantitative Economics, 7*(2), 613—636.

Investment Company Institute. (2021). *Investment company fact book 2021.*

Israeli, D., Lee, C. M. C., & Sridharan, S. A. (2017). Is there a dark side to exchange traded funds? An information perspective. *Review of Accounting Studies, 22*(3), 1048—1083.

Ji, M. (2017). Are robots good fiduciaries? Regulating robo-advisors under the investment advisers act of 1940. *Columbia Law Review, 117*(6), 1543—1583.

Jurich, S. N. (2021). Does off-exchange trading decrease in the presence of uncertainty? *The Quarterly Review of Economics and Finance, 81,* 201—213.

Kim, S. D., Cotwright, M., & Chatterjee, S. (2019). Who are robo-advisor users? *Journal of Finance Issues, 18*(2), 33—50.

Koshoev, A. (2018). Synthetic versus physical exchange traded funds. Spillover and asymmetric-volatility effects. *Journal of Advanced Studies in Finance (JASF), 9*(17), 15—23.

Krause, T., & Tse, Y. (2013). Volatility and return spillovers in Canadian and US industry ETFs. *International Review of Economics & Finance, 25,* 244—259.

Krauss, A., Krüger, P., & Meyer, J. (2016). *Sustainable finance in Switzerland: Where do we stand?* Swiss Finance Institute White Paper.

Kumar, R. (2021). Active vs. Smart beta ETFs: Two sides of active management. *The Journal of Index Investing, 11*(4—1), 25—40.

La Monica, P. R. (2021). *The first bitcoin ETF finally begins trading.* https://edition.cnn.com/2021/10/19/investing/bitcoin-etf-proshares-bito/index.html. Retrieved 13 November 2021.

Lee, W. (2017). ETF risk management. *Journal of the Korean Data and Information Science Society, 28*(4), 843—851.

Lee, J. (2019). New revolution in fund management: ETF/Index design by machines. *Global Economic Review, 48*(3), 261–272.

Lee, W., & Ma, Q. (2018). Discovering expert traders on social trading services. *Journal of Advanced Computational Intelligence and Intelligent Informatics, 22*(2), 224–235.

Lettau, M., & Madhavan, A. (2018). Exchange-traded funds 101 for economists. *Journal of Economic Perspectives, 32*(1), 135–154.

Liebi, L. J. (2020). The effect of ETFs on financial markets: A literature review. *Financial Markets and Portfolio Management, 34*(2), 165–178.

Lintner, J. (1965). The valuation of risk assets and the selection of risky investments in stock portfolios and capital budgets. *Review of Economics and Statistics, 47*, 13–37.

Lintner, J. (1969). The aggregation of investors' diverse judgements and preferences in purely competitive markets. *Journal of Financial and Quantitative Analysis, 4*, 346–382.

Lord, J. (2021). *UBS launches SPI ESG ETF.* https://www.etfstrategy.com/ubs-launches-spi-esg-etf-sustainable-ethic. Retrieved 18 November 2021.

Madhavan, A. N. (2016). *Exchange-traded funds and the new dynamics of investing.* Oxford University Press.

Madhavan, A. N., & Sobczyk, A. (2016). Price dynamics and liquidity of exchange-traded funds. *Journal of Investment Management, 14*(2), 1–17.

Malkiel, B. G. (2016). *A Random Walk down Wall Street: The Time-tested Strategy for Successful Investing.* W.W. Norton & Company.

Markowitz, H. (1952). Portfolio selection. *The Journal of Finance, 7*(1), 77–91.

Markowitz, H. (1959). *Portfolio selection: Efficient diversification of investments.* Yale University Press.

Marszk, A. (2017). Structure of the US investment company industry over the period 2000 to 2017: Substitution analysis. *Zarzędzanie i Finanse, 15*, 157–174.

Marszk, A., & Lechman, E. (2018). Tracing financial innovation diffusion and substitution trajectories. Recent evidence on exchange-traded funds in Japan and South Korea. *Technological Forecasting and Social Change, 133*, 51–71.

Marszk, A., & Lechman, E. (2019a). *Exchange-traded funds in Europe.* Academic Press.

Marszk, A., & Lechman, E. (2019b). New technologies and diffusion of innovative financial products: Evidence on exchange-traded funds in selected emerging and developed economies. *Journal of Macroeconomics, 62.*

Marszk, A., Lechman, E., & Kato, Y. (2019). *The emergence of ETFs in Asia-Pacific.* Springer.

Marszk, A., Lechman, E., & Kaur, H. (2017). Financial markets diffusion patterns. The case of Mexican investment funds. *Equilibrium. Quarterly Journal of Economics and Economic Policy, 12*(1), 83–100.

Mateus, C., Mateus, I. B., & Soggiu, M. (2020). Do smart beta ETFs deliver persistent performance? *Journal of Asset Management, 21*(5), 413–427.

Mateus, C., & Rahmani, Y. (2017). Physical versus synthetic exchange traded funds. Which one replicates better? *Journal of Mathematical Finance, 7*(04), 975–989.

Maurer, F., & Williams, S. O. (2015). Physically versus synthetically replicated trackers. Is there a difference in terms of risk? *Journal of Applied Business Research, 31*(1), 131–146.

Meinhardt, C., Mueller, S., & Schoene, S. (2015). Physical and synthetic exchange-traded funds: The good, the bad, or the ugly? *The Journal of Investing, 24*(2), 35–44.

Meyer, J., & Hess, K. (2018). Investments for development in Switzerland: A sub-type of impact investing with strong growth dynamics. In K. Wendt (Ed.), *Positive impact investing* (pp. 177–195). Cham: Springer.

Meziani, A. S. (2016). *Exchange-traded funds: Investment practices and tactical approaches.* Palgrave Macmillan.

Miller, G. S., & Skinner, D. J. (2015). The evolving disclosure landscape: How changes in technology, the media, and capital markets are affecting disclosure. *Journal of Accounting Research, 53*(2), 221–239.

Mossin, J. (1966). Equilibrium in a capital asset market. *Econometrica, 35*, 768—783.

Nikbakht, F., Pareti, K., & Spieler, A. C. (2016). Exchange-traded funds. In H. K. Baker, G. Filbeck, & H. Kiymaz (Eds.), *Mutual funds and exchange-traded funds: Building blocks to wealth* (pp. 153—168). Oxford University Press.

Oehler, A., Horn, M., & Wendt, S. (2016). Benefits from social trading? Empirical evidence for certificates on wikifolios. *International Review of Financial Analysis, 46*, 202—210.

Oser, D., & Marti, M. (2021). ESG reporting and due diligence obligations introduced in Switzerland. *International Financial Law Review.*

Pagano, M., Sánchez Serrano, A., & Zechner, J. (2019). Can ETFs contribute to systemic risk? *Reports of the Advisory Scientific Committee, 9.*

Pan, K., & Zeng, Y. (2017). *ETF arbitrage under liquidity mismatch. 59.* ESRB Working Paper Series.

Park, Y. K., Jung, H. J., & Choi, H. S. (2014). Index funds and Exchange traded funds; Substitutability and reasons for the coexistence. *International Information Institute (Tokyo). Information, 17*(10(B)), 5109—5114.

Pelster, M., & Breitmayer, B. (2019). Attracting attention from peers: Excitement in social trading. *Journal of Economic Behavior & Organization, 161*, 158—179.

Pessina, C. J., & Whaley, R. E. (2021). Levered and inverse exchange-traded products: Blessing or curse? *Financial Analysts Journal, 77*(1), 10—29.

Phoon, K., & Koh, F. (2018). Robo-advisors and wealth management. *The Journal of Alternative Investments, 20*(3), 79—94.

Piccotti, L. R. (2018). ETF premiums and liquidity segmentation. *Financial Review, 53*, 117—152.

Puschmann, T., Hoffmann, C. H., & Khmarskyi, V. (2020). How green FinTech can alleviate the impact of climate change—the case of Switzerland. *Sustainability, 12*(24).

Reith, M., Fischer, M., & Lis, B. (2020). Explaining the intention to use social trading platforms: an empirical investigation. *Journal of Business Economics, 90*(3), 427—460.

Röder, F., & Walter, A. (2019). What drives investment flows into social trading portfolios? *Journal of Financial Research, 42*(2), 383—411.

Samuelson, P. A. (1974). Challenge to judgment. *The Journal of Portfolio Management, 1*(1), 17—19.

Shanmuganathan, M. (2020). Behavioural finance in an era of artificial intelligence: Longitudinal case study of robo-advisors in investment decisions. *Journal of Behavioral and Experimental Finance, 27.*

Shapiro, C., & Varian, H. R. (1998). *Information rules: A strategic guide to the network economy.* Harvard Business School Press.

Sharpe, W. (1964). Capital asset prices: A theory of market equilibrium under conditions of risk. *The Journal of Finance, 19*(3), 425—442.

Sherrill, D. E., & Upton, K. (2018). Actively managed ETFs vs actively managed mutual funds. *Managerial Finance, 44*(3), 303—325.

Singhvi, S. (2021). Understanding the emerging role and importance of robo-advisory: A case study approach. In *Fourth Industrial revolution and business dynamics* (pp. 37—51). Singapore: Palgrave Macmillan.

Sironi, P. (2016). *FinTech Innovation: From robo-advisors to goal based investing and gamification.* Wiley.

Stankevičienė, J., & Petronienė, I. (2019). Bond mutual funds vs. Bond exchange traded funds: Evaluation of risk adjusted performance. *Administrative Sciences, 9*(2), 31.

Steiner, J., Ferro, M., & Widmer, O. (2021). ESG developments and the impact on financial institutions in Switzerland. *International Financial Law Review.*

Stüttgen, M., & Mattmann, B. (2021). *IFZ Sustainable Investments Studie 2021: Nachhaltige Fonds und Klimarisiken.* Institut für Finanzdienstleistungen Zug IFZ.

Swiss Funds & Asset Management Association, & Swiss Sustainable Finance. (2020). *Sustainable asset Management: Key messages and recommendations of SFAMA and SSF.*

Swiss Sustainable Finance. (2016). *Sustainable Investment in Switzerland. Excerpt from the sustainable investment market report 2016.*

Swiss Sustainable Finance. (2017). *Sustainable investing: A unique opportunity for Swiss Private wealth Management. Ten arguments and practical tools for client advisors.*

Swiss Sustainable Finance. (2019a). *Transforming finance for a better world.*

Swiss Sustainable Finance. (2019b). *Swiss Sustainable Investment Market Study 2019.*

Swiss Sustainable Finance. (2020). *Swiss Sustainable Investment Market Study 2020.*

Swiss Sustainable Finance. (2021). *Swiss Sustainable Investment Market Study 2021.*

Swiss Banking. (2020). *Sustainable finance in Switzerland: From pioneer to a premier international hub.*

Tan, G. K. S. (2020). Robo-advisors and the financialization of lay investors. *Geoforum, 117,* 46–60.

Thomadakis, A. (2018). *The European ETFs market: What can be done better?* Centre for European Policy Studies.

Todorov, K. (2021). *The anatomy of bond ETF arbitrage.* BIS Quarterly Review.

Uzsoki, D. (2020). *Sustainable investing: Shaping the future of finance.* International Institute for Sustainable Development.

Waeger, D., & Mena, S. (2019). Activists as moral entrepreneurs: How shareholder activists brought active ownership to Switzerland. *Research in the Sociology of Organizations, 63,* 167–186.

Wang, J., Kang, H., Xia, F., & Li, G. (2018). Examining the equilibrium relationship between the Shanghai 50 stock index futures and the Shanghai 50 ETF options markets. *Emerging Markets Finance and Trade, 54*(11), 2557–2576.

Wiandt, J., & McClatchy, W. (2002). *Exchange traded funds.* John Wiley & Sons.

Wohlgemuth, V., Berger, E. S., & Wenzel, M. (2016). More than just financial performance: Trusting investors in social trading. *Journal of Business Research, 69*(11), 4970–4974.

Zawadzki, K. (2020). The performance of ETFs on developed and emerging markets with consideration of regional diversity. *Quantitative Finance and Economics, 4*(3), 515–525.

CHAPTER 3

Sustainable investing—main concepts. Sustainable investing ETFs: methodological and theoretical background

3.1 Terminology and historical background

The first issue that needs to be deliberated as the introduction to the further discussion of sustainable investing (or sustainable investment—both names will be used interchangeably) is the clarification of the concept, necessary to provide the theoretical background. We present and compare some of the most popular definitions (our selection is by no means exhaustive), showing their rather high level of homogeneity, allowing for the formulation of the definition that will be applied throughout the remainder of the book. After the overview of the terminological issues, we present a synopsis of the history of sustainable investing, adopting a global perspective and showing their development in various regions; we focus on the milestones from the last few decades, even though, as we show, the roots of sustainable investing can be traced at least a few centuries back.

3.1.1 Sustainable investing: definitions

Before the discussion of the various conceptualizations of sustainable investing (investment), it is necessary to underline that it is not the only term used to denote this category of financial products and services; there are multiple labels utilized by the financial professionals and, to a lesser extent, researchers. However, the closer analysis shows that some of the terms used only partially overlap with sustainable investing concept whereas the others are essentially the names of various subcategories of the broad category of sustainable investing—therefore, we discuss the latter in more

Sustainable Investing
ISBN 978-0-12-823871-4
https://doi.org/10.1016/B978-0-12-823871-4.00008-8

detail in the subsequent section. The terms at least to some degree syn-onymous to sustainable investing are mentioned below.

The discussion of the definitions and explanations of the sustainable investing needs to be preceded by an important stipulation—even though, as it will be shown below, the definitions of sustainable investing are similar, this does not necessarily mean that unambiguous identification of such financial products and services is easy or even possible: the problem is the difficulty to clearly define "sustainability," as noticed in the report by Eurosif (Eurosif, 2018).[1] However, the in-depth discussion of this issue lies outside the scope of this book—we will, though, address its selected di-mensions in multiple subsequent parts of the book, in particular with regard to the methodological aspects (in this chapter) and the impact of sustainable investing (in Chapter 5).

The most broadly used and most frequently referred to definitions of sustainable investing can be found in the reports and other documents published by the organizations which regard promoting the issues of sus-tainable investing as their main or at least important goal. These definitions may also be perceived as the most influential due to their adoption by the financial companies that manage sustainable investing financial products. However, it needs to be emphasized that to a large extent the denotations applied by the financial companies are a result of self-identification ap-proaches based on the selected (and not always disclosed) criteria. This problem may be resolved in the course of the implementation of the country- or region-wide regulations, including the unambiguous taxon-omies and linked limitations imposed on the terminology used (see the relevant sections of this chapter).

Global Sustainable Investment Alliance, that is, an organization facili-tating the cooperation of various entities promoting sustainable investing, defined in its annual report (the most comprehensive presentation of the global market) sustainable investment as "an investment approach that considers environmental, social and governance (ESG) factors in portfolio selection and management" (Global Sustainable Investment Alliance [GSIA], 2021, p. 7); moreover, GSIA considered "responsible investment"

---

[1] To make it even more complicated, there are also other, to some extent competing, similar concepts applied in certain contexts such as "sustainable consumption corridors" (Di Gulio, 2019; Di Giulio & Fuchs, 2016).

and "socially responsible investment" as synonyms for sustainable investment (albeit with possible regional differences in the applications of these terms).[2] Very similar in-kind, yet more detailed, definition was used by the Eurosif (2018, p. 12), the partnership of the European national forums for sustainable investment. In its two-part definition Eurosif explained it as, first, "a long-term oriented investment approach which integrates ESG factors in the research, analysis and selection process of securities within an investment portfolio," and, second stated its execution and effects as combining "fundamental analysis and engagement with an evaluation of ESG factors in order to better capture long term returns for investors, and to benefit society by influencing the behavior of companies." The third key definition is the one suggested in the influential reports by the Swiss Sustainable Finance (SSF) and cooperating organizations that stated that sustainable investment can be understood as "any investment approach integrating ESG factors into the selection and management of investments" (Swiss Sustainable Finance [SSF], 2017, p. 182; SSF, 2021, p. 75); SSF regards responsible investment as analogous to sustainable investment.

Definitions suggested in the academic literature are to a large extent comparable to the aforementioned presented in the reports by financial organizations—consequently, we present merely a few definitions. For instance, Busch et al. (2016) explained sustainable investments as investments that take into account ESG factors in the investment decisions. Puaschunder (2016) defined socially responsible investment as an approach that considers both maximizations of profits and social aims. Kölbel et al. (2020) clarified sustainable investment as investments that consider ESG information. In one of the early studies on sustainable investing, Paetzold and Busch (2014) defined it by dividing into two forms: first being focus on or exclusion of certain industries, and, second, in line with the more recent view as integrating ESG factors into investment decisions. Hawley (2016) explained responsible investment as behaviors and investment strategies incorporating at least to some extent the ESG factors (the ones being material in a certain context) or investments based on various moral, political or religious belief systems.

Based on the overview of the definitions of sustainable investment presented in the preceding paragraphs, it is possible to list its key attribute that will serve as our understanding of the concept in the remainder of the

---

[2] For more on the topic of responsibility in the economic and financial context see, for example, Lucas (1993).

book. The fundamental feature of **sustainable investing (investment)** can thus be defined as **taking into consideration ESG factors in the investment decisions including but not limited to the selection of securities (or other assets), portfolio management and any associated research.** This definition clearly underlines the crucial role of the umbrella factors known as ESG in sustainable investing strategies, thus the issue of ESG should be clarified before further discussion. ESG consists of the following elements (the list of issues taken into account is not exhaustive—only the most important and common elements are mentioned) (Baier et al., 2020; Boerner, 2007; Ezeokoli et al., 2017; Inderst & Stewart, 2018; Kofman & Payne, 2017; Matos, 2020; Whitelock, 2019):

- E—environmental: climate change, air pollution, carbon emissions, water pollution, environmental management, environmental standards, pollution control, waste and recycling, biodiversity management;
- S—social: human rights, labor standards, diversity policies, employee engagement, gender policies, public health, product safety, community relations, supply chain labor standards;
- G—governance: audit and control, whistle-blowing system, board composition, board independence, executive compensation, corruption policies, business ethics, stakeholder engagement, responsible marketing.

Consequently, in the remainder of the book, we use the terms "ESG investing" or, later, "ESG ETFs" as synonyms for the labels such as "sustainable investing (investment)." Possibility to use it as synonymous term applies also to "(socially) responsible investing," in line with the aforementioned approaches adopted by the leading organizations; nonetheless, as we show in the historical overview it is an older and to some extent different concept—therefore we will not use it interchangeably with sustainable investing. Similar stipulation applies to "ethical investing" [3]—as explained by Silvola and Landau (2021), ethical and sustainable investing are to some extent different concepts: the former can be understood as investments with potentially lower expected returns than conventional ones albeit consistent with the investor's values whereas the latter (in line with

---

[3] "Ethical investing," "ethical funds" or "ethical finance" should not be mistaken with "ethics of finance" (or financial markets) that deals with analysis of the actions of participants of the financial system from the ethical perspective (see, among others, Baquero-Herrera, 2021; Bhala, 2019; Bonvin & Dembinski, 2002; Dembinski, 2017; Ferrero et al., 2021; Foo, 2019; Hendry, 2013; O'Hara, 2016; Scalzo, 2019).

the previously discussed definitions) as taking ESG factors into consideration in investing decisions.

To continue the terminological discussion, it should be added that even though the ESG (sustainable investing) approach with regard to the terminology has undoubtedly become the most popular and used among academics and professionals, there were some earlier similar attempts. For example, in another approach, suggested several years ago by Bonini and Emerson (2005), before the advent of the current ESG framework, the suggested strategy of a company is to create "blended value," that is, a blend of economic, social, and environmental value; the blended value can be maximized by focusing jointly on five aspects: CSR, sustainable development, social investing, social enterprise, and strategic/effective philanthropy.

It should also be added that sustainable investing is a part of **sustainable finance**, that is, a broader category within the financial system, defined by SSF (2020) as various types of financial services that take into consideration the ESG criteria while making business or investment decisions, with the aim of achieving the lasting benefit not only for their clients but also society at large; it includes subcategories such as ESG in asset management, green bonds, impact investing, active ownership or lending taking into account the ESG risk factors. In a comprehensive definition, Migliorelli (2021) explained sustainability "as finance to support sectors or activities that contribute to the achievement of, or the improvement in, at least one of the relevant sustainability dimensions" (p. 2).

Another term frequently used to denote certain elements within the sustainable finance category is "green finance"; "climate finance" is a similar term (Bracking, 2015; Vanderheiden, 2015). As noted by Zhang et al. (2019), both terms remain vaguely defined and they are frequently mixed. Still, the former may be explained as an investment aimed at achieving positive environmental effects and the latter as a subset of the green finance linked to activities mitigating climate changes and their consequences. Moreover, a much less recognized term, "blue finance," refers as, defined by Shiiba et al. (2022), to financial investments or instruments that contribute to the conservation of the ocean environment and related resources (or boost the blue economy).

As our book has a more empirical rather than theoretical focus, we do not continue the complicated and frequently ambiguous theoretical discussion of the various concepts—for in-depth and up-to-date review see, for example, Migliorelli (2021); for a more historical perspective (i.e., at the beginning of the current century), see Dunfee (2003) or Sandberg et al. (2009) (for the late 2000s) and for the extensive overview of the changing attitude toward ESG issues in the mainstream finance see the article by Starks (2021). However, there is one important issue that we need to emphasize, in particular in the context of the methodological discussion (see Section 3.6) and further empirical study. Even though the definition of sustainable investing is quite clear, it does not take into account one fundamental issue, that is, whether the fact these investments take into consideration ESG factors does actually mean that they contribute in any substantial and measurable way to the process of sustainable development (in any dimension). Only fulfilling the aforementioned aim should lead to labeling certain financial products or services as being "sustainable" (or "socially responsible," etc. if we use the synonymous terms). Nonetheless, in the practice of the academic studies or in the applicatory perspective such assessment and justified use of the sustainable investing term is hindered by a large number of factors such as the problems with identification of the possibly affected sectors of the economy or society, also in the international perspective. We aim to address this issue and thus provide some insights into the actual sustainability of the studied investment funds by conducting the empirical study whose results are presented in Chapter 5. The issue covered in this paragraph is complemented by the discussion of the issues such as greenwashing in Section 3.5.

3.1.2 History of sustainable investing: summary

In spite of the fact that sustainable investing has attracted substantial attention from the investment community in the last several years, its history is much longer. In the longest perspective, its roots can be traced back to various religious- and faith-linked investments, including the ones aligned with the Jewish faith system (dating back even a few thousand years ago) or the Religious Society of Friends (Quakers) as well as Methodist Church (more recent yet both still dating back to the 18th century) (Busch, Bruce-Clark et al., 2021; Camilleri, 2017; Hawley, 2016; Lewis & Kaleem, 2019). Apart from the investing approaches linked to religious principles (Berry, 2016), the historical background of the contemporary sustainable investing can be identified in the various movements (above all in the United States) in the second half of the 20th century such as the ones focused on the environmental or civil rights (Schueth, 2003; Townsend, 2020), in particular the activist movements of the 1960s and 1970s. These movements consisted of, among others, the boycott of certain companies or shareholders' actions undertaken in an attempt to limit the actions of corporations, in some ways preceding certain types of modern sustainable investing as presented in Table 3.1. The boycotts were conducted also against certain countries such as South Africa and included the limitation or withdrawal of investment from such economies; another factor was the pressure of the trade unions on the pension stocks (Busch, Bruce-Clark et al., 2021; Child, 2015; Hawley, 2016; Paul & Aquila, 1988). Similar processes could be observed in the other regions, for example, in Scandinavia, which remains one of the global sustainable investment leaders (for the history of the Scandinavian sustainable investing see Bengtsson, 2008).

An important, more recent step in the development of sustainable investing was the introduction and increased prominence of socially responsible investing (SRI) in the 1980s and 1990s (Statman, 2000; Townsend, 2020). In comparison to sustainable investing, SRI has been (and partially still is—see the next comment) to a higher extent focused on applying exclusion criteria and negative screens. According to Townsend (2020), SRI can be perceived as the traditional, US model whereas ESG investing is more common in the European markets; one of the milestones in the development of the US SRI model was the establishment of the Forum for Sustainable and Responsible Investment (US SIF Forum) (CFA Institute, 2020; Morningstar, 2020). The next and to a high degree accompanying process to the emergence of SRI was the growing interest in CSR, initially and still predominantly in the form of self-regulation of the large companies from the developed economies. The basic idea behind CSR is the assumption that companies should take into account in their actions the positive impact on the society (Gomes, 2019); in another explanation, CSR can be understood as the requirement for a company to combine economic and social responsibilities (Giles, 2015). In the CSR framework, the firm's social responsibilities are distinguished from economic responsibilities; with the former linked to the nonmarket dimension of its activity (Gomes, 2019).

The report by CFA Institute (2020) divided the history of sustainable investing into three stages:

1. beginnings (up to 2006): investment industry focused above all on the governance issues;
2. developing (2006—19): initiated by the launch of the UN Principles for Responsible Investment (PRI) in 2006—investment industry began taking ESG issues into consideration;

Table 3.1 Key sustainable investing approaches.

Category	Description
ESG integration	Inclusion of ESG factors (risks and opportunities) in financial analysis of potential investments in an explicit and systematic manner.
Negative/exclusionary screening	Exclusion from the investment portfolio the assets (in terms of companies, sectors, countries, etc.) due to their activities being assessed as controversial or unacceptable.
Corporate engagement and shareholder action/ESG engagement and ESG voting	Investments aimed at influencing the behavior of corporations within the shareholders' activism.
Norms-based screening	Screening (selection) of investments against minimum standards of business (issuer) practices, by referring to broadly accepted international norms.
Sustainability themed/thematic investing	Investments in themes or assets that contribute to some particular aspects of sustainable development.
Best-in-class/positive screening	Focus on the relative terms: sectors, companies, or projects selected based on their relatively more positive ESG results than their peers.
IImpact and community investing	Impact investing: investments aimed at reaching a measurable, positive social and environmental impact alongside a financial return. Community investing: broader type than impact investing (impact investing is a type of community investing).

Source: own elaboration based on Barber, B. M., Morse, A., & Yasuda, A. (2021). Impact investing. Journal of Financial Economics, 139(1), 162–185, Caseau, C., & Grolleau, G. (2020). Impact investing: Killing two birds with one stone? Financial Analysts Journal, 76(4), 40–52, Eurosif. (2018). European SRI study 2018, Ezeokoli, O., Layne, C., Statman, M., & Urdapilleta, O. (2017). Environmental, social, and governance (ESG) investment tools: A review of the current field. Summit Consulting, LLC, Gabriel, K. (2019). Verantwortlich Investierende. Motive, Massstäbe und Handlungsoptionen von Kapitalanlegern. In M. Stüttgen (Ed.), Ethik von Banken und Finanzen (pp. 57–75). Nomos Verlag, Global Sustainable Investment Alliance. (2021). Global sustainable investment review 2020, Kofman, P., & Payne, C. (2017). A matter of trust: The practice of ethics in finance. Melbourne University Press, Krosinsky, C. (2017). The seven tribes of sustainable investing. In C. Krosinsky, & S. Purdom (Eds.), Sustainable investing: Revolutions in theory and practice (pp. 7–10). Routledge, Silvola, H., & Landau, T. (2021). Sustainable investing: Beating the market with ESG. Palgrave Macmillan, Swiss Sustainable Finance. (2020). Swiss sustainable investment market study 2020, Swiss Sustainable Finance. (2021). Swiss sustainable investment market study 2021, Vartiak, L. (2017). Global sustainable and responsible investment activities and strategies of companies. New Trends and Issues Proceedings on Humanities and Social Sciences, 4, 77–87, Vinueza-Peter, L. (2020). How far is the sustainable fund market in Europe?. On the Competitive Position of the German Asset Management Industry. BVI Bundesverband Investment und Asset Management, Zagst, R., Krimm, T., Hörter, S., & Menzinger, B. (2011). Responsible investing: Verantwortlich investieren. FinanzBuch Verlag.

3. mainstreaming (2019–): ESG investing becomes mainstream in the investment industry due to the new regulations and the impact of Covid-19 pandemic.

According to Desmartin (2016), five stages can be identified: ethical funds in the 1920s, engagement of shareholders in the 1960s, social and environmental focus in the 1980s, first funds focused on the sustainable development in the 1990s, and, finally, sustainable investing becoming part of the mainstream finance, with the broad integration of ESG aspects and development of the international initiatives (in the first decade of the 21st century).

As we focus in the book on the investment funds, in particular sustainable investing ETFs, it is important to mention that the first sustainable investing mutual fund was started in 1971 by Pax World (in line with the roots of the sustainable investing it was founded by two antiwar ministers (Child, 2015)),[4] and 1990 marked the introduction of the pioneering capitalization-weighted index covering sustainable investments, known most recently as MSCI KLD 400 Social Index (CFA Institute, 2020).

The changing attitudes toward what is currently known as sustainable investing can also be identified with regard to the scope of financial products and services included in this category. Initially, sustainable investing was possible exclusively through the financial products available privately, to a narrow group of investors,—this changed, for example, with the launch of the first sustainable mutual funds.

The increasing inclusion of sustainable investing in the mainstream financial industry has resulted in some reservations concerning their actual impact and potentially too strong focus on the financial aspects that should by assumption be supplementary or secondary—as Child (2015) noticed, in the past entities involved in the sustainable investments (or in the preceding investments), in particular in terms of their establishment and sale, were mostly motivated by the underlying ethical causes whereas more recently it has become to a higher extent a value-seeking decision; the linked process has been the emergence of the types of ESG investing other than the most "strict" such as exclusion (Woods & Urwin, 2010), more relaxed in terms of ethical principles including, for example, ESG integration. However, from the other perspective, Krosinsky et al. (2012) claimed that the long-

---

[4] In other sources, Pioneer Fund (launched in 1928 in Boston) was identified as the first ethically inspired fund (López Ortega, 2019).

term outcome of the rising popularity of sustainable investing should be replacing the mainstream investments rather than resembling them.

3.2 Categories of sustainable investing

After presenting an overview of the key attributes of sustainable investing, in this section, we outline its key categories. It should be stressed though, that we do not present in this section the specific financial instruments that can be used as sustainable investing tools (it is the subject of Section 3.4) but rather the approaches that can be implemented in various financial products and services.

According to GSIA (2021), there are seven main types of sustainable investments: ESG integration, corporate engagement and shareholder action, norms-based screening, negative/exclusionary screening, best-in-class/positive screening, sustainability themed/thematic investing, and impact investing and community investing. Highly similar categories (with slightly different names) are used by Eurosif (2018). The list of sustainable investing approaches in the reports published by SSF (2020, 2021) is somewhat different. It consists of eight elements: six almost identical to the abovementioned—best-in-class, ESG integration, exclusions, impact investing, norms-based screening, sustainable thematic investing and two different—ESG engagement and ESG voting; the latter may, though, be considered as two parts of corporate engagement and shareholder action. Table 3.1. includes a brief presentation of the aforementioned approaches, followed by a more in-depth discussion in the subsequent paragraphs; the approaches are listed in descending order in terms of the global assets managed within these strategies according to 2020 data presented in GSIA (2021).

The first among the approaches listed in Table 3.1, ESG integration is globally the most frequently utilized approach with regard to sustainable investing (GSIA, 2021; Kotsantonis et al., 2016). One of the apparent reasons for the relative popularity of this strategy is its rather general nature and thus the possibility to apply it among many asset classes and specific financial instruments and services (Kaiser, 2020). More specific types of ESG integration strategies include systemic inclusion or consideration of ESG in the financial models (the most frequent subcategory), systemic use of ESG information in the portfolio construction, tracking of the index based on ESG integration criteria (strategy utilized by the passive funds, both ETFs and mutual funds), and use of ESG integration indices as the benchmark in active management (highly infrequent type of approach) (SSF, 2021).

The second type of sustainable investing strategy, that is, negative/exclusionary screening, can also be considered the oldest approach within the contemporary ethically linked investing, as discussed in the preceding section, with the financial products and services based on faith-linked exclusion decisions as the historically first launched. The exact choice of the categories of assets or specific assets excluded has evolved in line with the changing groups of the users of this investment approach as well as changes in the societal attitudes toward certain actions, companies, places, issues, etc (Matteini, 2018). The extremely broad diversity of this category is reflected in the exclusion criteria applied to eliminate certain assets, based on some values or norms, excluding, among others, certain product categories (frequent examples are tobacco, coal, oil, or weapons), companies exhibiting certain practices (such as bribery, corruption, violation of human or labor rights, animal testing, pornography). In the last several years, the exclusions linked to climate change mitigation have become the most frequently applied yet also some new types of negative lens seem to emerge such as excluding securities of companies with the low ESG scores (SSF, 2021). In the other dimension, in terms of country-level exclusions, the negative screenings applied based on the international sanctions (e.g., imposed by the UN), should not be regarded as part of the ESG strategies as they are simply legally binding for all entities (SSF, 2021).

The actions undertaken in the third category of sustainable investing, that is, various types of ESG engagement, may include voting (including proxy voting) during shareholders' meeting in line with the established ESG guidelines, filing or cofiling shareholder proposals, and direct engagement in the corporate management (consisting of communicating with senior management and/or boards of companies) (Bénabou & Tirole, 2010; GSIA, 2021; Hart & Zingales, 2017). The framework of SSF distinguishes between the activity in the form of voting based on ESG versus influencing the corporate management as two separate types of sustainable investing; both of them are considered to be postinvestment sustainable investing approaches (SSF, 2021).

The fourth type is norms-based screening. The norms taken into consideration in the screening include the standards or declarations issued by the international organizations such as the UN (e.g., UN Global Compact, Rio Declaration on Environment and Development or UN Guiding Principles on Business and Human Rights), Organization for

Economic Cooperation and Development (OECD) or International Labor Organization as well as the norms suggested by the NGOs such as Transparency International (Elsenhuber & Skenderasi, 2020; GSIA, 2021). The violations of the norms may result in asset managers excluding the securities from their portfolios (Scholtens, 2014). Interestingly, according to GSIA (2021), norms-based screening was the only category that has declined in terms of assets over 2016–20. It is the category almost exclusive to the European market (the only other significant market is Canada), as evidenced by the lack of reporting on this type by the United States and Australasian financial corporations.

Thematic investing covers usually the environmental and social aspects (governance is less common)—GSIA's report listed areas such as sustainable agriculture, green buildings, lower carbon tilted portfolio, gender equity, and diversity (GSIA, 2021). Another approach is to build a multithemed portfolio covering various sustainability topics, combining social and environmental elements, including the financial products based on certain ESG indexes (Bender et al., 2017; SSF, 2021).

Best-in-class approach, from an implementation perspective, includes both investing in assets with ESG ratings above a certain level and avoiding assets under this selected level (Margot et al., 2021; Verheyden et al., 2016).

Impact investing is the most distinctive category, by some even considered as a separate element of sustainable finance rather than simply another sustainable investing approach as shown by the aspects covered in the definitions of this type of investment. GSIA (2021) emphasized that impact investing requires measuring and reporting against the declared social and environmental impact, showing and proving the intentionality of the investor and the covered asset/investee, as well as demonstrating the contribution. Busch, Bruce-Clark et al. (2021) defined impact investments as "investments that focus on real-world changes in terms of solving social challenges and/or mitigating ecological degradation" (p. 32), stressing the ambiguity of this term, based on, for example, available market data. According to Ezeokoli et al. (2017), an important attribute of impact investing is the emphasis on social and environmental effects, regardless of the financial performance with regard to benchmark. Another important feature of impact investing, underlined by Brock and Knorz (2020) is the fact that it is not a separate asset class but rather an approach than can be utilized with regard to all asset classes. Finally, Glänzel and Scheuerle (2016) distinguished "finance first impact investing" (understood as aimed at reaching ecological and social as well as financial aims) from "impact first impact investing," the latter focused primarily on the formation of quantifiable social impact, with the financial benefits being an additional benefit. Impact investing, due to its rather specific characteristics and more in-depth engagement into the ESG issues than in case of the other ESG investing approaches (with the exception of community investing), is currently associated with the substantially developed institutional environment, with an important role of organizations such as Global Impact Investing Network or Global Steering Group for Impact Investment (Brock & Knorz, 2020). For the history of impact investing, see Trelstad (2016) and for a recent analysis of selected key aspects, see Mazzullo (2021).

Yet another specific category that may be considered a part of the sustainable investing category is community investing (Cameron, 2007; Puaschunder, 2016; Schueth, 2003), frequently regarded jointly with impact investing (as explained in Table 3.1, it is usually considered a broader term than impact investing). It covers, among others, investments or provision of financial services aimed at satisfying key needs of the underserved low-income groups as well as development and social venture capital funds. GSIA (2021) explained community investing as a sustainable investment in which the funds are specifically directed to traditionally underserved individuals or communities; the other possibility is the provision of financing to companies with a strong social or environmental purpose.

In a rather infrequent and unusual methodology, Ezeokoli et al. (2017) distinguished "index-based ESG investing" as a separate category, understood as building and managing an investment portfolio to track selected established index covering environmentally and socially responsible companies. However, such an approach seems redundant and slightly confusing as investment strategies based on indexes may be utilized in all types mentioned in Table 3.1, as evidenced by the substantial and still increasing heterogeneity of the global sustainable investing ETFs market. The extension of such classification would require a comparison of the passive and active ESG investment approaches.

Apart from the above-presented approach, another way to consider the discussed types of sustainable investing is to regard them all as the steps in the increasingly more sustainable investing process, starting from the most basic methods such as negative screening, through relatively more advanced including ESG integration, ending in impact investing or corporate engagement as the most advanced and fully ESG-aligned types (Brock & Knorz, 2020). In yet another perspective, Derwall et al. (2011) divided the entire SRI movement into two categories: values-orientation (focused on negative screens applied to exclude controversial stocks) versus profit-motivated (using mostly positive screening).

The classification of sustainable finance (covering also sustainable investing) by Schoenmaker and Schramade (2019) consists of three stages (called sustainable finance 1.0, 2.0, and 3.0) and additionally "finance as usual" as the preceding stage in the typology. In finance as usual the value created is for shareholders, in sustainable finance 1.0 it is refined shareholder value (maximization of financial value taking into account the environmental and social impact), in 2.0 stakeholder value is created (optimization of the integrated value), and in the most advanced 3.0, the focus is on the common good value (optimization of the environmental and social impact subject to the financial aspects). Combining the most common classification (presented in the majority of this section) with their approach, Schoenmaker and Schramade (2019) regarded exclusion strategies as a 1.0 type, ESG integration as 2.0, and impact investing, among others, as the most advanced 3.0.

Further classification of responsible investing can be found in the article by Dembinski et al. (2003) who divided them into four categories based on the types of ethical concerns of the investors: value- or conviction-based (investor disapproves of some practices or systems and thus refuses to support or contribute to them), fructification oriented (investment aimed at achieving profit, including a long-term partnership, usually in unquoted companies or initiatives), impact- or consequence-based (the purpose is to make the practices and activities of financial intermediaries and public companies consistent with the investor's ethical requirements), and ethics as financial selection (in this case ethics is not the motivation behind the actions but rather serves as a selection criterion for the portfolio—the assumption being that the companies respecting ethical values generate more favorable financial performance than the nonethical ones).

3.3 Sustainable development policies: global and European outlook

This section presents the key developments in the sustainability-linked policies on the global, regional, and, in some cases, country-specific level. It needs to be stressed that in this section we do not discuss various methodologies utilized to identify and classify sustainable (ESG) investments—they are covered in Section 3.4. The key topic of this section are global- or regional-level (national a lower extent) policies that boosted the introduction and affected the development of sustainability-related financial products and services. Due to the substantial dynamics of the discussed regulatory framework, with continuous launch and revision of associated documents, we present the state up-to-date as of late 2021 and early 2022. Moreover, due to the extensive scope of many policies, we focus on their key elements to provide sufficient background for further discussion.

From the historical perspective, one of the milestones in the global discussion concerning sustainability and sustainable development was the 1992 Rio de Janeiro UN Conference on Environment and Development, with the participation of 172 countries (CFA Institute, 2020; Cohen, 2020; Grubb et al., 2019). However, sustainable investing, in particular with regard to the ESG investment funds, has started its rapid development a bit later, we, therefore, do not discuss the Rio de Janeiro summit as being of limited significance (still, it was one of the factors boosting the emergence and initial growth of the contemporary sustainable investing).

Probably the key and most influential document with regard to the development of the global sustainable investment industry is 17 Sustainable Development Goals (SDGs), accepted by the UN member states in 2015, aimed to be fulfilled by 2030 (CFA Institute, 2020; Fu et al., 2019); the document that covers SDGs is entitled the 2030 Agenda for Sustainable Development (or UN Agenda 2030; La Torre & Chiappini, 2021). SDGs are formulated in a way that corresponds (in the opinion of their creators) to the key challenges faced by the global community, including climate change, poverty, armed conflicts, inequality, and environmental degradation (Randers et al., 2019; Wuelser et al., 2020). Moreover, to make the goals quantifiable and to be able to assess their completion, each SDG is accompanied by specific aims that are expected to be reached by the completion date (i.e., 2030), their total number is 169, measured using 231 indicators (GSIA, 2021). 17 SDGs are the following (La Torre & Chiappini, 2021; United Nations General Assembly, 2015; Wuelser et al., 2020):

Goal 1. End poverty in all its forms everywhere;

Goal 2. End hunger, achieve food security and improved nutrition, and promote sustainable agriculture;

Goal 3. Ensure healthy lives and promote well-being for all at all ages;

Goal 4. Ensure inclusive and equitable quality education and promote lifelong learning opportunities for all;

Goal 5. Achieve gender equality and empower all women and girls;

Goal 6. Ensure availability and sustainable management of water and sanitation for all;

Goal 7. Ensure access to affordable, reliable, sustainable, and modern energy for all;

Goal 8. Promote sustained, inclusive, and sustainable economic growth, full and productive employment, and decent work for all;

Goal 9. Build resilient infrastructure, promote inclusive and sustainable industrialization, and foster innovation;

Goal 10. Reduce inequality within and among countries;

Goal 11. Make cities and human settlements inclusive, safe, resilient, and sustainable;

Goal 12. Ensure sustainable consumption and production patterns;

Goal 13. Take urgent action to combat climate change and its impacts;

Goal 14. Conserve and sustainably use the oceans, seas, and marine resources for sustainable development;

Goal 15. Protect, restore and promote sustainable use of terrestrial ecosystems, sustainably manage forests, combat desertification, and halt and reverse land degradation and halt biodiversity loss;

Goal 16. Promote peaceful and inclusive societies for sustainable development, provide access to justice for all, and build effective, accountable, and inclusive institutions at all levels;

Goal 17. Strengthen the means of implementation and revitalize the Global Partnership for Sustainable Development.

The topic of SDGs is well covered both in academic literature and policy documents as well as reports of financial corporations; therefore, we do not contribute more attention to this topic, focusing on the relatively less known or more recent developments. As for the historical background, SDGs were preceded by the eight Millennium Development Goals, concluded in 2015 (Berrou et al., 2019; Jacob, 2017).

Even though SDGs and related regulations are determined and implemented at the state level, there are also some attempts to encourage both companies and investors to adopt self-regulation in this field (GSIA, 2021). One of the key initiatives is the UN Global Compact (established in the early 2000s (Lauesen, 2017)) and the regional associated organizations, engaged in the development of the guidance for business-level SDG implementation (Fussler et al., 2017; Orzes et al., 2020). UN Global Compact is the UN initiative whose target is to encourage businesses worldwide to implement the universally accepted principles concerning, among others, environmental protection, human rights, and labor in their operations; signing companies declare to publish reports showing their progress in fulfilling the 10 adopted principles (SSF, 2020).

To increase the sustainability of the corporations and also, in a linked dimension, of the financial investments, it is necessary to gain insight into the various attributes of companies in the context of the nonfinancial reporting. Even though the issues of methodologies and reporting linked to sustainability are presented above all in Section 3.5, some issues will be covered here due to their global-level importance. Because of their extensive and complicated nature, we cover merely the fundamental aspects.

Two of the global leaders in terms of developing the sustainability standards are Sustainability Accounting Standards Board and Global Reporting Initiative—as noted by Busco et al. (2020) both organizations have similar aims but operate in a different way.

Sustainability Accounting Standards Board (SASB) is a US-based nonprofit organization (Busco et al., 2020), established in 2011. The key aim of the SASB standards is to identify and evaluate the ESG factors affecting the financial performance of companies and thus significant for investors (Fagerström et al., 2017). Consequently, industry-specific and market-informed codified ESG standards were developed and published in 2018, based on detailed discussion with all interested market participants such as companies and investors. An important element of the standards is the classification of companies into sectors and, at a more detailed level, into industries, to address the problem of the differences (in many cases deep) with regard to the materiality of sustainability issues, observable in various sectors of the economy.

The second aforementioned organization, Global Reporting Initiative (GRI), was established in 1997 to ensure the accountability of companies to the rules of responsible environmental actions (Brown et al., 2009; CFA Institute, 2020). The focus of GRI is slightly different compared to SASB because its target audience is broader—it consists of various types of stakeholders interested and potentially affected by the externalities (positive and negative) resulting from the corporate actions (SASB targets investors); therefore, it provides reporting guidelines on the ESG issues material for these stakeholders and materiality is understood as social impact (Busco et al., 2020). From another perspective, SASB concentrates on the issues that are financially important now whereas GRI refers to the potentially significant in the future.

There are also some merging (i.e., codification) initiatives among the organizations focused on the ESG standards. For instance, in 2020 a number of organizations focusing on the ESG standards, including both GRI and SASB as well as the International Integrated Reporting Council (IIRC) signed a document entitled "Statement of Intent to Work Together Toward Comprehensive Corporate Reporting," demonstrating the intent to develop joint standards (CFA Institute, 2020). Even more substantial step, undertaken in 2021, was the merger of IIRC and SASB to form the Value Reporting Foundation, aimed at creating an integrated sustainability reporting framework (Starks, 2021).

Returning to the core issue of this section, that is, sustainable development policies, an interesting and at the same time influential approach to the issue of sustainable development, with some policy implications was suggested by Raworth (2017) and is known as Doughnut Economic Model. It can be regarded as a way to visualize the issue of sustainability through the combination of the concepts of the social and planetary boundaries (the former as complementary aspect) (Wuelser et al., 2020). The inner ring of the doughnut corresponds to human well-being (consistent with the dimensions covered by the SDGs) and the border (outer ring) of the doughnut represents the ecological ceiling, that is, the nonexceedable planetary boundaries. In line with the doughnut economic model, the sustainable economy is understood is as meeting its social goals without transgressing the ecological dimensions.

There are also international policy developments that are linked to specific aspects covered by ESG, above all the climate change. They do not necessarily directly affect the activities of investment funds but in some cases rather the actions of companies whose financial assets are held in the portfolios. Selected, key initiatives are discussed in the subsequent paragraphs.

Probably, the sustainability area attracting most attention over the last several years is climate and climate-related issues—this increasing interest has resulted in a number of important government-level and other initiatives. One of the most prominent examples is the Paris Agreement, agreed on during the COP21 summit in Paris in 2015, aimed at strengthening the global response to the threats posed by the climate change, in particular limiting the global increase of air temperature to under $2°C$; it can thus be regarded as multilateral climate agreement (Rhodes, 2016). The key aspect of the agreement which entered into force in 2016, is the commitment of the signing countries to reach net-zero emissions of the greenhouse gases by

2030 and lowering them by half by 2030 (Robbins, 2016). One of the elements leading to reaching this aim is aligning flows of finance with the climate-related targets. Apart from the commitment of the governments, there is also declaration on the corporate level, with the net-zero pledges by certain companies (Döbeli, 2021); the other potential impact on the corporations is through the state-enacted legislation resulting from the implementation of the Paris Agreement in a certain country. There is also similar self-regulation imitative for the asset management companies, entitled Net-Zero Asset Owners Alliance (NZAOA) that involves setting decarbonization goals by the members, with the final aim of the 100% decarbonization of the held portfolios, as well as enabling climate-related investments leading to net-zero emissions (Eurosif, 2021; SSF, 2021). Furthermore, the initiative Climate Action 100+, the global investor engagement initiative on climate change, currently consists of more than 600 investors aiming to impact the companies whose securities they held in their portfolios to improve their climate change governance, cut their emissions, and expand the climate-related financial disclosures (Climate Action 100+, 2021). Finally, Carbon Disclosure Project, an element of cooperation between SASB and GRI (Weber & ElAlfy, 2019), focuses on the disclosures related to the climate issues of companies and cities.

Another important example is the OECD Guidelines for Multinational Enterprises that provide the legal background for the actions against multinational companies violating certain aspects of sustainability; these actions resulted in clarifications of the guidelines, setting certain ESG standards for the affected companies (Lauesen, 2017; Rasche, 2021). UN Guiding Principles on Business and Human Rights (endorsed by the UN in 2011) is a further example of the international imitative which in some way has become linked to the financial sector and, as a result, sustainable investing—one of its most recent recommendations is the inclusion of the financial institutions to reach the stated aims, referring in particular to human rights (SSF, 2021; Weber & ElAlfy, 2019); as already mentioned the principles already affect the ESG investing sector as they are a common part of the norms-based screening.

The most recent development in the global sustainability policies (as of the writing of this chapter) is the November 2021 summit in Glasgow COP26. The decisions agreed on the Glasgow summit include (BBC, 2021): declaration of further cuts in the carbon-dioxide emissions, declaration to reduce the use of coal, increased support for developing economies with regard to the energy transition, and decreasing subsidies to fossil fuels.

Apart from the regulations adopted and imposed by the governments or as self-regulation of the financial industry, some role in the sustainable transformation of the financial sector in the climate field is attempted to be played by the central banks. Probably the most notable example is the Network For Greening the Financial System (NGFS) that was established in 2017 (Busch, Ferrarini & Hurk, 2021). It is an international body that consists not only of central banks but also of financial supervision authorities from more than 100 countries (as of early December 2021 according to the NGFS's website)—their cooperation is aimed at coordinating and defining the best sustainability-related practices and actions of central banks and regulators (Vaze et al., 2019).

The other sphere of the financial (including investing) activities which has become increasingly more regulated (in most cases self-regulated) by the international documents is the reporting of various types of climate-related information by the companies. We discuss the fundamental aspects with regard to this sphere in the methodological Section 3.5. However, continuing the preceding discussion of the climate-related issues one element needs to be presented here. In 2015 Financial Stability Board (organization aimed at ensuring global financial stability) established the Taskforce on Climate-related Financial Disclosures (TCFD), whose recommendations were released in 2017 (Eccles & Krzus, 2019; GSIA, 2021; Weber & ElAlfy, 2019).[5] The key aspect and requirement expected within TCFD are for the company to present in its reports the influence on the global climate—TCFD provides recommendations on the proper way to disclose information on the climate-related risks and opportunities as well as disclosures related to the other ESG elements such as governance and risk management. The fundamental issue expected to be solved through the broad implementation of TCFD is the increased consistency and comparability of the climate-related information provided by the companies. From the perspective of sustainable investing such development can be expected to improve the processes of the selection and management of investment portfolios taking into account the climate-related ESG factors. Another step in ensuring the consistency of the ESG reporting is the launch of the Taskforce on Nature-related Financial Disclosures, similar to TCFD albeit focused on the nature-related risks and aimed at, among others,

---

[5] For a detailed overview of the TCFD framework, see Bopp and Weber (2020).

setting international biodiversity reporting standards (Petrie, 2021). The EU-level reporting regulations cover to some extent the elements of TCFD—they are discussed in the subsequent parts of this section. Moreover, it should be noted that TCFD disclosures have also been adopted in the other European countries. For instance, the UK government has made the TCFD reporting mandatory for some financial institutions such as pension schemes; it can be added the UK authorities have also imposed the reporting requirements concerning the assessment of social risks and opportunities by these entities (SSF, 2021).

As our study concentrates on the European sustainable investing funds, it is also necessary to discuss the European-level regulations—as the vast majority of the European ETFs are primary listed or domiciled in the EU-member states, we focus on the regulations imposed by the EU[6]; regulations and policies concerning the two major non-EU ETFs markets (i.e., United Kingdom and Switzerland) are discussed in the relevant case studies.

EU-level regulatory framework linked to sustainable development is broad and continues to expand—we present the most relevant documents, discussing their key implications in the context of sustainable investments. Undeniably, one of the milestones in the planned transition of the EU economies toward higher sustainability is the EU Action Plan on Sustainable Finance, further abbreviated to "EU Action Plan" (Bernardini et al., 2021; Maltais & Nykvist, 2021; Silvola & Landau, 2021). The key elements of the EU Action Plan (full name: "Action Plan: Financing Sustainable Growth"), adopted by the European Commission in March 2018, are transparency, reporting, and disclosure, embraced to provide a common reference framework (taxonomy) for the activities that contribute to the environmental sustainability (Forum Nachhaltige Geldanlage, 2021; Moreira, 2021). More formally, the three key aims of the EU Action Plan are (SSF, 2021):

1. reorienting capital flows toward a more sustainable economy (through, e.g., the establishment of relevant taxonomies and integrating sustainability into acts governing financial investments);
2. mainstreaming sustainability (including, e.g., Sustainable Finance Disclosure Regulation, discussed later)
3. fostering transparency (for instance, through the Non-Financial Reporting Directive (NFRD), also known as Corporate Sustainability Reporting Directive (CSRD)).

[6] In-depth discussion can be found in Busch, Bruce-Clark et al. (2021).

The EU Action Plan was redeveloped in July 2021 as the Renewed Sustainable Finance Strategy, to align with the goals of the European Green Deal (Eurosif, 2021); for more details on this plan see the subsequent paragraphs.

In the context of the reporting and accounting requirements, the fundamental EU-level regulation is CSRD. The core goal of CRSD is imposing the requirement for companies to disclose nonfinancial information related to their activities, including the information about the impact of sustainability issues on their business and, as the other side of the relationship, their influence on the society and environment (Döbeli, 2021; Gal, 2020). Furthermore, the directive aims to ensure similar levels of quality (e.g., in terms of assurance) for financial and sustainability reporting. CSRD applies to large public-interest companies (Moreira, 2021).

Another fundamental development in the EU is the European Green Deal (henceforth, Green Deal) (Busch, Ferrarini & Grünewald, 2021; Busch, Ferrarini & Hurk, 2021), accompanied by the European Green Deal Investment Plan. Green Deal targets to enable the EU-member countries to reach net-zero greenhouse emissions, decouple the economic growth from the use of resources, and make the environment pollution free by 2050, by focusing on the specific areas including (the list is not exhaustive, only the elements most important in the context of the financial system are mentioned) (Claeys et al., 2019; Döbeli, 2021): green projects financing, investments in smarter and more sustainable transports, reaching greener industry, facilitating just transition, climate law and pact, promotion of clean energy, and increasing the energy efficiency of homes.

The European Green Deal Investment Plan is aimed at mobilizing at least one trillion EUR of sustainable investments over the next 10 years (Busch, Ferrarini & Hurk, 2021); the increased spending in this sphere from the EU budget is expected to accompany the private sustainable investments (they key role in this process will be played by the European Investment Bank). The overall assumption of the plan is to create a framework to increase both public and private investments necessary for the transition to the European economy being more green, competitive and inclusive as well as climate-neutral. The plan is linked to another element of the European Green Deal, that is, the Just Transition Mechanism targeted at mobilizing at least 100 billion EUR over 2021–27 to alleviate the socio-economic impacts of the green transition in the most affected European regions (European Commission [EC], 2020a).

Two more EU investment programs are linked to sustainable investing (Eurosif, 2021). First, InvestEU is aimed at boosting sustainable investments, innovation, and fostering job creation in Europe through the InvestEU Fund with c. 370 billion EUR of public and private investments out of which a minimum of 30% must be linked to climate aims. Second, Next Generation EU (NGEU), is the post-Covid-19 stimulus package, worth c. 2 trillion EUR—within the current EU financial perspective of 2021−27 30% of the funds are to be allocated to climate-related aims.

Furthermore, since 2020 EC is strongly advocating for another potentially groundbreaking initiative, that is, 2030 Climate Target Plan, setting the target of the minimum 55% of the greenhouse gas emissions reduction target by 2030 compared to the 1990 levels (EC, 2020b). The complex legislative proposals were adopted in 2021 (they are known as "Fit-for-55 Package" Eurosif, 2021; Köhl et al., 2021; Ovaere & Proost, 2021) and they are strongly linked to some other EU-level policy actions presented in this section such as the EU Green Deal. The further development of the 2030 Climate Target Plan, as well as its implementation, remains to be seen. Additionally, in March 2020 EU adopted another sustainability-related action plan, devoted to circular economy (Döbeli, 2021).

The next discussed element of the EU legislation is in fact linked to both issues described in this section and the ones presented in the context of the methodologies in the subsequent sections. The EU Taxonomy Regulation (discussed in detail in Section 3.5.) is the framework for the future EU taxonomy establishing criteria to assess the environmentally sustainable aspects of economic activities. The other important elements of the ESG framework, that is, no significant harm and social taxonomies, are under preparation (GSIA, 2021).

Some EU-level policy developments are not linked to the introduction of the new directives or other types of legislation but rather amendments made to the already binding. For instance, the planned changes to the Markets in Financial Instruments Directive II (MiFID II) involve the modification of the suitability rules adhered to during portfolio management and provision of investment advice by introducing the necessity to take into account the ESG preferences of the clients.

Apart from the EU-level regulations, there are also certain policy developments with regard to the non-EU countries analyzed in our study, in particular Switzerland and the United Kingdom. We present them in relevant case studies covering these countries. Nonetheless, some other, rather unique country-level ESG regulatory attempts can be mentioned—in the Netherlands, the assessment of the local financial sector's exposure to the biodiversity loss has been conducted by the Dutch central bank (SSF, 2021) and in France institutional investors are required to report annually on various climate-related issues (Mésonnier & Nguyen, 2020).

As the focus of our book and underlying study is on Europe, we do not address specifically the US policy developments. Still, it does not constitute a large gap as many of the initiatives that we labeled as global refer in some way also to the US economy, including the financial system. Among some recent important developments is the accession of the US central bank, that is, FED, to the NGFS in 2020 and the establishment of the committees dedicated to sustainable finance (SSF, 2021). Moreover, the US government decided to once again become a member of the already discussed Paris Agreement. Another development, of not only the United States but also global importance, is the relaunch of the sustainable finance working group of the G20 group, which will be led by the United States and China and focus on the promotion of transparency of the climate-related financial risks and, more generally, sustainable finance.

Finally, it should be added that sustainable development policies have in recent years been adopted not only on a global level or in North America and Europe but also in the key emerging economies. Interestingly, the South African stock exchange rather than, for example, the United States or European ones, was on a global scale the first one to require the listed companies to cover sustainability in their reports (CFA Institute, 2020). In India, the guidelines concerning noneconomics responsibilities of companies were issued in 2011 whereas in China the regulations and strategies concerning green finance were launched in 2016. In yet another region, in Latin America, Mexico enacted the Code of Best Corporate Practices (del Carmen Briano Turrent, 2019).

3.4 Sustainable investing: investment opportunities

In the previous sections, we outlined different aspects of sustainable investment, starting with its definition, through the categories, to linked policies. This section is devoted to presenting briefly the possibilities to include the sustainability-related financial products in the investment portfolios; this discussion is continued to a large extent in chapters four and five, with regard to the sustainable investing ETFs. It should be stressed that we focus on the types of ESG investing opportunities linked at least to some extent to the capital markets (either available in the form of or holding securities in their portfolios)—we do not include the other types in our discussion such as sustainable retail financial products offered for the banks' clients or, on the quite opposite side, the venture capital or various state-backed pools of funds as well as special banks focusing on the sustainable investing present in some countries, for example, Germany. Our discussion does not cover carbon markets and transition assets as well. A more detailed overview of taking ESG issues into consideration in the investment process can be found in Hayat and Orsagh (2015).

The first category is equities, that is, investments into single equities, portfolios of equities, or indexes based on the ESG criteria, that is, in line with one of the aforementioned sustainable investing strategies (Hebb, 2012; Hebb et al., 2016). As they are to a large extent covered within the respective types of investment funds, we do not discuss them further for more details see, e.g., Berry and Junkus (2013); He et al. (2021, p. 786); Morrow (2014); Paetzold and Busch (2014); Paetzold et al. (2015); Ouenniche et al. (2016).

Possible sustainable investment opportunities consist also of fixed income (debt) securities, with the green bonds among the key examples. However, the group of sustainability-related debt securities is much more diversified and consists of the following financial instruments: green bonds, social bonds, sustainability bonds, and sustainability-linked bonds. According to Driessen (2021), the issuance of sustainable debt securities reached a record-high level of about 465 billion USD in 2019 (majority of this value were green bonds), meaning over 1.1 trillion USD in cumulative bond issuance up to that year.

The key aspect of green bonds refers to the use of the proceeds from their issuance that should be aimed at financing climate-related or, more broadly, environmental goals (Eurosif, 2018). First green bonds were issued by the European Investment Bank in 2007, followed by the World Bank in 2008 (Birindelli et al., 2021). Green bonds are issued by various entities, including the institutions such as International Finance Corporation (member of the World Bank Group). Defining and classifying green bonds is linked to various ambiguities, therefore some attempts to formalize this process can be noticed such as the adoption of the Green Bond Principles (Driessen, 2021) or country-level regulations (SSF, 2021). For example, in China green bonds' project directory was introduced in 2015. An international perspective, International Capital Markets Association developed guidelines for green, social, and sustainability-linked bonds focusing on the use of the proceeds from the issuance of the bonds. In the European dimension, the European green bond standard was announced in 2020. Among the other types of fixed income sustainability-related securities, social bonds are a category of bonds in which proceeds are used in line with the social aims as stated by the Social Bond Principles (e.g., increasing food security); they remain less popular than green bonds (J.P. Morgan, 2019; Schoenmaker & Schramade, 2019). Sustainability bonds are similar to the two aforementioned categories, as their proceeds should be used for sustainability aims. However, sustainability-linked bonds constitute a different group as they revolve around the idea that the payments are based on the issuer's key performance indicators with regard to the ESG criteria (Liberadzki et al., 2021). Finally, social impact bonds, despite their name, are not bonds but can be explained as contracts aimed at reaching social outcomes (with regard to, e.g., education) through bilateral agreement based on the "pay for performance model" (Clifford & Jung, 2017; Schoenmaker & Schramade, 2019); they combine the use of private investments with the addressing of the welfare expenses subject to public budget constraints (Proietti, 2021).

The third and the last presented possibility to utilize sustainable investing strategies is through investment funds, in particular mutual funds and ETFs. Sustainable investing mutual funds are mutual funds with the ESG focus (understood in various ways—see Section 3.2.), adopting various ESG investing strategies (Humphrey, 2016; Statman & Glushkov, 2016). As they are the key focus of our book, it is necessary to provide here a brief explanation of the sustainable investing ETFs. Following the concepts of the sustainable investments (see Section 3.1.), **sustainable investing** (ESG, responsible investing, etc.—many synonymous labels can be used) **ETFs** can be defined in rather simple terms as the category of ETFs that pronounces **to follow a declared type of sustainable investing approach** within the construction and management of the fund's portfolio; in the vast majority of cases, it means **following a certain ESG index** due to the passive nature of the majority of described funds. The importance of ESG for the ETFs markets is best symbolized by the statement of the BlackRock's, ETFs provider being the global ETFs market leader, CEO's Larry Fink that "climate risk will lead to a significant reallocation of capital" (CFA Institute, 2020, p. 12). Moreover, in 2020, Larry Fink provided clear support of BlackRock for the sustainability reporting standards by stating that "BlackRock believes that SASB provides a clear set of standards for reporting sustainability information across a wide range of issues" as well as "for evaluating and reporting climate-related risks, as well as the related governance issues that are essential to managing them, the TCFD provides a valuable framework" (Busco et al., 2020, p. 120). Apart from mutual funds and ETFs, also pension funds may in some way employ a sustainable investing profile (Woods & Urwin, 2010).

3.5 Sustainable investing: methodological dilemmas. Literature review

In this section, we discuss various methodological aspects of the identification and classification of sustainable investments, in particular the ones related to sustainable investment funds. We present the regulatory documents rather than commercial initiatives (the latter are omitted due to the extensive nature of this topic and a significant rate of changes—we provide, though, some references to exhaustive overviews). Moreover, we discuss the issues concerning misleading or false ESG information. Our presentation is based on the in-depth literature review, conducted to provide insight into the topic, with the overview being as objective and up-to-date as possible yet without the details that are secondary in the light of the book's key focus on investment funds. In the final part of this section, we present the methodological approach to the identification and categorization of sustainable investing ETFs that we applied in our book, in particular in the empirical study (discussion continues in chapters four and five). It should be added that some methodological aspects were already covered in Section 3.3 to supplement the discussion of the policy developments (e.g., SASB, TCFD).

One of the oldest initiatives is the United Nations Environment Program Finance Initiative (UNEP FI), started after the Rio de Janeiro summit, being a joint initiative of the UNEP and financial corporations. Among the most relevant and recent effects of this partnership is the Sustainable Financial Roadmap Initiative, which, on the global level, developed an integrated approach to boost the transformation of the financial system in the direction of higher sustainability (GSIA, 2021). On the regional level, it consists of the local Sustainable Finance Roadmaps.

The milestone in the development of the modern responsible investment was undeniably the introduction and increasing adoption of the PRI backed by the UN, established in 2006. PRI is a network of institutional investors, with voluntary participation. The signatories of the PRI declared to uphold the following principles in their investment actions (Hebb et al., 2016; Majoch et al., 2017; Weber & ElAlfy, 2019):

1. Incorporate ESG issues into investment analysis and decision-making processes.
2. To be active owners and incorporate ESG issues into their ownership policies and practices.
3. To seek appropriate disclosure on ESG issues by the entities in which they invest.
4. To promote acceptance and implementation of the Principles within the investment industry.
5. To work together to enhance their effectiveness in implementing the Principles.
6. To report on their activities and progress toward implementing the Principles.

PRI-related guidelines continue to be developed as evidenced by the introduction of the framework concentrating on human rights (SSF, 2021). An important result of the PRI movement has been increased awareness of and application of the sustainable investing rules among institutional investors because, as observed by Woods and Urwin (2010), it allowed for overcoming their previous reservations concerning socially responsible investments. For many years the direction was unequivocal—the investment companies joined PRI by agreeing to uphold the PRI principles and there were no delistings; however, this has recently changed which strengthens the significance of the declarations. As of 2021, there are almost 4 thousand signatories of PRI, managing approximately 120 trillion USD of assets.

Another important methodology related to the ESG ETFs is the EU Sustainable Finance Disclosure Regulation (SFDR), aimed at increasing the comparability and understanding among investors of the sustainability profile of, among other, investment funds (Buschm 2021; Ferrarini et al., 2021, p. 576; Gortsos, 2021; Mezzanotte, 2021). More generally, the aim of SFDR is to impose requirements increasing transparency concerning sustainability-related disclosures at the following levels: entity (i.e., financial institution), financial product, and financial service (SSF, 2021). SFDR is binding for both participants of financial markets and financial advisors (Döbeli, 2021). The key requirement of SFDR with regard to sustainable investing is the necessary reporting by investors and advisors of the integration of sustainability risks and promotion of sustainability elements by the managed or offered financial products. SFDR entered into force by the end of 2019 and became binding since March 10, 2021 for various entities.

It may be added that the SFDR rules are to some extent similar to SASB (for more on this issue, see Section 3.3). Finally, the development of the exact articles of SFDR and accompanying documents has been subject to the lobbying activities, influencing the final form of the regulations (Cato, 2022); the same applies to other elements of the EU-level sustainability methodologies (Schütze & Stede, 2021).

In what can be perceived as a substantial step in the methodological dimension, SFDR introduces important definitions and classifications. According to SFDR, sustainable investment strategies can be explained as strategies in which ESG opportunities, risks, associated values, and impact are the central part of the investment process. Sustainable investment strategies are further divided into (Döbeli, 2021):

- general ESG focus—concentrating on promoting environmental or social features, with good governance attributes;
- sustainable impact focus—concentrating on activities contributing to environmental or social targets, with good governance attributes and implementing the principle of do no significant harm.

In April 2022, EC adopted the key document for the implementation of the SFDR—the technical standards (Regulatory Technical Standards (RTSs)) concerning the disclosure of the sustainability information, thus being detailed guidelines to the provisions applied from 2021, providing the rules to be followed by, among others, the asset managers (Glow, 2022b). RTSs are predicted to become binding from the beginning of 2023. Exact RTS articles are predominantly consistent with the earlier drafts of the document published in 2021 or earlier, consulted with various entities, so the financial companies have mostly already adopted their methodologies accordingly.

RTSs are crucial from the methodological perspective of sustainable investing, as they supplement the core standards, imposing disclosures with regard to the negative effects of investments in terms of sustainability, based on 18 indicators (nine environmental, five social, two referring to investments in supernationals and sovereigns, and the final two dedicated for real estate investments) (Busch, 2021; Chance, 2020; Dario et al., 2021; Gortsos, 2021). As GSIA (2021) noticed, the implementation of SFDR can have a profound effect on the popularity of some categories of sustainable investments, including negative/exclusionary screening, norms-based screening, and ESG integration, as the related ESG assessments will by default take into account in the SFDR-governed financial products. Finally, it should be added that SFDR is strongly linked to the EU Sustainable Finance Action Plan, published in 2018 (Moreira, 2021).

Currently, the core result of the SFDR adoption is the creation of a common standard for the sustainable investment funds, using the following designations (Busch, 2021; Eurosif, 2021; Moreira, 2021)[7]:

- article 8 (light green) describes financial products (in this case: investment funds) promoting environmental and/or social characteristics;
- article 9 (dark green) represents funds following a sustainable investment objective (with the subcategory of funds aimed at reducing carbon emissions).

More generally, SFDR (in article 2) defines sustainable investment as "an investment in an economic activity that contributes to an environmental or social objective, where the company does not harm other objectives, besides having good governance practices" (Eurosif, 2021, p. 34). What is important, SFDR applies also to the financial products managed by the non-EU financial corporations—it covers all products offered on the EU financial markets (Moreira, 2021).

Despite the substantial progress with regard to the identification and classification of ESG investments due to SFDR, there are certain important weaknesses of this taxonomy, including (Eurosif, 2021): insufficient precision of the definition of sustainable investing, problematic classification, lack of required minimum levels of the ESG assets in the portfolio, possibility to label investment products as green and belonging to the same ESG category despite extremely different shares of investments aligned with the rules (potentially merely 1% is sufficient); the interpretation is open to the providers of the products and highly divergent approaches are used.

One of the currently and potentially also in the nearest future most influential public-backed methodological document is currently under development and implementation in the EU. It is known as the EU Taxonomy Regulation and is a result of the political agreement between the European Council and Parliament (it is, though, mostly implemented by the EC), attempted to become the first official classification system for the sustainable economic activities with regard to the environmental aspects (EC, 2021; Marini, 2019; Pacces, 2021; Schütze & Stede, 2021; Silvola & Landau, 2021). A more recent background of the EU Taxonomy

---

[7] Additionally, article 6 is simply non-ESG financial products. Therefore, the common classification is to divide the financial products into four groups: articles 6, 8, 9, and not reported.

Regulation is providing support for the implementation of the European Green Deal (see Section 3.3, for more details).

EU Taxonomy Regulation (henceforth, "Taxonomy") can be briefly explained as a taxonomy system that will be used to categorize economic activities as "green" through the examination of six environmental objectives as well as "do no significant harm" requirement (compliance with one criterion cannot result in significant violation of the other) and a minimal social safeguard clause (Gortsos, 2021; SSF, 2021).[8] The six environmental objectives are (EC, 2021; Gortsos, 2021; Moreira, 2021): climate change mitigation, climate change adaptation, the sustainable use and protection of water and marine resources, the transition to a circular economy, pollution prevention, and control, and the protection and restoration of biodiversity and ecosystems. Generally, the Taxonomy includes the criteria for the classification of such activities and sets the requirements and criteria for the financing of sustainability aims (FNG, 2021; Marini, 2019). One of the fundamental assumptions of Taxonomy is the inclusion of the concept known as double materiality, meaning that financial aspects should be reported accompanied by the environmental and social factors, addressing a two-way relationship, that is, both the effects of companies' activities on the environmental and social issues and the effects of nature and society on the value of the company in the financial terms (the taxonomy provides guidance on this topic) (Gortsos, 2021; Schoenmaker, 2021).[9] Two subcategories also covered by the Taxonomy are *enabling* and *transitional* activities, that is, special groups not adhering to the outlined criteria of sustainability.

The more direct aim of the Taxonomy is to increase the volume of sustainable investment and introduce the European Green Deal through the way of providing investors, companies and policymakers with the appropriate definitions of the economic activities being sustainable with regard to the environmental aspects; more broadly, it should result in higher security for investors involved in sustainable investing (with regard to the environment), decrease the scale of greenwashing, lower the level of market fragmentation, improve the switching between compliant and noncompliant investments and, with regard to the corporations, boost their

---

[8] Exact four conditions that need to be met can be found in the Taxonomy documents.

[9] Single materiality covers the latter element only—impact of nature and society on the company; it will serve as the basis for the International Sustainability Standards to be developed by the IFRS Foundation (Schoenmaker, 2021).

efforts to involve in climate-related actions (EC, 2021; Marini, 2019). The Taxonomy will cover a number of entities but from the perspective of the book's aims and topic, the key affected are participants of financial markets offering financial products that will be required to either state in what way and to what extent the offered investment contribute to the economics activities compliant with the environmental taxonomy or state that they do not invest in such activities. Moreover, on the company reporting level, there will be a requirement to present similar information with regard to the company's activities in case of companies required to comply with the NFRD (i.e., large companies). For the other, smaller companies, the system is planned as voluntary yet strongly recommended due to, for example, possible easier access to financing.

Taxonomy regulation entered into force in July 2020; they were preceded by the work of the Technical Expert Group focusing on sustainable finance, conducted over 2018–20 (EC, 2021). The first binding elements ("delegated act") of the Taxonomy, referring to the climate change issues, were disclosed and adopted by the EC in April 2021 which means that the first group of the technical criteria of assessment was enacted starting from January 2022. However, the Taxonomy's implementation is substantially behind schedule as initially the acts covering all six objectives were planned to be adopted by the end of 2021. In July 2021, another delegated act concerning methodology and presentation of information was published as a supplement to the Taxonomy. Taxonomy is strongly linked to the SFDR as it provides guidance for necessary classifications. The implementation of the Taxonomy is associated with legal acts referring to specific parts of the investment industry such as the EU Eco-label for the retail types of investment funds, for example, UCITS equity funds (Busch, Bruce-Clark et al., 2021); nevertheless, the current Eco-label qualification criteria in practice hinder its application to any of the major funds available in Europe (Eurosif, 2021). The remainder (i.e., nonenvironmental part) of the Taxonomy is still under preparation by the EU Platform on Sustainable Finance (the EC's experts group, created within the Taxonomy's regulation), in particular with regard to the social aspects of the sustainability.

Despite the apparent benefits linked to the Taxonomy, there are also some issues that may limit its actual usefulness and meaning for the financial sector (Eurosif, 2021). The first limitation is still a very low share of investors using the Taxonomy in the course of investment decisions (it may obviously improve in the future). Second, the criteria within the Taxonomy seem too narrow in the context of the portfolio's diversification—only a small share of total investable universe could qualify as aligned with the taxonomy. Moreover, what needs to be taken into account is that the correct and meaningful adoption of the discussed taxonomy is to a large extent dependent upon the scope and quality of ESG data provided by the companies in their reports, thus the importance of the acts such as CRSD (FNG, 2021). Further problematic issue concerns private companies, in particular the small and medium ones that generally do not publish ESG information and potentially imposing such requirements on these entities may result in high costs affecting their financial standing.

EU Taxonomy affects also the public taxonomical attempts undertaken in the other European and non-European countries. For example, the UK authorities aim to adopt a green taxonomy based on the EU ideas (SSF, 2021). Similar yet slightly less comprehensive green taxonomies are discussed or planned to be launched in the countries such as Canada, Singapore, or South Africa. This indicates the far-reaching (also in geographical terms) implications of the EU ESG-linked methodological efforts. Yet another example of international cooperation with regard to the sustainable finance taxonomy development is the International Platform on Sustainable Finance consisting of several members (Gonzalez, 2021).

Apart from the global and EU-level guidelines discussed in the preceding paragraphs, there are also national (or regional) ESG guidelines in Europe used to identify and provide ESG labels to investment funds in some European countries such as the Nordic Region, German-speaking countries or France—according to GSIA (2021) as of 2021 c. 1500 European investment funds (with more than 800 billion EUR in assets) had at least one such label.

Among the most recent developments in the ESG methodological sphere is the decision made during the COP26 conference in Glasgow to establish the International Sustainability Standards Board (ISSB), with the headquarters in Frankfurt in Germany, whose fundamental duties will include a publication of a set of global ESG norms, scheduled for 2022 (foundation of the ISSB was announced in the early November 2021 yet preparatory actions were undertaken already in 2020 (Butcher, 2020)). First, two sustainability standards of ISSB were published for consultation at the end of March 2022, with the focus on the general sustainability disclosure requirements and climate-related reporting (Glow, 2022a). ISSB is governed by the International Reporting Financial Standards (IFRS) Foundation, that is, the key provider of the globally accepted financial reporting standards (Hodge, 2021). According to the statement on the

IRFS Foundation's website the aim of the new standards boards is "to deliver a comprehensive global baseline of sustainability-related disclosure standards that provide investors and other capital market participants with information about companies' sustainability-related risks and opportunities to help them make informed decisions" (International Reporting Financial Standards Foundation, 2021). It is still much too early to assess the scope or the possible significance of this initiative, in particular in terms of their alignment with the country-level or regional standards (Glow, 2022a).

Yet another, industry-level set of ESG disclosure standards was issued in November 2021 by the CFA Institute, to be followed by more detailed documents in 2022 and next years (CFA Institute, 2021). Moreover, there are also important initiatives linked to the ESG investing also in the developed countries in the other regions than Europe or the United States such as the Responsible Investment Association Australasia, which provides guidance for retail clients interested in such investment strategies (Homa-nen, 2019).

The increased interest in the sustainable investments, demonstrated by, for example, the rising assets allocated to the ESG financial investment products, has resulted in the substantial activity of the companies delivering various types of financial data—they offer an increasing number of ESG scores and rankings as well as detailed ESG assessment of certain corporations or financial products. We do not discuss them in our book as even a brief presentation and comparison of some of the most popular commercial ESG ratings, with the particular focus on the methodologies applied to the investment funds, would constitute a lengthy topic—it could be a topic of the other book (at least one). It should be borne in mind that the rate of revisions, changes, and at times overhauls of the methodologies is in some cases extremely high—we present the state in 2020/2021 according to the available literature. Some major commercial ESG scores and ranking include (EC, 2020c; Ezeokoli et al., 2017; Silvola & Landau, 2021)[10]:

- Morningstar Sustainability Rating,
- SocialFunds.com,
- MSCI ESG Fund Ratings,
- Sustainalytics.

There are some very detailed in-depth analyses of the ESG ratings including EC (2020c), Eccles et al. (2016), Escrig-Olmedo et al. (2010), and

---

[10] We limit our list to the ones with the ESG scores applied to investment funds rather than, for example, companies.

Ezeokoli et al. (2017). A significant issue of the discrepancies in the ESG ratings and the associated consequences was examined by Gibson Brandon et al. (2021). Again, it should be emphasized that due to a large number of such methodologies, in Chapter 5, we discuss the one utilized in our empirical analysis and present its key elements, that is, ESG scores provided by Refinitiv.

The large amounts of data covered within the ESG methodologies have resulted in increased digitalization of the ESG evaluation process and the emergence of companies offering related services such as GreenDelta or Clarity AI, in particular in the FinTech sector (Vergara & Agudo, 2021). Nonetheless, it should be underlined that human input remains necessary to evaluate the context.

Due to the fact that the vast majority of ESG ETFs globally are passive equity funds, it is necessary to provide a brief overview of the sustainable investing indexes, that is, indexes "representing a portfolio of shares from local, regional, or multinational companies selected on the basis of ESG factors" (de Souza Cunha & Samanez, 2013, p. 21). The history of the ESG-compliant indexes of the equity markets is rather short. The first ESG capitalization-weighted index, Domini 400 Social Index (currently MSCI KLD 400 Social Index) was launched in 1990 (Morningstar, 2020). Another major ESG equity index, Dow Jones Sustainability Indices (DJSI), was introduced in 1999, and FTSE4Good Index in 2001 (CFA Institute, 2020). The landscape of the ESG indexes is currently very broad and highly diversified and includes, among others, the following "families" of indexes (as of 2017; however, the changes over the next years covered mostly, e.g., names): Thomson Reuters Corporate Responsibility Indices, FTSE4Good Indices, Calvert Responsible Indices, MSCI ESG Indices, Dow Jones Sustainability Indices, Morningstar Global Sustainability Indices. Finally, it should be added that an active approach to sustainable investing is rather infrequent and requires further scrutiny (Schoenmaker, 2018). The key drawbacks of ESG investing based on the sustainability indexes are their focus mostly on the liquid, large companies with high availability of data on their ESG performance (thus other entities are neglected), and the lack of investor's engagement apart from the selection of the index as other sustainability-related actions are undertaken by the index providers (Silvola & Landau, 2021).

The issue of the European ESG indexes is covered in a vast number of publications including, for example, Bernardová et al. (2020), Brzeszczyński et al. (2021), Janik and Bartkowiak (2015, 2022), Lydenberg and White

(2016), Śliwiński and Łobza (2019). ESG disclosures requirements concerning the European benchmarks are covered within the regulations of the EU Action Plan (with the exception of currency and interest rates benchmarks); they also led to the creation of the two EU climate benchmarks (Moreira, 2021).

The fact that there are many methodologies applied to sustainable investing and their number and complexity seem to be still increasing has resulted in some serious concerns expressed by both academics and financial practitioners. These stipulations focus on the actual sustainability of the financial products and services labeled as sustainable by their providers and other entities engaged in their distribution. Paradoxically, the high number of possible ways to evaluate sustainability could have in some way contributed to these problems—the interested parties can screen various criteria to find the ones that are met by their actions. Most concepts mentioned in this part of the chapter are well-known therefore we limit our discussion to the key aspects. The reason for their emergence is above all the ambiguity, complexity, and at times conflicting aspects of the definitions and standards of sustainable investing. The most popular and broadly recognized term is "greenwashing." It stems and still is observed above all in the consumer goods industry, and can be explained as providing misleading information about the services, products (including financial products and services), policies, or aims of the company with regard to their positive impact on the environment (Migliorelli, 2021). "Sustainable washing" is the concept of greenwashing extended to all types of sustainable investing, not only the environmental-linked ones. These issues may also apply to specific types of sustainable investment—similar term, that is, "impact washing," was used by Busch, Bruce-Clark et al. (2021) with regard to the impact investments. Tinelli (2016) distinguished between "green" (related to environmental issues) and "blue" washing (related to the UN-based or social standards).

More generally, Ezeokoli et al. (2017) listed the following four main issues of critique with regard to the selection of the ESG investments:

1. too inclusive: too inclusive ESG selection criteria, resulting in possibility to include the vast majority of the listed companies in the investment portfolio based on some selected ESG scoring system;
2. dubious criteria: criteria used being too subjective as well as based on narrow or conflicting viewpoints in ideological or political terms;

3. quality of information: problems with verification, comparison, and standardization of the ESG information, in most cases gathered from the examined companies themselves;

4. too much focus on short-term performance: the practice of screening investments first for performance and in the second step for ESG factors linked to short-term returns, thus excluding companies with high ESG scores and long-term focus.

The report by Eurosif (2021) mentioned the following drawbacks of the commercial ESG ratings: high discrepancies with regard to their methodologies, lack of understanding of the rating process by neither the rated companies nor the investors utilizing the scores, the general concept based on measuring the exposure of the company's financial value to the ESG factors instead of the ESG impact of the company's actions (i.e., insufficient focus on the positive impact of the company on the economy and society as well as environment, etc.), and, last but not least, aggregate scores potentially hiding serious ESG risks and negative impact in certain areas. Lack of comparability is by some authors regarded as more substantial problem than greenwashing with regard to ETFs, hindering the comparisons between funds and constituting a much more significant barrier for the investors (Clements, 2022).

As in our analysis we focus on the sustainable investment funds, it is necessary to briefly mention the issue of the ESG ratings of the funds—in vast majority of cases, their sustainability scores are based on the scores of the securities held in their portfolios; therefore, they provide valuable insight into the sustainability-related attributes of certain funds (Silvola & Landau, 2021). However, the exact assessment of the fund's sustainability profile is hindered by the differences in the ESG scoring methodologies, the relative attributes of the fund's ratings (i.e., they are presented in relation to the benchmark funds—their selection affects the ESG performance of the scrutinized funds), and ambiguities concerning in particular the thematic ESG funds. Thematic funds invest in companies from certain industries or address selected sustainable development issues—their securities may have low ESG scores even though they are fully consistent (due to deficiencies in some ESG aspects) with the aims of the funds, thus leading to an overall lower score of the fund (Zhang, 2021).

Finally, after discussing the complex and in some aspects controversial issue of the ESG methodologies applied to sustainable investing, we present the methodological approach that is used in our analysis. As our study focuses on the European ESG ETFs, due to the planned introduction of the

EU-level taxonomies (which probably to some extent will also be used by the other European countries), the development of the proprietary methodology seems redundant. Already, SFDR from March 2021 requires to report the sustainability status of the funds. In our methodology we use the status of the funds in the (Refinitiv) Lipper's database—we extract data on "ethical funds" that we qualify as sustainable investing (ESG) funds. Additionally, in case of insufficient information or other uncertainties, we cross-check our list by referring to the other sustainability rankings as well as reports of ETFs.

3.6 Sustainable investing ETFs in the European countries: case study (II)—Germany

In the second case study of sustainable investing ETFs in a single country, we discuss the German market that constitutes an interesting and, at the same time, important case due to the size of the German economy and, accordingly, also the financial sector. German market for investment funds, including ETFs, is among the largest in the world and Europe, in particular with regard to the UCITS and AIF funds in case of which Germany is the biggest market in Europe (Eurosif, 2021). Even though in terms of sustainable investing Germany ranks slightly worse than Switzerland (for more details on this country see the first case study), it can still be regarded as one of the regional and global leaders with regard to this part of the financial system. Our discussion of Germany follows the structure used in the Swiss case: it begins with the overview of sustainable investing in Germany, followed by a brief presentation of the German sustainable investing funds, and concludes with the outline of the German sustainable investing ETFs market segment (the last element is further discussed in Chapter 4).

One of the distinctive features of the German financial system, affecting also the sustainable investing sector, is its substantial diversity in terms of the financial institutions; however, the key role is played by banks, either public or cooperative (as well as private) (Eurosif, 2016). The significant diversity can be also noticed with regard to the asset management companies in terms of their number or the range of the financial products offered. However, consistently with the overall structure of the German financial system, sustainable investment sector is shaped above all by the banks which offer a broad variety of the linked financial products; substantial activity with regard to sustainable investing applies also to the state-owned financial institutions such as KfW (Kreditanstalt für Wiederaufbau) (Eurosif, 2016).

The other important bank-related impact on the sustainable investment is the activity of the specialist banks with the sustainability focus, often with a long history and a wide range of applied sustainable strategies. Moreover, in the early stages or years preceding contemporary ESG investing, the funds or other institutions linked to churches or religious organizations were of particular significance in Germany.

To fully understand the German sustainable investing sector, it is necessary to provide some insight into its surroundings, in particular in terms of the legal aspects. Some of the key legal acts concerning sustainable investing in Germany include (Vinueza-Peter, 2020): first, acts directly linked to the sustainable investments such as the Reform Act on Accounting Regulations (enacted in 2004—it required reporting of nonfinancial together with financial issues potentially affecting the financial performance); second, linked indirectly (i.e., through the impact on the assets potentially to be included in the sustainable investing portfolios): Act on Equal Participation of Men and Women in Leadership Positions in the Private and the Public Sector (since 2015—introduction of quotas for either men or women in case of their underrepresentation in publicly listed companies at the nonexecutive board level), Remuneration Transparency Act (since 2017—enacted to promote equality with regard to the remuneration by imposing transparency of remuneration policies of certain companies). There are also some regulations concerning specific segments of the German sustainable investing funds market—for instance, one section of the Insurance Supervision Act enacted by the German Federal Financial Supervisory Authority BaFin (2002) requires the pensions funds to disclose to the beneficiaries whether and how they take into consideration ESG issues (Vinueza-Peter, 2020). In 2019 BaFin and German central bank (Deutsche Bundesbank) published the guidelines for the financial institutions with regard to the climate- and other types of ESG-related risks (Bopp & Weber, 2020). These and other policy developments as well as the initiatives such as The Hub for Sustainable Finance Germany (Bassen & Zwick, 2018) constitute a significant change compared to the institutional framework a few years earlier—as noted in 2016 by Glänzel and Scheuerle, the conditions used to be less favorable. With regard to the assets held within the sustainable investing strategies (albeit also in the conventional portfolios), one of the key developments in the 2010s was the withdrawal of the German government from nuclear energy and its associated effects on the potential investments (Neher, 2016).

Obviously, due to the membership in the EU, German regulations include also the elements following the key ideas of the EU-level principles such as the 'Guidance Notice on Dealing with Sustainability Risks' published by BaFin, indicating that sustainability risks should be considered together with the other types of investment risks (Vinueza-Peter, 2020). In mid-2021, BaFin announced the plans to impose regulations aimed at providing a clear definition of the sustainable investing fund and thus preventing greenwashing with regard to the German funds, following the spirit of the SFDR and EU Taxonomy (Fischer & Raabe, 2021). The requirements are planned to apply to all retail funds referring to sustainability, for example, in their names or marketing materials, and the three possible frameworks include: (I) investing a minimum of 75% of the portfolio in the sustainable assets (additional requirement is that no investment may violate any ESG objective), (II) utilizing sustainable investing strategy (see, e.g., approaches presented in Table 3.1) to at least 75% of the portfolio, or (III) tracking sustainable index. The regulation is planned to be temporary, to be replaced by the EU-broad definition and classification system (see the previous section). There are also some policy actions aimed at boosting the popularity of certain types of sustainable investing, for example, impact investing—examples include Bundesinitiative Impact Investing launched in 2020 (Brock & Knorz, 2020).

To complete the overview of the German sustainable investment industry it is indispensable to provide data on its size and structure. According to the 2021 report by the Forum Nachhaltige Geldanlage (FNG), the size of the sector at the 2020 year-end was approximately 335 billion EUR (Forum Nachhaltige Geldanlage [FNG], 2021). Fig. 3.1 demonstrates the structure of the sector. As it may be clearly noticed, the German ESG investing industry is dominated by two categories: funds and mandates, similarly to the case of Switzerland. However, in contrast with Switzerland, the position of mandates is relatively stronger and they are the leading type. Comparison of the total value of the assets managed within German sustainable investing financial products to the aggregate either global (35 trillion USD) or European (12 trillion USD) market shows that Germany accounts for rather small of the total industry, in particular when taking into account the size of the German economy or the corresponding values for Switzerland. However, the methodological inconsistencies hinder formulating more in-depth and robust conclusions.

German sustainable investments sector is a quite frequent (in relation to the other countries) topic of the academic studies. Some of the issues

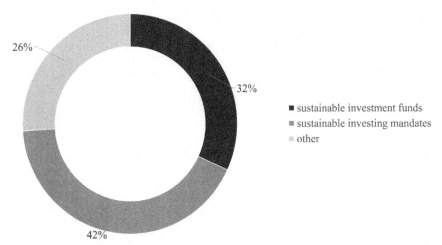

Figure 3.1 Structure of the assets of sustainable investing financial products in Germany in 2020. *(Source: own elaboration based on FNG (2021).)*

covered include the relationship between risk measures and sustainability indexes (Öcal & Kamil, 2021), impact investing in Germany (Brock & Knorz, 2020), readiness of German households to investing into sustainable assets (Gutsche & Ziegler, 2019; Gutsche & Zwergel, 2020), inclusion of the ESG assets in the portfolio of robo advisor (Nakajima et al., 2021), performance of German green mutual funds (Fernández et al., 2019), motivations and attitudes of the German mutual fund users toward sustainable funds (Wins & Zwergel, 2016), and impact of the inclusion of German companies in the sustainability equity indexes on their stock performance (Oberndorfer et al., 2013).

The second aspect discussed in this study is one specific part of the aforementioned sustainable investment industry in Germany, that is, investment funds following the ESG strategies. To ensure consistency with the previous case study, we report in Fig. 3.2 the statistics on the sustainable investing presented in the report by the FNG; it covers three European German-speaking countries (i.e., also Austria) and the data for Switzerland are identical with the ones discussed in the relevant case study, extracted from the publications of the Swiss Sustainable Finance. As it may be clearly noticed, the growth of the assets of the ESG funds over 2005—2020 has been impressive—the first noted value was merely c. 2.6 billion EUR and the total assets remained below 10 billion EUR until 2011; however, the rapid development started in approximately 2017 (year-end value of more

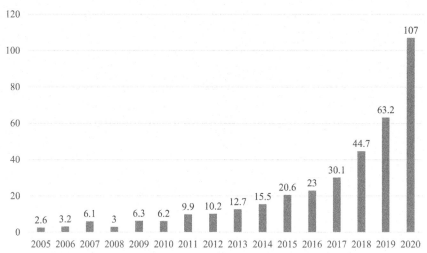

Figure 3.2 Assets of sustainable investing investment funds in Germany: 2015–20 (EUR billion). *(Source: own elaboration based on FNG (2021).)*

than 30 billion EUR) and the final reported value of assets exceeded for the first time 100 billion EUR. The report by FNG (2021) linked the very dynamic growth since 2018 to the already discussed EU Action Plan; in terms of the sources of inflow of capital to the ESG funds, the report stressed the significantly increased interest among the retail investors. However, putting again the discussed values in the comparative perspective shows that the German sustainable investing funds sector remained rather small either in relation to the global assets of the ESG funds (compare the respective values to Switzerland) or with regard to the total assets of all types of funds in Germany (approximately 4 trillion USD in 2020). In terms of the ESG strategies applied the cited report showed that exclusions and norm–based screening are the most frequent. Finally, it should be added that data on the German ESG funds reported by the Bundesverband Investment und Asset Management provide a somewhat different picture— according to the end-of-year data for 2020 German sustainable open-end funds managed 147 billion EUR of assets, out of which 91 billion EUR were held in retail funds and the remainder in the special funds (Vinueza-Peter, 2021). Due to the methodological differences, it is difficult to compare the values obtained from the different sources.

The structure of the main users of sustainable investing funds in Germany has evolved. Initially, mostly institutional entities invested in the ESG funds, above all pension funds, churches, and insurance companies

(Vinueza-Peter, 2020). However, over the next years, the other types of entities became active in this market and currently the group of investors is substantially diversified. Still, according to the 2020 year-end data, the institutional investors remained the main group of investors in the German sustainable investment funds and mandates, with the church-linked institutions, charities, and insurance companies corresponding for almost half of invested assets by institutional investors; on the other side, the share of retail clients in the total market was below 20% (FNG, 2021). Another example of entities utilizing ESG investing is German foundations (Stühlinger, 2018). Moreover, in a broader perspective, also state-linked funds, such as the German Federal Government's Special Pension and Care Funds, replicate ESG indexes within their sustainable finance strategies (Euronext, 2021).

The final part of our study is the analysis of the selected aspects of the German sustainable investing ETFs, using the criterion of the primary listing location; sustainable funds are identified using the classification of the Lipper's database, with additional cross-checks if necessary. Additionally, we use data on all ESG ETFs listed on the German stock exchanges, also the funds that are not primarily listed in this country. With regard to the primary listed funds we present exclusively the ESG ETFs listed on Xetra as our screening shows that there are no such funds listed on the other German stock exchanges (e.g., Stuttgart Stock Exchange).

According to the data as of the end of September 2021, the total net assets of the ESG ETFs primary listed in Germany were at c. 60.5 billion USD—these assets were managed by almost 200 (194) funds that could be classified as sustainable investing. However, some funds reported no data on assets, or the values were reported as zero which means that the actual number of German ESG ETFs was closer to 175. Most assets were managed by the passive equity funds, the position of bond funds and, even more clearly, active funds was weaker. The most common domicile locations were Ireland and Luxembourg, with no primary listed German ESG ETFs domiciled in Germany. Comparing the assets of ESG ETFs to the previously discussed assets of all sustainable investment funds (see Fig. 3.2) shows their strong position in the aggregate market—however, significant methodological differences mean that this result must be interpreted with much caution. Nevertheless, the position of Germany as one of the key ESG ETFs markets in Europe (see chapter four) is undeniable.

Table 3.2 presents the classification of the 10 largest German ESG ETFs. What is important, the largest fund (as well as the eighth in the ranking) is a

Table 3.2 The largest sustainable investing ETFs primary listed in Germany (according to the assets under management). September 2021 data.

Name of the fund	Total net assets (bln USD)	Asset class of exposure (Lipper's classification)	Benchmark	Provider	Inception date	Total expense ratio (%)
SPDR Bloomberg SASB US Corporate ESG UCITS ETF	5.68	Bond USD Corporates	Bloomberg SASB U.S. Corporate ESG Ex–Controversies Select Index	State Street Global Advisors	October 23, 2020	0.15
UBS ETF (LU) MSCI World Socially Responsible UCITS ETF (USD) A-dis	3.53	Equity Global	MSCI World SRI Low Carbon Select 5% Issuer Capped Total Return Net	UBS	August 19, 2011	0.22
Xtrackers MSCI USA ESG UCITS ETF 1C	3.52	Equity US	MSCI USA Low Carbon SRI Leaders Index	DWS Investment	May 8, 2018	0.15
iShares MSCI USA ESG Enhanced UCITS ETF USD (Acc)	3.24	Equity US	MSCI USA ESG Enhanced Focus Index	BlackRock Asset Management Ireland	April 16, 2019	0.07
Xtrackers MSCI World ESG UCITS ETF 1C	2.90	Equity Global	MSCI World Low Carbon SRI Leaders Index	Concept Fund Solutions, DWS Investment	April 24, 2018	0.20
Xtrackers MSCI Japan ESG UCITS ETF 1C	2.21	Equity Japan	MSCI Japan Low Carbon SRI Leaders Index	Concept Fund Solutions,	April 24, 2018	0.20

				DWS Investment		
UBS ETF (LU) MSCI USA Socially Responsible UCITS ETF (USD) A-dis	1.96	Equity US	MSCI USA SRI Low Carbon Select 5% Issuer Capped Total Return Net	UBS	August 18, 2011	0.22
Xtrackers II ESG EUR Corporate Bond UCITS ETF 1D	1.85	Bond EUR Corporates	Bloomberg MSCI Euro Corporate Sustainable and SRI Index	DB Platinum Advisors, DWS Investment	October 18, 2010	0.16
Amundi MSCI USA ESG Leaders Select UCITS ETF DR (C)	1.82	Equity US	MSCI USA ESG Leaders Select 5% Issuer Capped Index (Total return index)	Amundi Luxembourg	May 15, 2020	0.15
CSIF (IE) MSCI USA ESG Leaders Blue UCITS ETF B USD	1.63	Equity US	MSCI USA ESG Leaders Index	Carne Global Fund Managers (Ireland	March 13, 2020	0.10

Source: own elaboration based on Lipper's and justETF databases as well as websites of the funds' providers.

bond fund, which is quite surprising taking into account the overall structure. As it can be clearly noticed, most among the largest ESG ETFs primary listed in Germany have the indexes of the US markets as their benchmarks and there are no funds with the exposure to either European or German stock market indexes; the only funds with the specific European exposure is the third to last fund on the list yet its asset class is corporate bonds. Such structure shows that investors utilizing the largest funds listed on the German stock exchanges use them for obtaining exposure to non-German assets. Most among the largest funds are relatively recent, with the oldest one launched in 2010 (and two more in 2011). The list of providers is quite diversified yet most common providers are German-linked asset management companies. Data provided in Table 3.2. evidence also another important attribute of the German sustainable investing ETFs market—its high degree of concentration. The top 10 largest funds account for c. 45% of the total assets (top 20 for approximately two-thirds) which shows that despite the apparently large number of such funds the market in fact consists of a relatively low number of big funds, followed by a diversified group of smaller ETFs.

From another perspective, taking into consideration all ESG ETFs listed on the German stock exchanges, there are more than 400 such funds, with varying primary listing locations. Their total assets exceeded as of September/October 2021 170 billion EUR. Out of 10 largest ESG ETFs in this dimension, only three are primarily listed in Germany, the remainder in, among others, the United Kingdom or on the Euronext exchanges. In terms of the structure, it is quite similar to the already discussed market exclusively for the primary listed ETFs.

All major European ETFs providers are present in the ESG segment of the German ETFs market, including BlackRock, State Street, UBS, Amundi, or asset management arms of the Deutsche Bank financial group. The covered benchmarks, that is, in most cases the tracked indexes, include the major ESG indexes (mostly equity), not necessarily of the German or even European stock markets. Obviously, there are also ESG ETFs with the exposure to the German equities through the indexes accounting for the sustainability factors—the examples include the funds launched by the major ETFs providers, that is, BlackRock, Lyxor, and Amundi, in 2020 and 2021 (Gonçalves, 2020; Gordon, 2021). Moreover, as a factor to some extent contributing to the market's development, it should be added that in some cases institutional investors cooperate with the ETFs providers to launch and develop ESG ETFs of their preference—see, for example, the partnership between Ilmarinen Mutual Pension Insurance based in Finland and one of the leading ETFs providers, Amundi, covering $500 million in sustainable investing ETF listed in Germany (Baker, 2021).

To supplement our discussion of the German ESG ETFs, another type of indicator can be mentioned. The importance of the ESG funds on the German ETFs market is also demonstrated by their growing share in total ETFs turnover—according to the leading exchange Xetra, the share of ESG ETFs in the total turnover of ETFs has increased in 2021 to c. 16% in comparison to 6% in 2021 (Chatterjee, 2021).

References

Climate Action 100+. (2021). *About climate action 100+*. https://www.climateaction100. org/about/.

Baier, P., Berninger, M., & Kiesel, F. (2020). Environmental, social and governance reporting in annual reports: A textual analysis. *Financial Markets, Institutions & Instruments, 29*(3), 93—118.

Baker, S. (2021). *ESG interest drives ETF expansion in Europe*. Pensions & Investments. https://www.pionline.com/esg/esg-interest-drives-etf-expansion-europe.

Baquero-Herrera, M. H. (2021). Ethics in finance as the result of a strong systemic commitment: Auribus Teneo Lupum. In L. San-Jose, J. Retolaza, & L. Van Liedekerke (Eds.), *Handbook on ethics in finance* (pp. 17—30). Springer.

Barber, B. M., Morse, A., & Yasuda, A. (2021). Impact investing. *Journal of Financial Economics, 139*(1), 162—185.

Bassen, A., & Zwick, Y. (2018). Sustainable finance in Germany — what are we waiting for? *German Almanac of Sustainability, 2018*, 1—8.

BBC. (2021). *COP26: What was agreed at the Glasgow climate conference?*. https://www.bbc. com/news/science-environment-56901261.

Bénabou, R., & Tirole, J. (2010). Individual and corporate social responsibility. *Economica, 77*(305), 1—19.

Bender, J., Sun, X., & Wang, T. (2017). Thematic indexing, meet smart Beta! Merging ESG into factor portfolios. *The Journal of Index Investing, 8*(3), 89—101.

Bengtsson, E. (2008). A history of Scandinavian socially responsible investing. *Journal of Business Ethics, 82*(4), 969—983.

Bernardini, E., Di Giampaolo, J., Faiella, I., & Poli, R. (2021). The impact of carbon risk on stock returns: Evidence from the European electric utilities. *Journal of Sustainable Finance & Investment, 11*(1), 1—26.

Bernardová, D., Kašparová, K., Fink, M., Ivanová, K., & Arkhangelska, T. (2020). Construction and significance of corporate social responsibility indices—from results to the essence. *Organizacija, 53*(3).

Berrou, R., Dessertine, P., & Migliorelli, M. (2019). An overview of green finance. In M. Migliorelli, & P. Dessertine (Eds.), *The rise of green finance in Europe* (pp. 3—29). Palgrave Macmillan.

Berry, L. (2016). Religious investors and responsible investment. In T. Hebb, J. P. Hawley, A. G. Hoepner, A. L. Neher, & D. Wood (Eds.), *The Routledge handbook of responsible investment* (pp. 474—484). Routledge.

Berry, T. C., & Junkus, J. C. (2013). Socially responsible investing: An investor perspective. *Journal of Business Ethics, 112*(4), 707—720.

Bhala, K. T. (2019). The philosophical foundations of financial ethics. In C. A. Russo, R. M. Lastra, & W. Blair (Eds.), *Research handbook on law and ethics in banking and finance* (pp. 2–24). Edward Elgar Publishing.

Birindelli, G., Trotta, A., Chiappini, H., & Rizzello, A. (2021). Environmental impact investments in Europe: Where are we headed? In M. La Torre, & H. Chiappini (Eds.), *Contemporary issues in sustainable finance: Creating an efficient market through innovative policies and instruments* (pp. 151–175). Palgrave Macmillan.

Boerner, H. (2007). Your company's ESG-environmental, social, and governance factors are mattering more now to institutional investors. *Corporate Finance Review, 12*(2), 40.

Bonini, S., & Emerson, J. (2005). *Maximizing blended value—Building beyond the blended value map to sustainable investing, philanthropy and organizations.*

Bonvin, J. M., & Dembinski, P. H. (2002). Ethical issues in financial activities. *Journal of Business Ethics, 37*(2), 187–192.

Bopp, R., & Weber, M. (2020). *Sustainable Finance: Auswirkungen des Klimawandels auf das Risikomanagement der Banken.* Schäffer-Poeschel.

Bracking, S. (2015). The anti-politics of climate finance: The creation and performativity of the green climate fund. *Antipode, 47*(2), 281–302.

Brock, P., & Knorz, J. (2020). Growth of impact investing (in Germany/and the European Union) generally and as a consequence of the Covid-19 pandemic. *The International Family Offices Journal, 5*(1), 6–14.

Brown, H. S., De Jong, M., & Lessidrenska, T. (2009). The rise of the global reporting initiative: A case of institutional entrepreneurship. *Environmental Politics, 18*(2), 182–200.

Brzeszczyński, J., Gajdka, J., & Schabek, T. (2021). How risky are the socially responsible investment (SRI) stocks? Evidence from the central and eastern European (CEE) companies. *Finance Research Letters, 42.*

Busch, D. (2021). Sustainability disclosure in the EU financial sector. In D. Busch, G. Ferrarini, & S. Grünewald (Eds.), *Sustainable finance in Europe. Corporate governance, financial stability and financial markets* (pp. 397–443). Palgrave Macmillan.

Busch, T., Bauer, R., & Orlitzky, M. (2016). Sustainable development and financial markets: Old paths and new avenues. *Business & Society, 55*(3), 303–329.

Busch, T., Bruce-Clark, P., Derwall, J., Eccles, R., Hebb, T., Hoepner, A., Klein, C. H., Krueger, P. H., Paetzold, F., Scholtens, B., & Weber, O. (2021). Impact investments: A call for (re) orientation. *SN Business & Economics, 1*(2), 1–13.

Busch, D., Ferrarini, G., & Grünewald, S. (2021). Sustainable finance in Europe: Setting the scene. In D. Busch, G. Ferrarini, & S. Grünewald (Eds.), *Sustainable finance in Europe. Corporate governance, financial stability and financial markets* (pp. 3–17). Palgrave Macmillan.

Busch, D., Ferrarini, G., & Hurk, A. V. D. (2021). The European commission's sustainable finance action plan and other international initiatives. In D. Busch, G. Ferrarini, & S. Grünewald (Eds.), *Sustainable finance in Europe. Corporate governance, financial stability and financial markets* (pp. 19–59). Palgrave Macmillan.

Busco, C., Consolandi, C., Eccles, R. G., & Sofra, E. (2020). A preliminary analysis of SASB reporting: Disclosure topics, financial relevance, and the financial intensity of ESG materiality. *Journal of Applied Corporate Finance, 32*(2), 117–125.

Butcher, D. (2020). IFAC pushes for new sustainability standards board. *Strategic Finance, 102*(4), 8-8.

Cameron, S. (2007). *Community investing in Canada.* Canadian Community Investment Network Cooperative.

Camilleri, M. A. (2017). *Corporate sustainability, social responsibility and environmental management: An introduction to theory and practice with case studies.* Springer.

del Carmen Briano Turrent, G. (2019). The need to make ethics part of finance: A new dimension in corporate governance in Latin America. In P. H. Dembinski, J. Kamerling, & V. Perret (Eds.), *Changing frontiers of ethics in finance. Ethics & trust in finance global prize awards 2012—2017* (pp. 411—419).

Caseau, C., & Grolleau, G. (2020). Impact investing: Killing two Birds with one stone? *Financial Analysts Journal, 76*(4), 40—52.

Cato, M. S. (2022). *Sustainable finance: Using the power of money to change the world.* Springer Nature.

CFA Institute. (2020). *Future of sustainability in investment management.*

CFA Institute. (2021). *Global ESG disclosure standards for investment products.*

Chance, C. (2020). EU regulatory developments. *Law and Financial Markets Review, 14*(2), 128—139.

Chatterjee, S. (2021). *ESG fever: Share of sustainable fund trading soaring in 2021.* https://www.reuters.com/business/sustainable-business/esg-fever-share-sustainable-fund-trading-soaring-2021-2021-07-14/.

Child, C. (2015). Mainstreaming and its discontents: Fair trade, socially responsible investing, and industry trajectories. *Journal of Business Ethics, 130*(3), 601—618.

Claeys, G., Tagliapietra, S., & Zachmann, G. (2019). *How to make the European green deal work.* Bruegel.

Clements, R. (2022). Why comparability is a greater problem than greenwashing in ESG ETFs. *William & Mary Business Law Review, 13*(2), 441—486.

Clifford, J., & Jung, T. (2017). Exploring and understanding an emerging funding approach. In O. M. Lehner (Ed.), *Routledge handbook of social and sustainable finance* (pp. 161—176). Routledge.

Cohen, M. J. (2020). Does the COVID-19 outbreak mark the onset of a sustainable consumption transition? *Sustainability: Science, Practice and Policy, 16*(1), 1—3.

Dario, C., Sabrina, L., Landriault, E., & De Vega, P. (2021). *DLT to boost efficiency for Financial Intermediaries. An application in ESG reporting activities.* Technology Analysis & Strategic Management. in press.

Dembinski, P. H. (2017). *Ethics and responsibility in finance.* Routledge.

Dembinski, P. H., Bonvin, J. M., Dommen, E., & Monnet, F. M. (2003). The ethical foundations of responsible investment. *Journal of Business Ethics, 48*(2), 203—213.

Derwall, J., Koedijk, K., & Ter Horst, J. (2011). A tale of values-driven and profit-seeking social investors. *Journal of Banking & Finance, 35*(8), 2137—2147.

Desmartin, J. P. (2016). Asset manager stakeholders: At the heart of supply and demand in responsible investment. In T. Hebb, J. P. Hawley, A. G. Hoepner, A. L. Neher, & D. Wood (Eds.), *The Routledge handbook of responsible investment* (pp. 510—519). Routledge.

Di Giulio, A. (2019). Wege zu nachhaltigem Konsum jenseits der kleinen Schritte. In C. Bohn, D. Fuchs, A. Kerkhoff, & Ch Müller (Eds.), *Gegenwart und Zukunft sozial-ökologischer Transformation* (pp. 25—54). Nomos Verlagsgesellschaft.

Di Giulio, A., & Fuchs, D. (2016). Nachhaltige Konsum-Korridore: Konzept, einwände, entgegnungen. In K. Jantke, F. Lottermoser, J. Reinhardt, D. Rothe, & J. Stöver (Eds.), *Nachhaltiger Konsum* (pp. 143—164). Nomos Verlagsgesellschaft.

Döbeli, S. (2021). *Marktentwicklung.* Swiss Sustainable Finance.

Driessen, M. (2021). Sustainable finance: An overview of ESG in the financial markets. In D. Busch, G. Ferrarini, & S. Grünewald (Eds.), *Sustainable finance in Europe. Corporate governance, financial stability and financial markets* (pp. 329—350). Palgrave Macmillan.

Dunfee, T. W. (2003). Social investing: Mainstream or backwater? *Journal of Business Ethics, 43*(3), 247—252.

Eccles, R. G., Herron, J., & Serafeim, G. (2016). Reliable sustainability ratings: The influence of business models on information intermediaries. In T. Hebb, J. P. Hawley,

A. G. Hoepner, A. L. Neher, & D. Wood (Eds.), *The Routledge handbook of responsible investment* (pp. 620–631). Routledge.

Eccles, R. G., & Krzus, M. P. (2019). Implementing the task force on climate-related financial disclosures recommendations: An assessment of corporate readiness. *Schmalenbach Business Review, 71*(2), 287–293.

Elsenhuber, U., & Skenderasi, A. (2020). ESG investing: The role of public investors in sustainable investing. *Evolving Practices in Public Investment Management, 45.*

Escrig-Olmedo, E., Muñoz-Torres, M. J., & Fernandez-Izquierdo, M. A. (2010). Socially responsible investing: Sustainability indices, ESG rating and information provider agencies. *International Journal of Sustainable Economy, 2*(4), 442–461.

Euronext. (2021). *Euronext's ESG WORLD 75 index chosen by the federal government of Germany's pension and Care funds.* https://www.euronext.com/en/about/media/euronext-press-releases/euronexts-esg-world-75-index-chosen-federal-government-germanys.

European Commission. (2020a). *Financing the green transition: The European green deal investment plan and just transition mechanism.* https://ec.europa.eu/commission/presscorner/detail/en/ip_20_17.

European Commission. (2020b). *Stepping up Europe's 2030 climate ambition. Investing in a climate-neutral future for the benefit of our people.* https://eur-lex.europa.eu/legal-content/EN/TXT/?uri=CELEX:52020DC0562.

European Commission. (2020c). *Study on sustainability-related ratings.* Data and Research.

European Commission. (2021). *EU taxonomy for sustainable activities.* https://ec.europa.eu/info/business-economy-euro/banking-and-finance/sustainable-finance/eu-taxonomy-sustainable-activities_en.

Eurosif. (2016). *European SRI study 2016.*

Eurosif. (2018). *European SRI study 2018.*

Eurosif. (2021). *Eurosif report 2021: Fostering investor impact. Placing it at the heart of sustainable finance.*

Ezeokoli, O., Layne, C., Statman, M., & Urdapilleta, O. (2017). *Environmental, social, and governance (ESG) investment tools: A review of the current field.* Summit Consulting, LLC.

Fagerström, A., Hartwig, F., & Cunningham, G. (2017). Accounting and auditing of sustainability: Sustainable indicator accounting (SIA). *Sustainability: The Journal of Record, 10*(1), 45–52.

Fernández, M. S., Abu-Alkheil, A., & Khartabiel, G. M. (2019). Do German green mutual funds perform better than their peers? *Business and Economics Research Journal, 10*(2), 297–312.

Ferrarini, G., Siri, M., & Zhu, S. (2021). *The EU sustainable governance consultation and the missing link to soft law.* European Corporate Governance Institute-Law Working Paper.

Ferrero, I., Roncella, A., & Rocchi, M. (2021). A virtue ethics approach in finance. In L. San-Jose, J. Retolaza, & L. Van Liedekerke (Eds.), *Handbook on ethics in finance* (pp. 77–96). Springer.

Fischer, M. R., & Raabe, M. (2021). *Germany: German regulator combats greenwashing by proposing guidelines on "sustainable" investment funds.* https://www.mondaq.com/germany/fund-management-reits/1100050/german-regulator-combats-greenwashing-by-proposing-guidelines-on-sustainable-investment-funds.

Foo, M. (2019). Ethics at the new frontiers of finance. In P. H. Dembinski, J. Kamerling, & V. Perret (Eds.), *Changing frontiers of ethics in finance. Ethics & trust in finance global prize awards 2012–2017* (pp. 65–78).

Fussler, C., Cramer, A., & Van der Vegt, S. (2017). *Raising the bar: Creating value with the UN global Compact.* Routledge.

Fu, B., Wang, S., Zhang, J., Hou, Z., & Li, J. (2019). Unravelling the complexity in achieving the 17 sustainable-development goals. *National Science Review, 6*(3), 386–388.

Gabriel, K. (2019). Verantwortlich Investierende. Motive, Massstäbe und Handlungsoptionen von Kapitalanlegern. In M. Stüttgen (Ed.), *Ethik von Banken und Finanzen* (pp. 57—75). Nomos Verlag.

Gal, J. (2020). Corporate governance of insurers in Germany. German national report. *Zeitschrift für die gesamte Versicherungswissenschaft, 109*(1), 41—64.

Gibson Brandon, R., Krueger, P., & Schmidt, P. S. (2021). ESG rating disagreement and stock returns. *Financial Analysts Journal, 77*(4), 104—127.

Giles, S. (2015). *The business ethics twin-track: Combining controls and culture to minimise reputational risk.* John Wiley & Sons.

Glänzel, G., & Scheuerle, T. (2016). Social impact investing in Germany: Current impediments from investors' and social entrepreneurs' perspectives. *VOLUNTAS: International Journal of Voluntary and Nonprofit Organizations, 27*(4), 1638—1668.

Global Sustainable Investment Alliance. (2021). *Global sustainable investment review 2020.*

Glow, D. (2022a). *Monday morning memo: The ISSB published its first two drafts for the IFRS sustainability disclosure standards.* https://lipperalpha.refinitiv.com/2022/04/monday-morning-memo-the-issb-published-its-first-two-drafts-for-the-ifrs-sustainability-disclosure-standards/.

Glow, D. (2022b). *The EU commission approved the technical standards for SFDR.* https://lipperalpha.refinitiv.com/2022/04/the-eu-commission-approved-the-technical-standards-for-sfdr/.

Gomes, R. (2019). Corporate market responsibility: Ethical regulation for orderly financial markets. In P. H. Dembinski, J. Kamerling, & V. Perret (Eds.), *Changing frontiers of ethics in finance. Ethics & trust in finance global prize awards 2012—2017* (pp. 279—295).

Gonçalves, P. (2020). *Amundi targets ESG companies in Germany with new DAX ESG ETF.* Investment Week. https://www.investmentweek.co.uk/news/4024711/amundi-targets-esg-companies-germany-dax-esg-etf.

Gonzalez, C. I. (2021). Overview of global and European institutional sustainable finance initiatives. *Banco de Espana Article, 3*, 1—16.

Gordon, J. (2021). *BlackRock launches darker green DAX ESG ETF.* https://www.etfstream.com/news/blackrock-launches-darker-green-dax-esg-etf/.

Gortsos, C. V. (2021). The taxonomy regulation: More important than just as an element of the capital markets union. In D. Busch, G. Ferrarini, & S. Grünewald (Eds.), *Sustainable finance in Europe. Corporate governance, financial stability and financial markets* (pp. 351—395). Palgrave Macmillan.

Grubb, M., Koch, M., Thomson, K., Sullivan, F., & Munson, A. (2019). *The 'earth summit' agreements: A guide and assessment: An analysis of the Rio'92 UN conference on environment and development.* Routledge.

Gutsche, G., & Ziegler, A. (2019). Which private investors are willing to pay for sustainable investments? Empirical evidence from stated choice experiments. *Journal of Banking & Finance, 102*, 193—214.

Gutsche, G., & Zwergel, B. (2020). Investment barriers and labeling schemes for socially responsible investments. *Schmalenbach Business Review, 72*(2), 111—157.

Hart, O., & Zingales, L. (2017). Companies should maximize shareholder welfare not market value. *Journal of Law, Finance, and Accounting, 2*(2), 247—275.

Hawley, J. P. (2016). Setting the scene: The basics and basis of responsible investment. In T. Hebb, J. P. Hawley, A. G. Hoepner, A. L. Neher, & D. Wood (Eds.), *The Routledge handbook of responsible investment* (pp. 16—33). Routledge.

Hayat, U., & Orsagh, M. (2015). *Environmental, social, and governance issues in investing: A guide for investment professionals.* CFA Institute.

Hebb, T. (2012). Introduction—the next generation of responsible investing. In T. Hebb (Ed.), *The next generation of responsible investing* (pp. 1—8). Springer.

Hebb, T., Hawley, J. P., Hoepner, A. G., Neher, A. L., & Wood, D. (2016). Introduction to the Routledge handbook of responsible investment. In T. Hebb, J. P. Hawley, A. G. Hoepner, A. L. Neher, & D. Wood (Eds.), *The Routledge handbook of responsible investment* (pp. 3−15). Routledge.

He, Y., Kahraman, B., & Lowry, M. (2021). *ES risks and shareholder voice.* European Corporate Governance Institute−Finance Working Paper.

Hendry, J. (2013). *Ethics and finance: An introduction.* Cambridge University Press.

Hodge, M. (2021). The ESG reporting journey: Take the first steps… before its too late. *The CPA Journal, 91*(8/9), 11−13.

Homanen, M. (2019). Voting with your wallet. *Financial Ethics Review, 46−47,* 157−167.

Humphrey, J. (2016). Socially responsible screening in mutual funds. In T. Hebb, J. P. Hawley, A. G. Hoepner, A. L. Neher, & D. Wood (Eds.), *The Routledge handbook of responsible investment* (pp. 667−676). Routledge.

Inderst, G., & Stewart, F. (2018). *Incorporating environmental, social and governance (ESG) factors into fixed income investment.* World Bank Group.

International Reporting Financial Standards Foundation. (2021). *About the international sustainability standards board.* https://www.ifrs.org/groups/international-sustainability-standards-board/.

Jacob, A. (2017). Mind the gap: Analyzing the impact of data gap in Millennium Development Goals'(MDGs) indicators on the progress toward MDGs. *World Development, 93,* 260−278.

Janik, B., & Bartkowiak, M. (2015). The comparison of socially responsible indices in Central and Eastern Europe. *International Journal of Environmental Technology and Management, 18*(2), 153−169.

Janik, B., & Bartkowiak, M. (2022). Are sustainable investments profitable for investors in Central and Eastern European Countries (CEECs)? *Finance Research Letters, 44.*

J.P. Morgan. (2019). *Decoding the elements of sustainable investing.* J.P. Morgan.

Kaiser, L. (2020). ESG integration: Value, growth and momentum. *Journal of Asset Management, 21*(1), 32−51.

Kofman, P., & Payne, C. (2017). *A matter of trust: The practice of ethics in finance.* Melbourne University Press.

Köhl, M., Linser, S., Prins, K., & Talarczyk, A. (2021). The EU climate package "Fit for 55"-a double-edged sword for Europeans and their forests and timber industry. *Forest Policy and Economics, 132.*

Kölbel, J. F., Heeb, F., Paetzold, F., & Busch, T. (2020). Can sustainable investing save the world? Reviewing the mechanisms of investor impact. *Organization & Environment, 33*(4), 554−574.

Kotsantonis, S., Pinney, C., & Serafeim, G. (2016). ESG integration in investment management: Myths and realities. *Journal of Applied Corporate Finance, 28*(2), 10−16.

Krosinsky, C. (2017). The seven tribes of sustainable investing. In C. Krosinsky, & S. Purdom (Eds.), *Sustainable investing: Revolutions in theory and practice* (pp. 7−10). Routledge.

Krosinsky, C., Robins, N., & Viederman, S. (2012). After the credit crisis−The future of sustainable investing. In T. Hebb (Ed.), *The next generation of responsible investing* (pp. 9−25). Springer.

La Torre, M., & Chiappini, H. (2021). Enhancing efficiency in sustainable markets. In M. La Torre, & H. Chiappini (Eds.), *Contemporary issues in sustainable finance: Creating an efficient market through innovative policies and instruments* (pp. 1−4). Palgrave Macmillan.

Lauesen, L. M. (2017). The landscape and scale of social and sustainable finance. In O. M. Lehner (Ed.), *Routledge handbook of social and sustainable finance* (pp. 5−16). Routledge.

Lewis, M. K., & Kaleem, A. (2019). *Religion and finance: Comparing the approaches of Judaism, Christianity and Islam.* Edward Elgar Publishing.

Liberadzki, M., Jaworski, P., & Liberadzki, K. (2021). Spread analysis of the sustainability-linked bonds tied to an issuer's greenhouse gases emissions reduction target. *Energies, 14*(23).

López Ortega, A. (2019). Online interbank funding Platform for social-impact projects. In P. H. Dembinski, J. Kamerling, & V. Perret (Eds.), *Changing frontiers of ethics in finance. Ethics & trust in finance global prize awards 2012−2017* (pp. 387−397).

Lucas, J. R. (1993). *Responsibility.* Oxford University Press.

Lydenberg, S., & White, A. (2016). Responsible investment indexes: Origins, nature and purpose. In T. Hebb, J. P. Hawley, A. G. Hoepner, A. L. Neher, & D. Wood (Eds.), *The Routledge handbook of responsible investment* (pp. 527−535). Routledge.

Majoch, A. A., Hoepner, A. G., & Hebb, T. (2017). Sources of stakeholder salience in the responsible investment movement: Why do investors sign the principles for responsible investment? *Journal of Business Ethics, 140*(4), 723−741.

Maltais, A., & Nykvist, B. (2021). Understanding the role of green bonds in advancing sustainability. *Journal of Sustainable Finance & Investment, 11*(3), 233−252.

Margot, V., Geissler, C., de Franco, C., & Monnier, B. (2021). ESG investments: Filtering versus machine learning approaches. *Applied Economics and Finance, 8*(2), 1−16.

Marini, V. (2019). Institutional initiatives to foster green finance at EU level. In M. Migliorelli, & P. Dessertine (Eds.), *The rise of green finance in Europe* (pp. 119−149). Palgrave Macmillan.

Matos, P. (2020). *ESG and responsible institutional investing around the world: A critical review.* CFA Institute Research Foundation Literature Reviews.

Matteini, C. (2018). Sustainable investing for institutions: A case study. *The CPA Journal, 88*(7), 16−18.

Mazzullo, A. (2021). Rethinking taxation of impact investments. In M. La Torre, & H. Chiappini (Eds.), *Contemporary issues in sustainable finance: Creating an efficient market through innovative policies and instruments* (pp. 37−59). Palgrave Macmillan.

Mésonnier, J. S., & Nguyen, B. (2020). *Showing off cleaner hands: Mandatory climate-related disclosure by financial institutions and the financing of fossil energy.* https://papers.ssrn.com/sol3/papers.cfm?abstract_id=3733781.

Mezzanotte, F. E. (2021). Accountability in EU sustainable finance: Linking the client's sustainability preferences and the MiFID II suitability obligation. *Capital Markets Law Journal, 16*(4), 482−502.

Migliorelli, M. (2021). What do we mean by sustainable finance? Assessing existing frameworks and policy risks. *Sustainability, 13*(2).

Moreira, M. (2021). *Refinitiv sustainable finance: Turning the art of ESG into science.* Refinitiv.

Morningstar. (2020). *ESG investing comes of age.* https://www.morningstar.com/features/esg-investing-history.

Morrow, D. (2014). A tool to construct your own sustainable portfolio. *Corporate Knights, 13*(4), 70−70.

Forum Nachhaltige Geldanlagen. (2021). *Marktbericht Nachhaltige Geldanlagen 2021 − Deutschland, Österreich und die Schweiz.*

Nakajima, T., Hamori, S., He, X., Liu, G., Zhang, W., Zhang, Y., & Liu, T. (2021). *ESG investment in the global economy.* Springer Nature.

Neher, A. L. (2016). Responsible investment in Austria, Germany and Switzerland. In T. Hebb, J. P. Hawley, A. G. Hoepner, A. L. Neher, & D. Wood (Eds.), *The Routledge handbook of responsible investment* (pp. 276−286). Routledge.

O'Hara, M. (2016). *Something for nothing: Arbitrage and ethics on wall street.* WW Norton & Company.

Oberndorfer, U., Schmidt, P., Wagner, M., & Ziegler, A. (2013). Does the stock market value the inclusion in a sustainability stock index? An event study analysis for German firms. *Journal of Environmental Economics and Management, 66*(3), 497—509.

Öcal, H., & Kamil, A. A. (2021). The impact of risk indicators on sustainability (ESG) and broad-based indices: An empirical analysis from Germany, France, Indonesia and Turkey. *International Journal of Sustainable Economy, 13*(1), 18—54.

Orzes, G., Moretto, A. M., Moro, M., Rossi, M., Sartor, M., Caniato, F., & Nassimbeni, G. (2020). The impact of the United Nations global compact on firm performance: A longitudinal analysis. *International Journal of Production Economics, 227.*

Ouenniche, A., Ouenniche, J., M'zali, B., & Pérez-Gladish, B. (2016). A portfolio analysis approach to assist socially responsible investors in making decisions. *International Journal of Operational Research, 27*(3), 469—501.

Ovaere, M., & Proost, S. (2021). Cost-effective reduction of fossil energy use in the European transport sector: An assessment of the Fit for 55 Package. *Working Papers of Faculty of Economics and Business Administration, Ghent University, 21*(1031), 1—31.

Pacces, A. M. (2021). Will the EU taxonomy regulation foster sustainable corporate governance? *Sustainability, 13*(21).

Paetzold, F., & Busch, T. (2014). Unleashing the powerful few: Sustainable investing behaviour of wealthy private investors. *Organization & Environment, 27*(4), 347—367.

Paetzold, F., Busch, T., & Chesney, M. (2015). More than money: Exploring the role of investment advisors for sustainable investing. *Annals in Social Responsibility, 1*(1), 195—223.

Paul, K., & Aquila, D. A. (1988). Political consequences of ethical investing: The case of South Africa. *Journal of Business Ethics, 7*(9), 691—697.

Petrie, M. (2021). *Environmental governance and greening fiscal policy: Government accountability for environmental stewardship.* Palgrave Macmillan.

Proietti, G. (2021). Profitable impact bonds: Introducing risk-sharing mechanisms for a more Balanced version of social impact bonds. In M. La Torre, & H. Chiappini (Eds.), *Contemporary issues in sustainable finance: Creating an efficient market through innovative policies and instruments* (pp. 61—78). Palgrave Macmillan.

Puaschunder, J. M. (2016). On the emergence, current state, and future perspectives of Socially Responsible Investment (SRI). *Consilience, 16,* 38—63.

Randers, J., Rockström, J., Stoknes, P. E., Goluke, U., Collste, D., Cornell, S. E., & Donges, J. (2019). Achieving the 17 sustainable development goals within 9 planetary boundaries. *Global Sustainability, 2.*

Rasche, A. (2021). The UN global compact and the OECD guidelines for multinational enterprises and their enforcement mechanisms. In I. Bentakes, & M. A. Stein (Eds.), *The Cambridge companion to business and human rights law* (pp. 195—214). Cambridge University Press.

Raworth, K. (2017). *Doughnut economics: Seven ways to think like a 21st-century economist.* Chelsea Green Publishing.

Refinitiv. (2022). *ESG Regulation (SFDR): Where are we heading in 2022?.*

Rhodes, C. J. (2016). The 2015 Paris climate change conference: COP21. *Science Progress, 99*(1), 97—104.

Robbins, A. (2016). How to understand the results of the climate change summit: Conference of Parties21 (COP21) Paris 2015. *Journal of Public Health Policy, 37,* 129—132.

Sandberg, J., Juravle, C., Hedesström, T. M., & Hamilton, I. (2009). The heterogeneity of socially responsible investment. *Journal of Business Ethics, 87*(4), 519—533.

Scalzo, G. (2019). Epistemological foundations for the relationship between ethics and finance. In P. H. Dembinski, J. Kamerling, & V. Perret (Eds.), *Changing frontiers of ethics in finance. Ethics & trust in finance global prize awards 2012—2017* (pp. 25—36).

Schoenmaker, D. (2018). Sustainable investing: How to do it. *Bruegel Policy Contribution, 23*, 1–12.

Schoenmaker, D. (2021). A new integrated-value assessment method for corporate investment. *Bruegel-Policy Contributions, 19*, 1–10.

Schoenmaker, D., & Schramade, W. (2019). *Principles of sustainable finance.* Oxford University Press.

Scholtens, B. (2014). Indicators of responsible investing. *Ecological Indicators, 36*, 382–385.

Schueth, S. (2003). Socially responsible investing in the United States. *Journal of Business Ethics, 43*(3), 189–194.

Schütze, F., & Stede, J. (2021). The EU sustainable finance taxonomy and its contribution to climate neutrality. *Journal of Sustainable Finance & Investment.* in press.

Shiiba, N., Wu, H. H., Huang, M. C., & Tanaka, H. (2022). How blue financing can sustain ocean conservation and development: A proposed conceptual framework for blue financing mechanism. *Marine Policy, 139*.

Silvola, H., & Landau, T. (2021). *Sustainable investing: Beating the market with ESG.* Palgrave Macmillan.

Śliwiński, P., & Łobza, M. (2019). Does relative performance of socially responsible investing increase with financial risk? *Problemy Zarzadzania, 17*(3), 212–228.

de Souza Cunha, F. A. F., & Samanez, C. P. (2013). Performance analysis of sustainable investments in the Brazilian stock market: A study about the corporate sustainability index (ISE). *Journal of Business Ethics, 117*(1), 19–36.

Starks, L. T. (2021). Environmental, social, and governance issues and the financial analysts journal. *Financial Analysts Journal, 77*(4), 5–21.

Statman, M. (2000). Socially responsible mutual funds (corrected). *Financial Analysts Journal, 56*(3), 30–39.

Statman, M., & Glushkov, D. (2016). Classifying and measuring the performance of socially responsible mutual funds. *The Journal of Portfolio Management, 42*(2), 140–151.

Stühlinger, S. (2018). Need of clarification: Current perceptions of impact investing in the German and Swiss foundation sectors. *CEPS Working Paper Series, 13*, 1–21.

Swiss Sustainable Finance. (2017). *Handbook on sustainable investments: Background information and practical examples for institutional asset owners.* CFA Institute Research Foundation.

Swiss Sustainable Finance. (2020). *Swiss sustainable investment market study 2020.*

Swiss Sustainable Finance. (2021). *Swiss sustainable investment market study 2021.*

Tinelli, M. L. (2016). Reflection: Responsible investment around the world. In T. Hebb, J. P. Hawley, A. G. Hoepner, A. L. Neher, & D. Wood (Eds.), *The Routledge handbook of responsible investment* (pp. 364–371). Routledge.

Townsend, B. (2020). From SRI to ESG: The origins of socially responsible and sustainable investing. *The Journal of Impact and ESG Investing, 1*(1), 10–25.

Trelstad, B. (2016). Impact investing: A brief history. *Capitalism & Society, 11*(2).

United Nations General Assembly. (2015). *Resolution adopted by the general assembly on 25 September 2015.*

Vanderheiden, S. (2015). Justice and climate finance: Differentiating responsibility in the green climate fund. *The International Spectator, 50*(1), 31–45.

Vartiak, L. (2017). Global sustainable and responsible investment activities and strategies of companies. *New Trends and Issues Proceedings on Humanities and Social Sciences, 4*, 77–87.

Vaze, P., Meng, A., & Giuliani, D. (2019). Greening the financial system. *Climate Bonds Initiative.*

Vergara, C. C., & Agudo, L. F. (2021). Fintech and sustainability: Do they affect each other? *Sustainability, 13*(13), 1–19.

Verheyden, T., Eccles, R. G., & Feiner, A. (2016). ESG for all? The impact of ESG screening on return, risk, and diversification. *Journal of Applied Corporate Finance, 28*(2), 47–55.

Vinueza-Peter, L. (2020). *How far is the sustainable fund market in Europe?. On the competitive position of the German asset management industry.* BVI Bundesverband Investment und Asset Management.

Vinueza-Peter, L. (2021). *Snapshot sustainability: The German sustainable fund market in Q4 2020.* BVI Bundesverband Investment und Asset Management.

Weber, O., & ElAlfy, A. (2019). The development of green finance by sector. In M. Migliorelli, & P. Dessertine (Eds.), *The rise of green finance in Europe* (pp. 53–78). Palgrave Macmillan.

Whitelock, V. G. (2019). Multidimensional environmental social governance sustainability framework: Integration, using a purchasing, operations, and supply chain management context. *Sustainable Development, 27*(5), 923–931.

Wins, A., & Zwergel, B. (2016). Comparing those who do, might and will not invest in sustainable funds: A survey among German retail fund investors. *Business Research, 9*(1), 51–99.

Woods, C., & Urwin, R. (2010). Putting sustainable investing into practice: A governance framework for pension funds. *Journal of Business Ethics, 92*(1), 1–19.

Wuelser, G., Chesney, M., Mayer, H., Niggli, U., Pohl, C., Sahakian, M., Stauffacher, M., Zinsstag, J., & Edwards, P. (2020). Priority Themes for Swiss sustainability research. *Swiss Academies Reports, 15*(5), 1–56.

Zagst, R., Krimm, T., Hörter, S., & Menzinger, B. (2011). *Responsible investing: Verantwortlich investieren.* FinanzBuch Verlag.

Zhang, L. (2021). ESG rating divergence: Beauty is in the eye of the Beholder. *The Journal of Index Investing, 12*(3), 53–63.

Zhang, D., Zhang, Z., & Managi, S. (2019). A bibliometric analysis on green finance: Current status, development, and future directions. *Finance Research Letters, 29*, 425–430.

CHAPTER 4

Sustainable investing ETFs: European market

4.1 Global sustainable investing industry: basic information

In the last several years, the global financial system has experienced an unprecedented increase in the flows of capital to various entities offering sustainable investing strategies. The exact assessment of the attributes of the global sustainable investing industry is hindered by a number of factors, above all insufficient reporting by the financial institutions and lack of common methodological standards, stemming from the issues such as varying understandings of the fundamental concept of sustainability. Regardless of the aforementioned stipulations, it is possible to gain some insights into the size and structure of this industry by taking into consideration the data provided by the global organizations focused on this topic—in this section, we discuss the information retrieved from all available biannual reports of the Global Sustainable Investment Alliance, GSIA (Global Sustainable Investment Alliance [GSIA], 2013, 2015, 2017, 2019, 2021). GSIA gathers global data on the sustainable investing using relatively methodologically consistent information from the surveys by the regional sustainable investment forums; nonetheless, the exact comparisons by regions and over time are impossible due to some discrepancies between regional organizations and changes over time; data presented covers all key financial systems but it should be emphasized that surveys are not conducted in all countries (GSIA, 2021).

According to the most recent data published by the GSIA as of the writing of this chapter (GSIA, 2021), the global assets of sustainable investments were on the turn of 2019 and 2020 at the record-high level of over 35 trillion USD. Fig. 4.1 covers the geographical structure of the assets of sustainable investments in 2020. As it may be clearly noticed, the North American region (exclusively the United States and Canada were covered

Sustainable Investing
ISBN 978-0-12-823871-4
https://doi.org/10.1016/B978-0-12-823871-4.00002-7

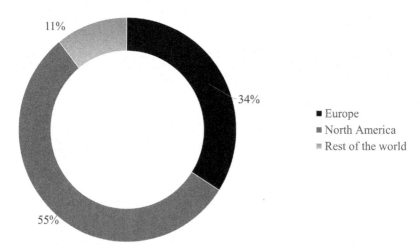

Figure 4.1 Global structure of the assets of sustainable investing financial products: assets by regions in 2020. *(Source: own elaboration based on Global Sustainable Investment Alliance (2021). Global sustainable investment review 2020.)*

in the study) was the largest in the world, with approximately 19.5 trillion USD of the sustainable investing assets, followed by Europe with about 12 trillion USD and much smaller value for the remaining regions, with aggregate share in the global assets of 11% (consisting above all of the assets of the Japanese sustainable investments). It can thus be stated that the vast majority of the sustainable investing assets globally were reported to be the elements of the portfolios of the financial institutions in the most developed countries with the largest financial systems, and the position of the other covered economies was negligible.[1]

As the results discussed above can directly be affected by the size of the financial sectors in the given economy, it is important to consider the relative dimension as well, that is, the share of sustainable investments in the total assets managed by the financial institutions in the examined regions. According to the GSIA (2021) the highest share (c. 62%) as of 2020 was reported for the Canadian market, followed by about 42% in case of

---

[1] Due to the increased financial flows to the emerging economies observed in the first several years of the 21st century, the position of their sustainable investing sectors may improve, for example, if the foreign investors begin taking into account the ethical factors as suggested by Dowell-Jones (2012). Some countries not examined in detail in the GSIA's reports albeit with already noticeable sustainable investing industries include Brazil, China, India, Singapore, and South Africa (CFA Institute & Principles for Responsible Investment, 2018, 2019a, 2019b).

Europe and 33% for the US sector; Japan was the last among the major markets with approximately 24% share. These values clearly prove that sustainable investments had a more prominent position in the European financial system than in the case of the remaining countries and regions, with the exception of Canada. Consequently, they show the significance of the European sustainable investing industry from a global perspective.

To gain insight into the key trends taking place in the global sustainable investing industry, we consider the data on their assets since 2012 (the earliest year with data available), as presented in Fig. 4.2. It unequivocally confirms the high dynamics of the studied market—between 2012 and 2020 the global assets have almost tripled, growing from ca. 13 trillion USD to over 35 trillion USD. However, as it may be clearly concluded, the rate of growth has evolved over the analyzed time period—the initial increase, between 2012 and 2014 had been the strongest, yet to some extent, it may be attributed to the broadening of the range of the surveyed financial institutions and other methodological aspects (albeit difficult to assess due to the lack of access to the primary datasets). Over 2014–16, the size remained

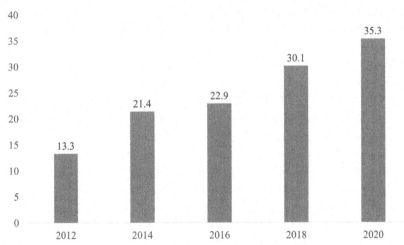

Figure 4.2 Global assets of the sustainable investing financial products: 2012–20 (USD trillion). *(Source: own elaboration based on Eurosif (2018). European SRI study 2018, Global Sustainable Investment Alliance (2013). Global sustainable investment review 2012, Global Sustainable Investment Alliance (2015). Global sustainable investment review 2014, Global Sustainable Investment Alliance (2017). Global sustainable investment review 2016, Global Sustainable Investment Alliance (2019). Global sustainable investment review 2018, Global Sustainable Investment Alliance (2021). Global sustainable investment review 2020, US SIF Foundation (2018). Report on US sustainable, responsible and impact investing trends, 2018.)*

stable and, most importantly, the rapid development has taken place since 2016, thus reflecting various trends contributing to the fast expansion of sustainable investment (see Chapter 3 for more details on the public policy developments boosting the rapid growth of, in particular, the European industry, and the other key factors, such as the activities of the financial organizations promoting ESG investing); one of the main trends seems increased access to the ESG-related information concerning financial investments.

Comparison of the values for 2020 to the GSIA's data for the previous years indicates some important changes in the geographical structure of the global assets that began to take place between 2018 and 2020 (GSIA, 2019, 2021). Up to 2018, Europe was the distinctive leader, accounting for at least half of the global assets (in the earlier years the share of Europe had been even higher, close to two-thirds (GSIA, 2013, 2015)). Over 2018–20, a dramatic overhaul could be identified with the substantial weakening of Europe's position in the global perspective, accompanied by an even more profound strengthening of the North American sector (the process identified already in the preceding time periods as discussed in the reports by the US SIF Foundation (2018, 2020) or even as early as at the very beginning of the 21st century (Schueth, 2003)); the position of the remaining regions has remained quite stable. However, import stipulation is necessary to put the aforementioned results implying the diminishing position of sustainable investments in the European region in the correct perspective. As stated in the 2021 GSIA's report (GSIA, 2021), the 2020 values reflect the modifications in the methodology applied with regard to the European sustainable investments resulting from the legal changes (for more on the topic see the relevant sections of Chapter 3), above all applying more strict definition of the sustainable investments, making the pre-2020 data inconsistent with the most recent indicators. This apparent decline of the European market should above all be attributed to the transition in terms of sustainable investment definitions inflicted by the European Sustainable Finance Action Plan—consequently, drawing robust conclusions concerning future prospects of the European market from this change is impossible.

The structure of the global sustainable investments may also be analyzed in other dimensions than the already mentioned ones, that is, in terms of the adopted investment strategies and the investors interested in such financial products. As the 2020 data showed, ESG integration was the most popular investment strategy globally, with over 25 trillion USD of assets managed within this approach (it has also been one of the most quickly increasing categories), followed by the negative/exclusionary screening (up to 2018 the most frequently deployed strategy), and corporate engagement/shareholder action. On the other side of the ranking, impact and community were by far the least popular approaches, with negligible assets in relation to the other strategies (GSIA, 2021). Examination of the popularity of investment strategies in the major regions uncovers some interesting between-region discrepancies—the US assets accounted for the vast majority of the ESG integration investments (c. 16 out of 25 trillion USD) yet in the case of the three next most broadly deployed approaches: negative/exclusionary screening, corporate engagement/shareholder action, and norms-based screening, Europe is the global leader. These results can at least to some degree be explained by the regulatory and policy factors as well as methodological differences—for instance, the norms-based screening strategies are not covered by the US surveys (thus the dominance of Europe and null position of US market) and the popularity of certain strategies in Europe stems from the legal requirements linked to the EU Sustainable Finance Disclosure Regulation (SFDR). The structure of the global sustainable investments in terms of their users has remained dominated by the most frequent institutional investors (75% share as of 2020) yet the share of retail users has more than doubled since 2012.

Finally, to briefly supplement our discussion, data on the size of the global sustainable investments may also be extracted from the other sources. The most important is the database of the Principles for Responsible Investment (PRI; for more on the PRI topic see Chapter 3), with the global values for 2006–21 (Principles for Responsible Investment [PRI], 2021). According to the end of March 2021 data, there were more than 3800 PRI signatories, with over 121 trillion USD of total assets under management, out of which approximately 600 were asset owners, managing slightly under 30 trillion USD of assets (the remainder were investment managers and service providers). The average annual growth rate of total assets was c. 22% over 2006–21, indicating high growth of the assets managed by the initiative's signatories. Due to the substantially different coverage and methodology, it is impossible to compare PRI's data to GSIA's yet both sources prove the undeniable development of sustainable investments globally. Moreover, it should be added that our discussion does not cover some rather specific types of investments linked to the sustainability issues that may also be included in the category of sustainable investments (or, more broadly, sustainable finance), for instance, financial instruments linked to the carbon markets (CFA Institute, 2020).

4.2 European sustainable investing industry: size, between-country differences

In the previous section, we presented the basic indicators on the global sustainable investing industry, showing, in particular, the between-region differences. This section covers the European sustainable investing industry—we examine its size, structure, and main trends; again, the key source of data deployed are the reports of the GSIA[2]; some secondary sources such as the data published by the PRI initiative are used as well. For the country-level data, we use the Eurosif reports on the European socially responsible investments.

According to the most recent report of the GSIA (2021), as of 2020 the total assets of sustainable investments in Europe reached approximately 12 trillion USD (see Fig. 4.3), that is, about one-third of the aggregate global assets—in the previous years, the share of Europe in the total assets was much higher (for a more detailed discussion of the global market, see the preceding section). However, as it was already mentioned, the level observed for Europe for 2020 is insufficiently comparable to the previous years because of the changes in the EU-level legislation. The values for the previous years are more consistent with the exception of 2012 (see the note below Fig. 4.3). The fast and stable growth of the European sustainability can be clearly identified for the years 2014—18; it is even more pronounced for 2012—14 but this result should be interpreted with caution. Still, in 2018 the assets were more than 3 trillion USD higher than in 2014. The conclusion becomes slightly less positive when we compare the growth rates noted for Europe with the other regions—in all cases, the pace of growth was much higher over 2014—18 than in Europe; the explanation seems related to the already high levels of assets in Europe in 2014 whereas in the other regions (including the United States) the size of the relevant market had been rather small. From the other perspective, even though the report by the PRI (2021) does not include the data on assets divided by regions, it conveys another significant indicator with more detailed data, that is, the number of signatories. In the key category of signatories in line with the main focus of our study, that is, the asset owners, there were approximately 360 European

---

[2] The scope of the GSIA's reports differs in terms of the number of the European countries covered, depending on the report's edition—the most recent 2020 edition covers 18 European sustainable investing sectors; the previous ones had more limited scope yet the differences applied to some rather minor markets thus not affecting substantially the conclusions reached.

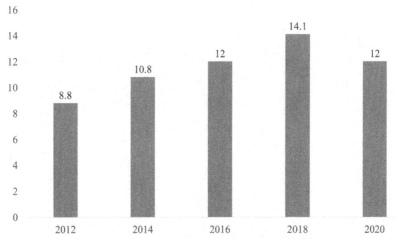

Figure 4.3 Assets of the sustainable investing financial products in Europe: 2012—20 (USD trillion). *(Source: own elaboration based on Global Sustainable Investment Alliance (2013). Global sustainable investment review 2012, Global Sustainable Investment Alliance (2015). Global sustainable investment review 2014, Global Sustainable Investment Alliance (2017). Global sustainable investment review 2016, Global Sustainable Investment Alliance (2019). Global sustainable investment review 2018, Global Sustainable Investment Alliance (2021). Global sustainable investment review 2020.)*

financial institutions (c. 60% of the global signatories in this category). Most European asset owners declaring compliance with the PRI were head-quartered in three groups of countries: the United Kingdom and Ireland, Nordic countries, and Germany and Austria.

The size of the European sustainable investments market should be examined not only with regard to the absolute values of the covered assets but also (potentially even more importantly in the context of their importance for the local investment industries) in relation to the total assets under management—see Fig. 4.4. In 2020, the share of sustainable investments was at the lowest level in the analyzed time period—this value is not entirely comparable to the previous years. Nevertheless, even over the 2014—18 time period, the decline had been quite significant, from close to 60% to under half of the aggregate assets; importantly, in all other major regions, the trend has been positive. The apparent negative conclusion concerning the relative importance of sustainable investments in Europe in the last decade should be mitigated, as suggested in GSIA (2019), by the possible explanation referring to a more correct classification of the investments as sustainable due to stricter definitions and standards.

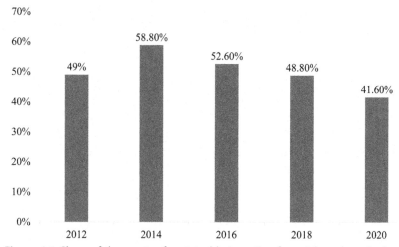

Figure 4.4 Share of the assets of sustainable investing financial products in the total assets under management, Europe: 2012–20 (%). *(Source: own elaboration based on Global Sustainable Investment Alliance (2013). Global sustainable investment review 2012, Global Sustainable Investment Alliance (2021). Global sustainable investment review 2020.)*

The analysis of the most recent structure of the European sustainable investments in terms of the utilized investment strategies is hindered by the lack of 2020 data derived from surveys as noted in GSIA (2021), thus the extrapolated data are utilized, presented in Fig. 4.5. Due to the fact that most financial companies employ multiple strategies, the values presented in Fig. 4.5 do not sum to the 2020 value shown in Fig. 4.3. The most frequent ESG investment strategy in Europe was unquestionably the negative screening approach—it was deployed in over three quarters of the investments in terms of assets. The common utilization of this strategy can be linked to the legal requirements imposed on most European financial institutions concerning the elimination of certain categories of industries or companies. Nevertheless, it is also the least advanced strategy as explained in Chapter 3, requiring the highly limited engagement of the managing company. The second most popular strategy (focused on the corporate actions) is quite opposite in this dimension as it is associated with the activity of the financial institutions during, for example, shareholders' meeting. ESG integration is relatively less common in Europe than in, for example, the United States. The fourth and the last among the frequent strategies, norms-based screening, is to some extent linked to the negative screening yet with the focus on the international standards. As it may be clearly

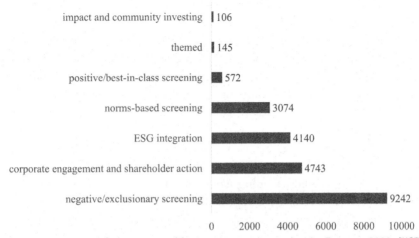

impact and community investing | 106

themed | 145

positive/best-in-class screening ▇ 572

norms-based screening ▇▇▇▇▇ 3074

ESG integration ▇▇▇▇▇▇ 4140

corporate engagement and shareholder action ▇▇▇▇▇▇ 4743

negative/exclusionary screening ▇▇▇▇▇▇▇▇▇▇▇ 9242

0   2000   4000   6000   8000   10000

Figure 4.5 Assets of the sustainable investment strategies in Europe: 2020 (USD billion, estimated). Note: 2020 values were obtained by the GSIA by extrapolation of the data from the previous edition of the report, from 2018. *(Source: own elaboration based on Global Sustainable Investment Alliance (2021). Global sustainable investment review 2020.)*

noticed in Fig. 4.5 impact and community investing, the two types of strategies potentially most strongly linked to the sustainability aims, remained "exotic" approaches, with a very low market share.

Additional dimension of the European structure is the split of the assets of sustainable investments between retail and institutional investors. The 2017 data was published by the Eurosif (2018). European SRI study 2018 shows high growth of the share of retail investors since 2013 (from c. 3% to over 30% of the total assets). Even though more recent indicators for Europe are not available, the further increase of retail users of sustainable investments on a global scale (mentioned in Section 4.1.) implies with a high possibility that a similar trend has taken place in Europe, taking into particular into account the fact that the examined indicator was already in the region above the global average and that the retail participation may have been boosted by the regulatory changes.

The structure of the European sustainable investments in terms of the country-level division is difficult to assess due to the lack of sufficiently disaggregated data that can be acquired from the sources used throughout this section. Some information on the major European markets can be found in the Eurosif's 2018 report (Eurosif, 2018); the most recent report does not include these data. The analysis of the 2017 data provided in the report indicates that the United Kingdom is undeniably the largest sustainable investments market in the European region, as evidenced by, among others, close to 3 trillion USD allocated to engagement and voting sustainable investing strategies or more than 2 trillion USD in both ESG integration and exclusions screening; it was also the second-largest market in Europe for the impact investments. Six next major European markets for ESG investments were Germany, France, Italy, the Netherlands, Sweden, and Switzerland. Switzerland was the regional leader in terms of negative/exclusions screening investments, with close to 2.5 trillion USD managed within such approach whereas France accounted for substantially more than half of the norms-based screening assets; a similar conclusion can be reached for Italy, a clear leader with regard to the impact investments. German market, consistently with the structure of the regional industry, consisted mostly of the negative/exclusions screening sustainable assets. Dutch and Swedish markets were highly diversified, with no clear leading category. Apart from the aforementioned, the other sustainable investing markets in Europe presented in the report included: Belgium, Denmark, and Spain (they can be characterized as mid-sized markets) as well as small markets of Austria and Poland (the latter with negligible sustainable investments).

As the conclusion of our discussion of the European sustainable investments we briefly outline some of the most recent key factors contributing to the development of this sector,[3] based on the overview provided in GSIA (2021):

- activity of the Eurosif in the promotion of sustainable investments;
- the growing number of sustainable financial products offered by the financial institutions, with increased diversity of their themes;
- growing interest from the retail investors, also related to growing disclosure requirements applied to financial advisors with regard to sustainability issues;
- collaboration of the financial institutions in establishing and promoting the cross-border sustainable finance credentials[4];
- EU-level regulatory and policy developments.[5]

---

[3] Discussion concerning factors in the earlier periods can be found in, for example, Hummels (2012).

[4] Country-level labels are also used in some European countries (Eurosif, 2016).

[5] In some cases country-level regulations may also affect the ESG ETFs markets (Deloitte, 2018). For more detailed information on certain policy aspects, see Chapter 3.

4.3 Sustainable investment funds in Europe

Following the discussion of the overall sustainable investing sector in Europe, in this section, we focus briefly on its subsector consisting of the investment funds with the sustainable (ESG) profile. Due to scarcity of data on the issue (most available sources include data for the entire sustainable investing sector, without more detailed decompositions) our presentation will be rather brief—it will be expanded with regard to our key category of investment funds, that is, exchange-traded funds (ETFs), in the next sections.

According to the report published by KPMG (2019), the assets of the ESG investment funds in Europe amounted in December 2018 to almost 500 billion EUR managed by close to 3000 funds (in both dimensions it meant an almost twofold increase in relation to 2012). The most frequent sustainable investing strategy deployed by these funds were various types of screening approaches that accounted for almost 90% in terms of assets; thematic funds were a much less common group. More than 60% of the European ESG funds (in terms of assets) were domiciled in one of the three countries: Luxembourg, France, or Sweden.

Another possible approach to identification and organization of the sustainable investment funds in Europe is through the application of the criteria of SFDR launched in March 2021—ESG funds are therefore the funds classified as either SFDR Article 8 or Article 9 compliant (for more on SFDR and related methodology see Chapter 3). According to the November 2021 report published by the European Fund and Asset Management Association (European Fund and Asset Management Association [EFAMA], 2021b), the total assets of the European sustainable investment funds exceeded slightly 4 trillion EUR in March 2021, out of which 3.7 trillion EUR were managed in the Article 8 funds (funds promoting sustainability) and the remainder by the Article 9 funds (funds with sustainability objective (Eurosif, 2021)). The share of Article 8 and 9 funds in the total assets of the European investment funds was at c. 24%. In terms of the geographical structure, the most frequent country of domicile was Luxembourg, followed by France and the Netherlands whereas according to EFAMA (2021a) the management locations of ESG funds were most frequently France, Sweden, the Netherlands, Germany, and Italy (when compared to the aggregate assets in a certain country, the highest share of

ESG funds was noted in the Nordic economies,[6] Belgium and the Netherlands); in terms of the asset classes, the distinctive first place belonged to the equity funds and the remainder mostly to bond and multiasset funds.

The usefulness of the above-mentioned data based on the SFDR articles is limited by its recent launch and lack of pre-2021 time series grounded in SFDR. Moreover, SFDR regulations do not cover the Swiss and UK investment funds; the other problem is the lack of SFDR labeling used by some asset managers. For both reasons the values presented in this paragraph in fact understate the total size of the European sustainable investment funds market—according to EFAMA (2021) the total assets of ESG funds in Europe in March 2021 were at ca. 6 trillion EUR. This result implies that investment funds account for more than half of the assets of all European sustainable investments (55% (EFAMA, 2021a)) and confirms the importance of the ESG funds in the context of the aggregate sustainable finance in Europe.

The third and final key report discussed in this section is the publication by Zeb and Morningstar (2021), adopting a perspective to some extent similar to the report by EFAMA, that is, with some discussion of the SFDR classification (yet not fully applied in the analysis; the preliminary results implied, though, results quite similar to the ones obtained by EFAMA). The total assets of the European sustainable funds were estimated at about 1.2 trillion EUR at the end of 2020 (data covered both the EU countries and the major non-EU European financial markets such as Switzerland or the United Kingdom). Their share in the total assets of the European investment funds was approximately 11% but in the case of the new capital flows to the funds, sustainable entities accounted for more than a half. With regard to the structure of the European sustainable investment funds, most funds had equity exposure and adopted an active investment approach. Luxembourg was the domicile for more than one-third of the European ESG funds, with France, Sweden, and Ireland at the second place, with highly similar values of assets. The results in terms of the shares in the total investment funds' assets show that the strongest position of sustainable funds was attained in the Netherlands, Sweden, and France. Moreover, similarly to the previously discussed studies, also this one showed the negligible role of the impact investments in comparison to the other types of ESG

---

[6] Nordic economies are perceived among the global leaders and innovators with regard to the sustainable investing (Reichenberg Gustafsson & Stewart, 2021).

strategies that may be regarded as less strict with regard to the sustainability aims.

As it can be clearly noticed, even after taking into consideration the dissimilar reporting periods, the levels of the sizes of the sustainable investment funds in Europe shown in the data sources presented in the preceding paragraphs are substantially different—this result proves the problem in the correct and reliable assessment of sustainable investments. Surprisingly high levels of sustainable investments funds market's size obtained using the SFDR classification as the base identification approach in relation to the other estimates could indicate some possible less strict utilization (by the asset management company conducting self-identification) or even some type of the sustainable washing problems. To sum up, as explained by Glow (2022b) and Le Sourd and Safaee (2021), as of 2021 and early 2022, the switch from conventional to the ESG investment funds was among the key trends shaping the European investment funds industry, influenced by the factors such as the enactment and implementation of the EU regulation, decisions of the funds' distributors to exclude non-ESG products from their offer, increased alignment of the corporations with the sustainable development principles, continuously growing demand from more ESG aware investors, and repurposing of the funds in line with the ESG rules by their providers.

To put the abovementioned results for Europe in a more global context, we also briefly discuss the sustainable investment funds markets in the second major region, in the United States. The US market had undergone a rapid expansion already in the early 2010s, with substantial year-to-year growth rates, resulting from a number of factors including the demand from the clients; in 2015 there were already more than 100 ESG domestic equity funds (Bialkowski & Starks, 2016). In 2017, the US sustainable investing funds managed c. 95 billion USD of assets—at that time the US sector was dominated by the ESG mutual funds rather than ESG ETFs (with the exception of the sector equity category, that is, mostly focused on the themed sustainable investments) (Hale, 2018). According to the most recent data on the US sustainable investing funds available (Hale, 2021), at the end of 2020 there were nearly 400 US investment funds with the ESG profile (out of which c. 110 were ETFs and the remainder mutual funds) with close to 250 billion USD—in terms of flows it was the first year when ESG ETFs exceeded (almost two-fold) mutual funds; 2020 was the year when all key indicators of the US investment funds market reached record-high levels. The size of the sustainable investment funds markets in the other regions (i.e., outside Europe or the United States) is more difficult to assess yet the available data indicate the much lower values of assets and their shares in the global market (socially responsible investment is a concept stemming from the US and European financial systems (Lean et al., 2015)).

4.4 European ETFs market: basic facts

Before the discussion of the European sustainable investing ETFs, we devote this section to the brief outline of the entire European ETFs markets, both at the regional and country levels, thus providing the background for the discussion in the subsequent section. We present the sizes of these markets (above all in terms of assets) and the key trends; unless stated otherwise all data used in this section were extracted from the Lipper's dataset and our own unique database was created. For reference purposes, to validate our approach, we also present the data acquired from the other sources.

To conduct the study, the first step was to identify all European countries with the local ETFs markets that is, with at least one ETF primary listed on the local stock exchange for at least 1 month; time period of the analysis is 2006–21. It was selected based on the availability of ESG ETFs in Europe, with almost no such funds before 2006. Due to the limited data availability for some countries, certain ETFs markets could thus be omitted yet they were some very small ones, with minimal activity—the lack of their inclusion does not affect significantly our conclusions. Consequently, in our analysis, we consider the following 17 countries as belonging to the European regional market: France, Germany, Greece, Hungary, Ireland, Israel, Italy, Latvia, Lithuania, Luxembourg, Norway. Poland, Russia, Spain, Switzerland, Turkey, and the United Kingdom. Two comments are necessary with regard to our sample. First, some of the listed countries are geographically only partially in Europe (or even entirely outside—the case of Israel)—still, we decided to include the local ETFs in our sample due to the strong economic and political links to the European countries. Nevertheless, the ETFs markets in these countries are relatively small thus their exclusion would not change substantially our conclusions and their inclusion extends the sample's size. Second comment refers to some rather specific cases of the stock exchanges operating in more than country, for which country-level data could not be acquired with sufficient reliability. Consequently, we adopted the following approach. Euronext data for the ETFs primary listed on the Paris segment are treated as values for France;

the remainder Euronext primary listed ETFs are considered separately as "Euronext_non_Paris." Similar approach, that is, joint label, was used for the ETFs primary listed on the Nasdaq Nordic stock exchange group—such ETFs are labeled as "Nordic" (the only Nordic country not covered in this category is Norway, with the own local stock exchange). As a result, the total composition of our sample is 17 countries and 2 combined entities.

The assets of the European ETFs amounted at the end of December 2006 to slightly below 75 billion USD (see Fig. 4.6). Over the next 15 years, the assets have increased (the only exception was minor declines over 2010−11 and 2017−18). The average annual growth rate was close to 23% and the highest increases could be noticed in the initial years of the examined time period. The final value of assets is over 1.4 trillion USD—the 1 trillion USD level was reached for the first time in August 2020. Results presented in Fig. 4.6. prove undeniable development of the European ETFs industry in the regional perspective, even during the periods of the increased financial stress or the Covid-19 global pandemic.

Analysis of the European ETFs market divided according to the countries of primary listing unveils the substantial heterogeneity of the ETFs industries in the region (see Fig. 4.7). There are four markets with the assets of ETFs exceeding 100 billion USD: United Kingdom (the largest ETFs market in Europe (over 46% share in total regional assets) and one of the largest in the world (according to our estimates, in September 2021

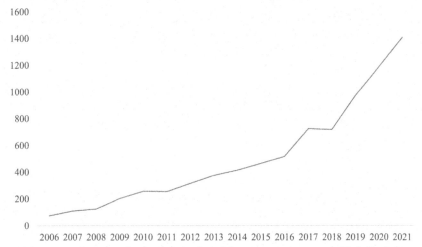

Figure 4.6 Total assets of ETFs primary listed in Europe: 2006−21 (USD billion). Note: 2021 data as of end of September 2021. *(Source: own elaboration based on the Lipper's database.)*

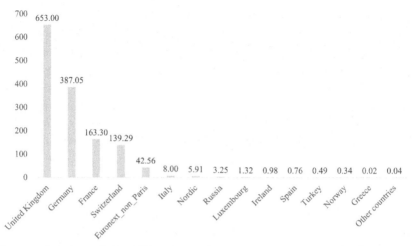

Figure 4.7 Assets of the ETFs primary listed in Europe: geographical structure (September 2021, USD billion). *(Source: own elaboration based on the Lipper's database.)*

only the US market was bigger)), Germany, France, and Switzerland. These four markets accounted for approximately 95.5% of the total European assets of ETFs. Euronext_non_Paris, that is, Euronext-listed ETFs (other than the ones listed primary on the Paris segment), accounted for c. 3% of the regional assets. The share of the remaining countries or exchanges did not exceed 1% and the level of 1 billion USD of assets was exceeded in four cases: Italy, Nordic exchanges, Russia, and Luxembourg. The observed discrepancies cannot be easily linked with the differences in the sizes of the economies—consider, among others, the differences between Switzerland and Italy.

European ETFs market can be compared to its counterparts in the other regions thus showing its importance on a global scale. According to our estimates, as of September 2021, the assets of ETFs primary listed in the United States were at approximately 6.6 trillion USD and the second North American market, Canadian, had the size of c. 250 billion USD. It can thus be stated that the European ETFs market corresponds to about one-fifth of the North American one. Still, aggregate European ETFs assets are much larger than in the case of the remaining regions (e.g., Asia Pacific (including Japan) or Latin America).

Finally, our statistics can be compared to the values presented in some of the globally leading and most frequently cited sources on the topic.

ETFGI's report (ETFGI, 2022) for November 2021 indicated that the total assets of European ETFs were at c. 1.5 trillion USD, the assets of the US ETFs amounted to c. 6.8 trillion USD, and the global assets were at approximately 9.7 trillion USD. According to the Refinitiv's annual report on the European ETFs (Glow, 2022a), the aggregate assets of the European were at about 1.33 trillion EUR at the end of December 2021, exceeding in 2021 for the first time the milestone of 1 trillion EUR. These results corroborate our approach as the differences seem rather negligible. The discussed discrepancies between the values provided by the broadly recognized sources and the ones obtained in our analysis can be explained through the methodological differences in particular in the classification of ETFs by country—we used the criterion of primary listing location whereas the other applied approaches included, for example, domicile; the other possible difference is the translation of the values between currencies and the applied exchange rates.

4.5 Sustainable investing ETFs in Europe market development patterns and dynamics—regional and country-specific evidence

In the previous sections of this chapter, we discussed some issues showing the selected aspects of the European sustainable investments, including the subsegment of investment funds with such exposure; we also showed the basic outline of the European ETFs market. All these elements can be regarded as the introduction to the current, core section of the chapter, in which we discuss the European sustainable investing (ESG) ETFs markets. In the first part of the section, we present selected methodological remarks concerning above all the identification of the sustainable investing ETFs, including the construction criteria of the sample of funds, used in our analysis in this section as well as subsequent chapters. The second part is devoted to the study of the European sustainable investing ETFs, analyzed at the regional level. We consider the following dimensions: the size and the key trends, geographical structure, and the largest funds, followed by the assessment of the diffusion of ESG ETFs. In the third part of the chapter, we discuss the corresponding country-level results, presenting briefly the European sustainable investing ETFs markets; more in-depth presentations of selected ETFs markets are covered in the case studies at the end of each chapter.

4.5.1 Methodological remarks

As it was already mentioned in Section 4.4, the core source of data on ETFs (regardless of their type) used in our analysis is the Lipper's database.[7] Data on the sustainable investing ETFs were also extracted from the afore-mentioned database, using the following criterion. All funds labeled in the database as "ethical" were assumed to be the ESG funds, based on the definition of the concept applied by the data provider[8]—ethical funds are understood by Lipper as funds investing exclusively in the securities assessed as ethical in line with the fund's mandate. We assume that "ethical" in this context means ESG-compliant. Examination of the database shows that in Lipper's all ESG (sustainable investing) funds are flagged as ethical.[9] Additionally, in some cases, secondary labeling was provided, allowing for the identification of the following types of ESG ETFs:

1. alternative energy: funds with the key investment focus on the securities of companies active in sectors such as renewable energy, clean energy utilities, industrials, and technologies[10];

---

[7] More information about the Lipper's database, including some methodological comments, can be found in Moreira (2021), Refinitiv (2019a, 2020a). As discussed in Chapter 3, other possible methodological approaches were also considered yet for varying reasons they were impossible to adopt. For instance, potentially most robust approach would be the use of the SFDR classification. However, due to its recent launch and lack of data for the non-EU markets its viability in the context of our study is highly limited.

[8] Definitions obtained through personal communication with the Lipper's provider—Refinitiv's customer service representative.

[9] Highly problematic issue is the reprofiling of the funds, for example, through the change of its benchmark from non-ESG to ESG one—such funds are classified by Lipper as ethical based on the most recent profile. Due to the impossibility of acquiring past identification of all funds, we need to assume that they could be identified as sustainable investing over the entire time period. However, in case this assumption was assessed as significantly affecting the results we conducted additional analysis of the past data—see, for example, the discussion for the Norway market in the case study in Chapter 5. Obviously, the reverse switches, from ESG to non-ESG, are also possible yet rare.

[10] Slightly different explanation is provided in Refinitiv (2019b).

2. green: funds with the main investment strategy (usually screening) based exclusively on environmentally friendly investments.

3. water: funds investing in water-related activities.[11]

Additional information on the particular funds that were examined in more detail was acquired not only from the Lipper's database but also from the other types of Refinitiv Eikon's (and related) services as well as supplementary sources such as the documents and websites of the funds' providers and other financial databases. In case of identified mistakes and for some secondary data, the justETF database was used to corroborate the results obtained from Lipper; furthermore, funds' ESG scores were also examined in these cases (for more on the ESG scores published by Refinitiv see the methodological discussion in Section 6.1.1. and Refinitiv (2020b, 2020c)).

The main indicators used throughout the section are total net assets (understood as equivalent to the assets under management) of the analyzed funds (expressed in common currency units, USD billions, for comparative purposes) and the share of their assets in the aggregate assets of all ETFs (i.e., ESG and non-ESG ones). Number of funds is used as a supplementary indicator.

The composition of the initial sample was presented in the previous section—it consisted of 19 countries and joint entities (see the discussion concerning, e.g., Euronext_non_Paris and Nordic markets in Section 4.4.), that is, all identified European ETFs markets. However, in the analysis presented in this section as well as in the two subsequent chapters our sample is restricted to the European ETFs markets with sustainable investing ETFs. We began construction of our sample by identifying all European ETFs markets with sustainable investing ETFs (labeled as such by Lipper) primary listed for at least 1 month in the time period analyzed. Following 11 markets were identified: Euronext_non_Paris, France, Germany, Italy, Luxembourg, Nordic, Norway, Russia, Switzerland, Turkey, and the United Kingdom. Nevertheless, we decided to drop the following markets from our sample for one of the two reasons: first, short time series and minimal levels of assets of the ESG ETFs (Russia and Turkey), and, second,

---

[11] Definition of the water funds was not provided yet it was formulated based on proprietary analysis. According to a different source concerning Lipper's classifications, not entirely overlapping with the already mentioned, equity water funds are defined as investing "in water related businesses including infrastructure and equipment such as water purification, irrigation, distribution and storage of water" (Refinitiv, 2019b, p. 12). Only four fully operational water ESG ETFs were identified in Europe in the Lipper's database, thus they constitute a negligible category in the region.

very high market shares of the sustainable investing ETFs in the total market caused by one or a few relatively very large funds (with possible reclassifications of the funds in the past; Luxembourg, Nordic, and Norway). The final sample consists therefore of six markets: Euronext_non_Paris, France, Germany, Italy, Switzerland, and the United Kingdom—most among the largest ETFs markets in the region. It should be added that in the regional-level analysis we consider data on all ESG ETFs primarily listed in Europe, not only on these six markets. It should be emphasized that the funds were classified by country according to their primary listing location—each ETF was thus attributed to one market only, there was no double counting.

In Section 4.4. we already declared the time period of the analysis as 2006–21.[12] The key selection criterion of the period was the availability of sustainability investing ETFs in Europe—their number before 2006 was negligible (in January 2006, there were only six such funds in Europe). Monthly data on assets (and the derived indicators) were used. In case of missing observations on the assets of certain ETFs, the value (or values) were extrapolated based on the levels in the preceding months.

Our analysis in some parts was split into two subperiods: first 2006–11, second 2012–21. The reason for such division is linked to the overall low size of the European ETFs markets up to 2011 (see Fig. 4.6) and thus the possible distortions in one of the key indicators utilized in the analysis, that is, the share of ESG ETFs in the total assets of ETFs. In the case of small ETFs markets, even one sustainable investing ETF can result in a substantial share even though it does not necessarily constitute convincing evidence for the significance of ESG ETFs for the local investment industry; moreover, the profile of the ETF could have been changed from non-ESG to ESG during the fund's lifetime.

The final element of our analysis consists of the application of the logistic growth model (for methodological details concerning all applied econometric tools see the outline in the Methodological annex), utilized to assess the spread paths and dynamics (diffusion) of various types of innovations, including the financial ones. In our study, we assume that sustainable investing ETFs can be regarded as an example of financial innovations in the context of the aggregate ETFs market due to their novel attributes (in terms of, e.g., focus on the ESG issues) when compared to the conventional (non-ESG) ETFs. Therefore, the diffusion of the sustainable

---

[12] To be more precise—January 2006–September 2021 (i.e., until the last month for which sufficient data could be gathered as of preparation of the study).

investing ETFs is understood in our analysis as their increasing share of the total ETFs market (consisting of both innovative and conventional) funds, measured in the perspective of the assets under management. We also refer to the more general concept of "development" of the ESG ETFs market—its level is measured using both the absolute (value of assets in USD billions) and relative (identical to diffusion) indicators.

4.5.2 Regional evidence

Our discussion begins with the results of the analysis conducted at the aggregate level of all European ETFs markets (i.e., 19 markets, including 11 markets with sustainable investing ETFs listed in the previous section). Fig. 4.8 presents the time trends for the two key indicators of the ESG ETFs markets development, and Table 4.1 covers their summary statistics, the latter divided into two subperiods.

As it may be clearly noticed in Fig. 4.8, the values of the assets of the European sustainable investing ETFs up to 2017 had been increasing rather slowly yet interrupted by rather infrequent and moderate declines. Taking into account the data for the first subperiod, 2006—11, the mean total European assets were at c. 6.4 billion USD, and the maximum levels were attained in 2011 (about 9.9 billion USD (see the first part of Table 4.1)).

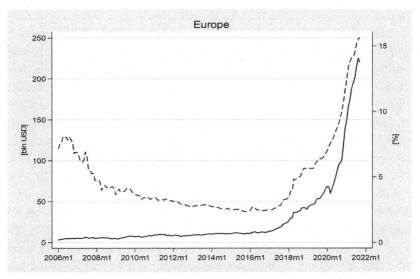

Figure 4.8 European assets of the sustainable investing ETFs and share of the sustainable investing ETFs in the total ETFs market. January 2006—September 2021 (monthly data). Note: raw data used; left-hand axis—assets of the sustainable investing ETFs (USD billion); right-hand axis—share of the sustainable investing ETFs in the total ETFs market (%); solid line—assets of the sustainable investing ETFs, dashed line—share of sustainable investing ETFs. *(Source: own elaboration.)*

Table 4.1 Assets of the sustainable investing ETFs and share of the sustainable investing ETFs in the total ETFs market: summary statistics for Europe. January 2006–September 2021 (monthly data).

Summary statistics: January 2006–December 2011.					
Variable	No. of obs.	Mean	Std. dev.	Min.	Max
Assets of the sustainable investing ETFs (billion USD)	72	6.38	1.71	3.18	9.87
Share of the sustainable investing ETFs in the total ETFs market (in %)	72	4.76	1.61	3.17	8.11

Summary statistics: January 2012–September 2021.					
Variable	No. of obs.	Mean	Std. dev.	Min.	Max
Assets of the sustainable investing ETFs (billion USD)	117	40.06	51.62	7.46	224.4
Share of the sustainable investing ETFs in the total ETFs market (in %)	117	4.78	3.46	2.33	15.65

Source: own calculations.

Rapid development has started in 2017 yet already since 2012 a noticeable shift had taken place with regard to the values of ESG ETFs' assets in Europe (compare the second and first part of Table 4.1). The average month-end value has increased to c. 40 billion USD in the second sub-period; from the minimum level of between 7 and 8 billion USD in 2012 to the maximum value of over 220 billion USD in the second half of 2021. If exclusively the period of the most pronounced growth is considered, that is, 2017–21, the scale of the European sustainable investing ETFs market development is even more impressive. The total assets of the European ESG ETFs in this time period have risen from about 13.5 billion USD to c. 220 billion USD—more than 15-fold during less than 5 years; the only, albeit short-lived, decline could be observed during the turmoil in the financial systems caused in the early 2020 by the events linked to the Covid-19 pandemic.[13] Therefore, 2017–21 can be unequivocally labeled as the take-off period of the European sustainable investing ETFs market.

---

[13] The slight decrease in the final month (September 2021) can be explained by missing observations for some funds as of preparation of the database.

The structure of the aggregate European sustainable investing ETFs market as of the end of September 2021 is presented in Fig. 4.9. The regional market is highly concentrated in terms of the primary listing locations—the three largest markets, the United Kingdom, Germany, and France, account for approximately 80% of the total assets (with the two formers having the share of over 60%). The remaining assets of the European ESG ETFs were managed mostly by the ETFs on the Swiss and Euronext_non_Paris markets (the aggregate share of the two countries was at c. 16%). Italian sustainable investing ETFs accounted for merely 1%, and the share of the other markets, not discussed separately (e.g., Norway), was close to 3%.

Such geographical structure of the European ESG ETFs market corresponds rather closely to the overall structure of the ETFs market in the region (compare Figs. 4.7. and 4.9), with a few minor differences in the sustainable segment such as a moderately weaker position of the UK market as the regional leader (and thus stronger position of both Germany and France). A similar observation applies to Switzerland—even though the Swiss sustainable investment industry (limited not only to the ETFs or the other types of investment funds) is still among the most developed in the region, its position on a European scale has decreased over the last several years in line with the growth of the other markets. Up to 2017, the share of

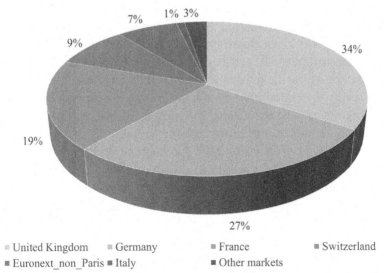

Figure 4.9 Assets of the sustainable investing ETFs primary listed in Europe: geographical structure (September 2021). *(Source: own elaboration.)*

the Swiss ETFs in the total European market had substantially exceeded 20%, reaching even 30%–40% levels in some periods (for instance, in 2008 and 2015–16)—it was the distinctive regional leader; for comparison, the share of the UK-listed funds had been substantially lower than the Swiss ones. However, since 2017 the UK market has surpassed quickly its Swiss counterpart; the same trend could be noticed for Germany and France.

In the second perspective, taking into consideration the share of sustainable investing ETFs in the total European ETFs market, the results of our analysis unveil to some extent different picture than for the values of assets. Still, the key trends are rather similar. The main dissimilarity can be noticed for the subperiod up to 2017 (see Fig. 4.8). In 2004, the share of ESG ETFs in total assets exceeded 8% yet over the next years the general trend was a decline, with the highest rate over 2007–09, continuing at a lower rate up to 2017. The explanation of this apparently surprising result can be formulated based on the arguments provided in Section 4.5.1. The overall size of the European ETFs markets had been relatively small up to 2012 and the calculated market shares are distorted by a relatively limited number of funds with substantial assets, labeled in the Lipper's database as ESG funds (in some cases they started to focus on the ESG issues much later as the funds changed their investment profile; however, such overhauls are not recorded in the database)—these results should thus be regarded with caution. In the subperiod 2006–11 (see Table 4.1) the mean market share of the ESG ETFs was at c. 4.8%. In the next subperiod 2021–21, it was almost identical—the minimum value for the second subperiod was even lower (2.33% vs. 3.17%). However, the comparison of the maximum values leads to dramatically different conclusions concerning the peak levels of development of the sustainable investing ETFs European markets in the two subperiods—in the latter, the relevant value exceeded for the first time 15%. Taking into consideration, the already identified period of rapid expansion of ESG ETFs in Europe starting from 2017, their market share has increased between January 2017 and September 2021 from 2.51% to the record-high 15.65%, with mean monthly value of 7.02%. The comparison of the market-level shares for our sample shows that the highest level as of September 2021 was attained by Euronext_non_Paris, of over 37%, followed by c. 28% in Italy and about 25% in France. The lowest, of c. 11.5%, was noted for the United Kingdom, thus showing that this largest market in the absolute terms, in the relative perspective remained much smaller (for more on the six markets see Section 4.5.3).

Additional insight into the data on the European market shares of the sustainable investing ETFs evolution and the overall attributes of this variable can be gained through the analysis of the distribution and monthly changes. Fig. 4.10. plainly shows that the vast majority of the values of the discussed variable over the 2006—21 time period remained below 5%, with the highest levels (over 10%) observed in just several months after 2019. Absolute changes in the monthly perspective presented in Fig. 4.11. confirm the conclusions reached based on the time lines in Fig. 4.8. Interestingly, the magnitude of the declines noted up to 2011 was generally higher than the increases since 2017 onwards. Fig. 4.8 shows that there were three distinct phases concerning the development of the ESG ETFs' market share variable: first, the stage of decline, second, the stage of stabilization, and, finally, the third phase of growth. It thus evidences the significant reverse of the apparent negative trend.

The European sustainable investing ETFs market can also be studied in other dimensions than presented in the preceding paragraphs—we present their brief overview, using the most recent September 2021 data.

There were close to 660 sustainable investing ETFs in Europe operating at the end of September 2021 (we take into account the funds with data on assets available), most of them (about 190) in the United Kingdom.

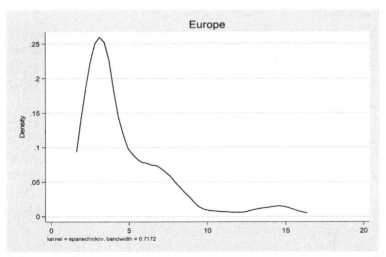

Figure 4.10 Share of the sustainable investing ETFs in the total ETFs market (%) distribution curves. Europe, January 2006—September 2021 (monthly data). Note: raw data used; kernel density nonparametric approximation applied; bandwidth set as default. *(Source: own elaboration.)*

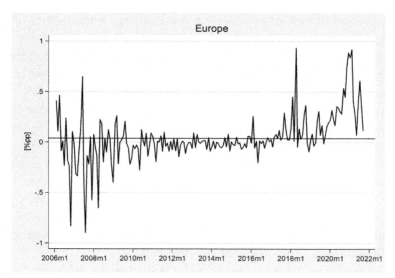

Figure 4.11 Month-over-month absolute changes in the share of the sustainable investing ETFs in the total ETFs market (%). Europe, January 2006–September 2021 (monthly data). *(Source: own elaboration.)*

Germany (174 funds) and France (113) were the second- and third-most frequent listing locations. There were also close to 100 funds primary listed in Switzerland and the number of funds in all remaining markets was much smaller.

The leading providers of the European ESG ETFs were (we consider jointly all country or regional branches or linked companies of certain provider) in terms of assets under management: BlackRock (over 80 billion USD), UBS (33 billion USD), Amundi (24 billion USD), DWS (16 billion USD), and Lyxor (14 billion USD).

In terms of the supplementary categories (alternative energy, etc.—see Section 4.5.1) there was one alternative energy ETF (with over 5 billion USD of assets; there were more such funds in the past yet their ceased operation or were transformed into other entities), 14 green ETFs (total assets close to 3 billion USD), and 4 water ESG ETFs (about 1.7 billion USD assets). Consequently, the second-level categories constituted less than 5% of the aggregate market in terms of assets.

Finally, Table 4.2 includes an overview of the five largest sustainable investing ETFs in Europe (according to the assets under management). They are mostly equity funds, listed on the largest ETFs markets in the region. Moreover, they are managed by well-established providers.

Table 4.2 The largest sustainable investing ETFs primarily listed in Europe. September 2021 data.

Name of the fund	Total net assets (bln USD)	Asset class of exposure (Lipper's classification)	Benchmark	Provider	Inception date	Primary listing ETFs market
iShares MSCI USA SRI UCITS ETF USD (Acc)	7.36	Equity US	MSCI USA SRI Select Reduced Fossil Fuel Index	BlackRock Asset Management Ireland	July 11, 2016	UK
SPDR Bloomberg SASB U.S. Corporate ESG UCITS ETF	5.68	Bond USD Corporates	Bloomberg SASB U.S. Corporate ESG Ex-Controversies Select Index	State Street Global Advisors	October 23, 2020	Germany
iShares Global Clean Energy UCITS ETF USD (Dist)	5.47	Equity Global	S&P Global Clean Energy Index TR	BlackRock Asset Management Ireland	July 6, 2007	UK
Amundi Index MSCI USA SRI UCITS ETF DR C	4.34	Equity US	MSCI USA SRI Filtered ex Fossil Fuels Index	Amundi Luxembourg	September 25, 2018	France
iShares MSCI Europe SRI UCITS ETF EUR (Acc)	4.13	Equity Europe	MSCI Europe SRI Select Reduced Fossil Fuel TR EUR	BlackRock Asset Management Ireland	February 25, 2011	Euronext_non_Paris

Source: own elaboration based on Lipper's database as well as websites of the funds' providers.

To supplement our discussion of the European ETFs market, we provide some brief data on the other regions, gathered using the same methodology as for Europe. The North American sustainable investing ETFs market consisted as of September 2021 of approximately 280 ETFs that gathered c. 113 billion USD in assets under management (above 200 US funds managing c. 108 billion USD assets and slightly under 80 Canadian funds with assets of below 5 billion USD). The share of the ESG ETFs in the total assets of North American ETFs slightly exceeded 1%. All other sustainable investing ETFs in the world (outside Europe or North America) had assets estimated at approximately 24 billion USD, that is, less than 4% in terms of the share in the total market. Consequently, Europe can be regarded as the undeniable global leader in terms of ESG ETFs' market development.

Our results presented in this section can be contrasted with the results obtained in the other studies. The Morningstar's report by Bryan et al. (2020) showed that in 2020 there were 162 sustainable ETFs in Europe, managing about 52 billion USD of assets whereas in the United States 83 ESG ETFs managed c. 35 billion USD (there were also 71 sustainable investing ETFs in the other countries).

According to the 2021 MSCI report, the assets of ESG ETFs exceeded 150 billion USD globally at the end of 2020; in 2015 they were at c. 6 billion USD (Mahmood, 2021). In terms of domicile, Europe accounted for about half of the sustainable investing ETFs (208 funds) and North America for the vast majority of the remaining funds. US market could be assessed as the global leader up to approximately 2014 when Europe became the forerunner. Twenty-six European ESG ETFs gathered assets exceeding 1 billion USD each.

Refinitiv's 2021 annual report on the European ETFs market (Glow, 2022a) demonstrated that ESG ETFs constituted at the end of 2021 a negligible part of the aggregate assets of the ETFs market, with a share of c. 6%. Nevertheless, their position has substantially strengthened during 2021. In terms of their exposure, sustainable investing ETFs were significantly more prevalent in the equity than bond segment (7.85 vs. 2.3% share), concentrated above all in the types of funds tracking major stock market indexes. Moreover, sustainable investing funds were offered by less than one quarter of the ETFs' providers.

Some noticeable differences between our study and the aforementioned can be linked above all to different definition and classification of the ETFs; the other reason is varying time periods. However, in terms of the values of assets, our estimates are quite close to those of the established financial companies.[14]

Another possible way to assess the size of the sustainable investing ETFs in the examined countries is to consider the size of their assets in relation to the capitalizations of the local stock markets. According to the most recent data available (as of the end of 2020), that could be obtained exclusively for the three countries, the highest levels were reached in Germany—the assets of the ESG ETFs corresponded to 1.4% of the German stock market's capitalization; the respective values for France were 0.55% and for Switzerland 0.65%. Consequently, it may be clearly noticed that the assets of the sustainable investing ETFs were even in 2020 still very low in comparison to the size of the most closely related part of the capital markets.

As the final part of this section, we discuss the conclusions that can be reached with regard to the European regional sustainable investing ETFs market with the application of the diffusion models. Estimates of the logistic growth diffusion model for this market are presented in Table 4.3. High R^2 of the model implies its high goodness of fit and allows for formulating some robust conclusion; the only misspecification was returned for the T_m parameter. The κ (upper asymptote) value of about 46% implies the substantial potential for the further increase in the market share of ESG ETFs in Europe—according to the trajectory assumed in the diffusion model if the current development trend continues, then the sustainable investing ETFs can account for about the half of the total ETFs' assets. Estimated value of ΔT indicates that it can take about 14 years for the sustainable investing

Table 4.3 European assets of the sustainable investing ETFs and the share of the sustainable investing ETFs in the total ETFs market: diffusion model estimates. January 2012–September 2021 (monthly data).

κ	T_m	α	ΔT	R2	Root MSE	No. of obs.
46.06 [17.5]	*753.3—misspecification*	0.06 [0.005]	170.7	0.98	0.45	117

Note: 3-parameter logistic growth model applied; estimation method—NLS. In parenthesis—standard errors generated from Gauss—Newton regression; constant term not included; in italics—results statistically insignificant or misspecifications returned.
Source: own estimates.

[14] For a detailed analysis of the global passive sustainable investing funds market as of 2018, see Bioy and Lamont (2018).

ETFs' share to grow from 10% to 90% of κ; in other words, despite the high growth rates, the already mentioned share of the half of the total market can be reasonably expected to be reached after 2030. In the nearest future, ESG ETFs will probably still remain the minority segment.

4.5.3 Country-level analysis

Following the presentation of the regional-level data, we devote this part of the section to the discussion of the country-level (to be more precise, market-level as we consider one market (joint-stock exchange) covering a few countries as well) analysis of sustainable investing ETFs. The outline of the presentation of the results is parallel to the analysis for the entire region.

The time lines of the two key indicators used to assess the development of the sustainable investing ETFs development drawn at the market level (see Fig. 4.12) prove that the overall trend with regard to the values of the assets of these investment funds was quite similar in all countries and also comparable to the regional-level evidence. The phase of the rapid development started in all countries in approximately 2017—on some markets a few months earlier (e.g., Germany) and on some relatively later (for example, Italy or Euronext_non_Paris). Two markets have rather unique time lines with regard to this indicator—France and Italy. In the former the phase of exponential growth was interrupted by the period of the slower growth and decline (in the first quarter of 2020)—French sustainable investing ETFs market was the most affected among the six studied by the period of financial distress linked to the emerging Covid-19 pandemic; still even there the decrease was short-lived and the rebound substantial. The case of the latter market is relatively similar yet the initial growth (since about early 2017) was less pronounced than in the case of France. The decline in the early 2020 in the Italian ETFs market was, however, almost negligible. The presented comparison shows that even those quite closely related ESG ETFs markets responded in a different way to some major events in the financial system.

The second variable presented in Fig. 4.12 is the share of the sustainable investing ETFs in the total assets of ETFs in the six analyzed markets. For the majority of markets under consideration, the trajectory of changes in the market shares of ESG ETFs has been similar to the trend with regard to the values of their assets (Table 4.4). Most noticeable differences between the two variables refer to the early years of the analyzed time period. As discussed in Section 4.5.2, the apparently high shares of sustainable investing

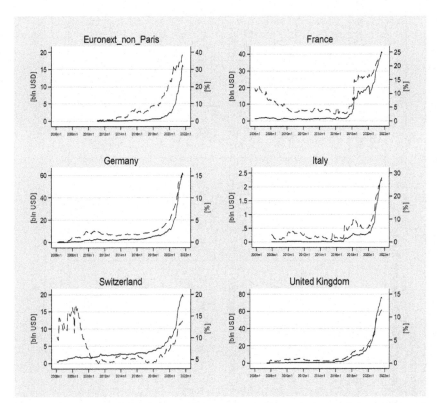

Figure 4.12 Assets of the sustainable investing ETFs and share of the sustainable investing ETFs in the total ETFs market. European markets, January 2006–September 2021 (monthly data). Note: raw data used; left-hand axis—assets of the sustainable investing ETFs (USD billion); right-hand axis—share of the sustainable investing ETFs in the total ETFs market (%); solid line—assets of the sustainable investing ETFs, dashed line—share of sustainable investing ETFs. *(Source: own elaboration.)*

ETFs can be explained to some extent through the distortions caused by the overall small size of the ETFs industries. Comparison of the results obtained for the two variables indicates that the development of the ESG ETFs markets should in some instances be assessed from the two perspectives as the high shares of these funds may be misleading. As a result, the majority of our analysis of their development focuses on the period 2012–21 when the values of the two variables have become more consistent with regard to their trends.

After the introductory remarks, we focus now on the presentation of the six sustainable investing ETFs markets (for more in-depth discussion see the end-of-the-chapters case studies). We discuss above all the 2012–21

Table 4.4 Assets of the sustainable investing ETFs and the share of the sustainable investing ETFs in the total ETFs market: summary statistics. European markets, January 2006–September 2021 (monthly data).

Summary statistics: January 2006–December 2011.

ETFs market	Variable	No. of obs.	Mean	Std. dev.	Min.	Max.
Germany	Assets of the sustainable investing ETFs (USD billion)	70	1.09	0.97	0.002	2.96
	Share of the sustainable investing ETFs in the total ETFs market (in %)	70	1.34	0.91	0.02	2.73
France	Assets of the sustainable investing ETFs (USD billion)	72	1.35	0.34	0.79	2.27
	Share of the sustainable investing ETFs in the total ETFs market (in %)	72	6.65	2.90	3.02	12.8
United Kingdom	Assets of the sustainable investing ETFs (USD billion)	54	0.39	0.25	0.01	0.83
	Share of sustainable investing ETFs in total ETFs market (in %)	54	0.65	0.26	0.05	1.03
Switzerland	Assets of the sustainable investing ETFs (USD billion)	71	1.59	0.52	0.45	2.71
	Share of the sustainable investing ETFs in the total ETFs market (in %)	71	10.36	4.42	4.13	17.61
Italy	Assets of the sustainable investing ETFs (USD billion)	49	0.01	0.006	0.004	0.021
	Share of the sustainable investing ETFs in the total ETFs market (in %)	49	2.82	1.25	0.99	4.75
Euronext_non_Paris	Assets of the sustainable investing ETFs (USD billion)	11	0.009	0.001	0.007	0.012
	Share of the sustainable investing ETFs in the total ETFs market (in %)	11	0.56	0.11	0.38	0.75

Summary statistics: January 2012—September 2021.

ETFs market	Variable	No. of obs.	Mean	Std. dev.	Min.	Max
Germany	Assets of the sustainable investing ETFs (USD billion)	117	8.98	13.78	1.65	61.93
	Share of the sustainable investing ETFs in the total ETFs market (in %)	117	3.66	3.53	1.41	15.62
France	Assets of the sustainable investing ETFs (USD billion)	117	9.13	11.18	0.84	41.27
	Share of the sustainable investing ETFs in the total ETFs market (in %)	117	8.77	7.00	2.44	25.03
United Kingdom	Assets of the sustainable investing ETFs (USD billion)	117	11.25	18.41	0.53	76.51
	Share of the sustainable investing ETFs in the total ETFs market (in %)	117	2.46	2.91	0.46	11.53
Switzerland	Assets of the sustainable investing ETFs (USD billion)	117	5.03	4.35	2.21	20.03
	Share of the sustainable investing ETFs in the total ETFs market (in %)	117	6.18	2.41	4.21	13.93
Italy	Assets of the sustainable investing ETFs (USD billion)	117	0.28	0.51	0.004	2.25
	Share of the sustainable investing ETFs in the total ETFs market (in %)	117	6.13	6.29	1.06	27.89
Euronext_non_Paris	Assets of the sustainable investing ETFs (USD billion)	117	1.69	3.40	0.008	16.27
	Share of the sustainable investing ETFs in the total ETFs market (in %)	117	10.49	10.79	0.53	38.64

Source: own calculations.

evidence as for the 2006–11 subperiod the dataset is rather limited (e.g., only 11 monthly observations could be gathered for Euronext_non_Paris; France is the only market with the complete dataset).

The German sustainable investing ETFs market is among the oldest in Europe—ETF known currently as "iShares DJ Eurozone Sust Screened UCITS ETF (DE)" was identified as the oldest in the group of still functioning funds (yet currently with rather small assets), launched in March 2006. In 2006–11, the German market remained rather small, with the mean assets of c. 1.1 billion USD, representing the average share of about 1.3% in the total German ETFs market. In the 2012–21 time period, the situation has become radically different—the mean values have increased to 9 billion USD and 3.7% respectively, with the maximum values of c. 62 billion USD and 15.6% reached in the second half of 2021. According to the most recent data available, there were more than 170 German ESG ETFs, domiciled mostly in Luxembourg and Ireland. The largest providers of these funds were Amundi, BlackRock, DWS, and UBS. In terms of exposure, the most frequent type of funds was equity ETFs with the benchmarks focused on foreign securities (e.g., US or global). For more details on the German market, see the case study in Chapter 3.

The oldest among the still active sustainable investing ETFs primary listed in France is "BNP Paribas Easy CAC 40 ESG UCITS ETF," started in March 2005. However, even though the fund is currently classified as "ethical" in the Lipper's database, until September 2021 it tracked a conventional index rather than ESG-focused. Consequently, the initial results concerning the assets of ESG ETFs on the French market should be regarded with caution. The average values of both indicators of the sustainable investing ETFs market development were in 2012–21 higher in France than in Germany; the difference is particularly substantial for the shares. In September 2021, the share of ESG ETFs exceeded 25%—one of the highest levels ever noted in the European region. There were more than 110 funds with such profile, domiciled almost exclusively in Luxembourg and France, provided by the majority by the financial institutions such as Amundi, BNP Paribas, and Lyxor. Their exposure was similar to the one noted for Germany yet with the more prevalent position of the bond funds. The case study of the French ESG ETFs market is presented at the end of this chapter.

The UK market is the largest in the region in terms of the values of assets managed by the sustainable investing ETFs in 2021 but in the dimension of their share it has remained the smallest among the six analyzed markets. The UK ESG ETF with the longest time series available in the Lipper's database is "Xtrackers MSCI ESG UK UCITS ETF," with data on assets acquirable for the period since July 2007 (fund incepted in June 2007). In September 2021, there were close to 200 operating sustainable investing ETFs in the United Kingdom, primarily listed on the London Stock Exchange. The funds' providers managing most assets within the presented category of ETFs were BlackRock (the distinctive leader—managing 56 out of 75 billion USD of assets), Invesco, LGIM Managers, UBS, and Wisdomtree among others. The exposure of the UK ETFs was highly diversified—some funds fell into the subcategories such as alternative energy or green ETFs; other thematic funds included the ones focused on cybersecurity or robotics. UK market is presented in the case study in this chapter.

The fourth market, that is, in Switzerland, differs from the abovementioned for a number of reasons—one of the most fundamental is the lack of EU membership; the United Kingdom is also no longer the EU-member state but it had been for the most of the 2006–21 time period. Due to its relative uniqueness, the Swiss market for the sustainable investing ETFs was discussed with most detail among all considered in the case study concluding Chapter 2. It can be added that the data on the Swiss market, similarly to France, suffers from certain weaknesses with regard to the individual funds, in particular when the largest ESG ETFs is concerned. According to the Lipper's database, the funds with most assets as of September 2021 was "Credit Suisse Real Estate Fund International A." It is classified as ethical by Lipper yet its ESG compliance requires additional scrutiny; moreover, the fund is not listed on the main Swiss exchange.

The Italian market is the smallest in our sample in terms of the assets' values indicators yet one of the most developed in the perspective of the share of ESG ETFs. It can be explained by considering its size—it is a relatively small market (when we consider the funds primary listed), with slightly above 70 ETFs of any type listed in September. However, more than 20 out of these about 70 ETFs were ESG funds. There were no sustainable funds managing assets exceeding 1 billion USD according to the most recent data—nine funds managed more than 100 million USD each. The largest ETF (about 400 million USD of assets under management) labeled as ethical by Lipper was "L&G ESG China CNY Bond UCITS ETF USD Dist," tracking the performance of the index covering ESG-compliant debt securities denominated in CNY. Almost all Italian funds labeled as ESG were domiciled either in Ireland or Luxembourg. The largest providers were LGIM Managers and UBS.

The sixth and the final market in our sample is at the same time the most specific one considered—Euronext_non_Paris, that is, covering all ESG ETFs listed on the Euronext apart from the ones listed on its Paris segment. It was the second-smallest market in 2012—21 in terms of the value of the assets but the most developed with regard to the share of ESG ETFs in the total ETFs market, in terms of both the average and maximum level of this variable. 38 out of 112 funds in September 2021 were sustainable investing ETFs. "iShares MSCI Europe SRI UCITS ETF EUR (Acc)" was the largest and oldest (incepted in February 2011—thus showing the short history of the ESG segment of the local ETFs market) of the ESG ETFs primary listed on this market, and, at the same time, the third biggest among all Italian ETFs, regardless of their ESG compliance. Almost all local ESG funds were domiciled in Ireland and they were provided almost entirely by BlackRock within the iShares brand. Their exposure was highly diversified.

Similarly to the regional-level evidence, we also consider the distribution curves (see Fig. 4.13) and monthly changes in the market share (see Fig. 4.14) of the sustainable investing ETFs for individual markets.

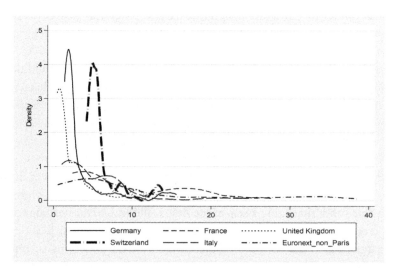

Figure 4.13 Share of the sustainable investing ETFs in the total ETFs market (%) distribution curves. European markets, January 2006—September 2021 (monthly data). Note: raw data used; kernel density nonparametric approximation applied; bandwidth set as default. *(Source: own elaboration.)*

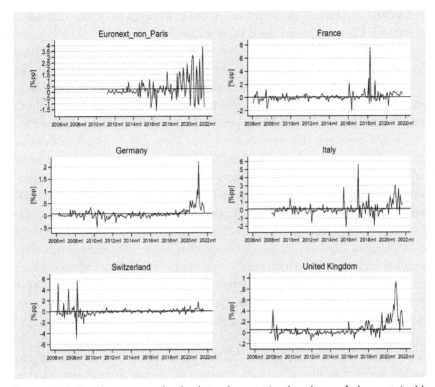

Figure 4.14 Month-over-month absolute changes in the share of the sustainable investing ETFs in the total ETFs market (%). European markets, January 2006–September 2021 (monthly data). *(Source: own elaboration.)*

Distribution curves of the studied variable plainly prove that the vast majority of the values of the ESG ETFs' shares on all markets in the 2006–21 time period were below the 10% threshold, thus representing a marginal part of the overall ETFs markets. The values exceeding 10% were noted between 2006 and 2011 exclusively for Switzerland and France (in the latter market for a few months), and the remainder represents the levels attained during the post-2017 phase of quick growth. The only market for which levels over 30% (close to 40%) were observed is Euronext_non_Paris—therefore to some degree, it was an outlier in this perspective.

The month-over-month absolute changes in the market share of ESG ETFs on the six markets (see Fig. 4.14) were most pronounced in the later years; the only exception is Switzerland. The highest variability is noticed for the Italian market, with the frequent ups and downs since 2018; for

Switzerland, excluding the initial years, the development of the sustainable investing ETFs market has been most stable.

In the last part of this section, we discuss the estimates of the diffusion models for the European sustainable investing ETFs markets (see Table 4.5). In contrast to the regional-level estimates (see Table 4.3), the results returned for the individual ETFs markets are in most cases impossible to interpret due to misspecifications generated by the model. Exclusively for France and (to some extent) Euronext_non_Paris some conclusions can be reached[15]; for the remaining markets, the reason for misspecifications is the extremely rapid development of the local sustainable investing ETFs markets observable in the final examined years (they were still in the early exponential phase of diffusion), hindering the identification of the parameters of the logistic growth process. What is important, only for France no over- or underestimates as well as other types of misspecifications were obtained for any of the parameters. R^2 of the model (0.88) is relatively high and it proves that the received estimates may be used to assess the diffusion process of the ESG ETFs in this market. The value of the estimated upper asymptote κ seems, though, relatively high—it appears rather improbable that it can be reasonably expected to be reached taking into account the 25% share observed in September 2021. The returned value of ΔT suggests that the growth from c. 8%–70% in terms of market share is projected to take over 12 years (i.e., it will conclude after 2030); a similar conclusion is implied by the estimated T_m parameter, describing the mid-point of the diffusion path in terms of months. The value of α (rate of diffusion) can be interpreted mostly in the comparative perspective—it is lower than for Euronext_non_Paris and substantially lower than in the case of the aggregate European market, potentially implying slower diffusion than for those two markets. In the case of the Euronext_non_Paris market, the returned estimates are more difficult to interpret. R^2 of the model estimated for that market (0.98) is as high as in the previously discussed model for the entire region. The upper asymptote κ is clear misspecification (share exceeding 100%). The other estimated parameters generally imply the continuation of the diffusion process, at a higher pace than in the case of the French market.

---

[15] What is worth noticing, both markets are part of the Euronext group of exchanges. Whether this is merely a coincidence or maybe a proof for, for example, similar factors shaping diffusion on both markets, remains to be verified.

Table 4.5 Share of the sustainable investing ETFs in the total ETFs market: diffusion model estimates. European markets, January 2012–September 2021 (monthly data).

ETFs market	κ	T_m	α	ΔT	R2	Root MSE	No. of obs.
Germany	*59,695,736 − misspecification;* exponential phase 77.9 [50.3]	*549.8 − misspecification*	0.042	104.4	0.93	n.a.	117
France	*24,729,367 − misspecification;* exponential phase	214.5 [34.3]	0.029 [0.003]	150.2	0.88	2.38	117
United Kingdom	*— misspecification;* exponential phase	*511.5 − misspecification*	0.045	97.5	0.98	n.a.	117
Switzerland	*12,773,143 − misspecification;* exponential phase	*1.616 − misspecification*	446.9	0.01	0.58	n.a.	117
Italy	*61,804,648 − misspecification;* exponential phase	*575.8 − misspecification*	115.3	0.068	0.85	n.a.	117
Euronext_non_Paris	238.06 [158.9]— Overestimates	232.1 [24.01]	0.036 [0.002]	119.6	0.98	1.65	117

Note: 3-parameter logistic growth model applied; estimation method—NLS. In parenthesis—standard errors generated from the Gauss–Newton regression; constant term not included; in italics—results statistically insignificant or misspecifications returned.
Source: own estimates.

4.6 Sustainable investing ETFs in the European countries: case study (III)—the United Kingdom

The third case study of the sustainable investing ETFs in Europe covers one of the regional and global leaders in terms of the ETFs market development—the United Kingdom. The UK financial system at large, including its financial markets, is among the largest in the world and the country may be regarded as one of the global financial centers. It seems, therefore, an interesting and important exercise, to assess the position of sustainable investing within this highly developed financial sector, consisting of both strong capital markets and other elements such as banking industry. However, a more detailed evaluation of the general attributes of sustainable investing in the United Kingdom is hindered by the lack of detailed data, available, for instance, for the countries discussed in the two previous case studies. Consequently, in the current case study, we provide less numerical evidence (with the exception of the sustainable investing ETFs data, gathered by us in a unique dataset) and concentrate rather on the landscape of the UK sustainable investment, discussing issues such as regulatory developments and other factors contributing to (or hindering) the expansion of this part of the financial system. Data sources and methodology are identical to the previous case studies.

According to the 2020 data, the total size of the UK investment management sector exceeded 9 trillion USD, being the biggest in Europe and second-largest in the world, behind only the United States (Investment Association, 2021). From the perspective of sustainability, according to the aforementioned study, close to half of the UK assets were managed taking into consideration the ESG issues. However, sustainability-focused investment strategies accounted for less than 3% of the total assets; impact investments had an even smaller share, of c. 0.5%. It means that the other approaches such as exclusions or ESG integration were much more common. Due to the insufficient data, it is difficult to assess the size of the UK sustainable investment funds—according to Owadally et al. (2021), their assets amounted to about 71 billion GBP in 2021.

Taking into consideration the history of sustainable investing in the United Kingdom, it can be assessed as quite long in comparison to the other economies. For example, the United Kingdom was one of the first countries in the world (and among absolute pioneers in Europe) in which the association of investors aimed at promoting sustainable investments was established, which took place in 1991 (Quak et al., 2014). The United

Kingdom was also a pioneer concerning the social impact bonds—first such financial instruments were launched in that country in 2010 (Méndez-Suárez et al., 2020). Historical perspective of the development of the concepts such as corporate social responsibility (CSR) and SRI in the United Kingdom is presented in, among others, Kinderman (2012) or McCann et al. (2003). It should be added that, historically, ethical investments in the United Kingdom until 1960s had been prevalently linked to religious organizations (Biehl & Atkins, 2016).

Over the last several years, there have been many important regulatory and policy developments linked to sustainable investing in the United Kingdom—we discuss briefly just a few selected topics based on their relevance for the ETFs markets (some issues were covered in Chapter 3). UK authorities have taken a number of steps related to the environmental policy, aimed at reduction of greenhouse gas emissions—they consist of, among others, Ten Point Plan (presenting the public investments plans in this sphere) as well as increased climate-related disclosure requirements for the financial institutions (Halper et al., 2021). In line with the aforementioned plan, in October 2021, the UK government adopted an action strategy directed at promoting sustainable investing and greening of the financial system. In the context of the investment funds, they address the matters including mitigation of greenwashing due to the improved disclosure requirements (clearer and more consistent) and promotion of more sustainably oriented flows of capital (HM Government, 2021). The first legal requirements focused on the largest asset managers, with the most attention devoted to the climate topics (rather than the other elements of sustainability), were planned to become binding in the early 2022 yet their scope is more limited than in the case of the EU-level SFDR methodology (Gerber et al., 2021). More generally, as stated in GSIA (2021), the UK authorities declared to cut the emissions of greenhouse gases to net zero by 2050, with substantial reduction already by 2035. Bank of England assesses the UK financial system through climate-related stress-testing framework (SSF, 2021).

Greenwashing seems to be an important problem with regard to the UK investment funds—according to the survey by the XPS Investment (2021), a substantial share of the UK funds (about one quarter in the case of equity funds) were unable to provide evidence for taking into account ESG issues in their investment process, despite their declarations concerning sustainability. Regulations concerning nonfinancial disclosures enacted in the past in the United Kingdom were to some extent based on the UN Guiding

Principles on Business and Human Rights (Ruggie & Middleton, 2019). There are also some specific ESG-related issues associated with the common law jurisdiction such as in the United Kingdom (Richardson, 2012). In more detailed ESG fields, concerning specific sustainability investing strategies, the 2020 UK code requires, among others, outcome-based reporting concerning the actions focused on voting and other types of shareholders' engagement (Eurosif, 2021). Finally, even though the SFDR classification is not binding for the UK funds, some providers decided to utilize this methodology, in particular with regard to climate-linked disclosures (John, 2021). These decisions stem from the marketing strategies and they are also aimed at facilitating the distribution of the funds in the EU countries. Another example of the convergence between the EU and UK sustainability frameworks is the planned introduction of the UK green taxonomy based to a high degree on its EU counterpart.

The total net assets of the UK primary listed sustainable investing ETFs reached as of the end of September 2021 (the last month of the time period analyzed) the level of about 75.3 billion USD (the record-high level, of approximately 76.5 billion USD, was noted 1 month earlier, in August 2021). What is worth noticing, is that there were 14 active ETFs primarily listed in the United Kingdom based on the information acquired from the Lipper's and justETF databases, the remainder were passive funds—the assets of the active ESG ETFs were minimal in comparison to their passive counterparts. Nevertheless, it was one of the few European ETFs markets with the active sustainable investing ETFs (the largest such segment in Europe according to our estimations). The development of the active category of the ESG ETFs may be yet another factor boosting the growth of the market as they will become competing alternatives for an increasingly larger group of mutual funds or other sustainable investments.

Ten biggest ESG ETFs primary listed in the United Kingdom are listed in Table 4.6. The biggest UK fund, "iShares MSCI USA SRI UCITS ETF USD (Acc)" was also the largest in Europe (see Table 4.2). Analysis of the investment profiles of the largest UK sustainable investing ETFs (see, e.g., asset classes or benchmarks in Table 4.6) shows that they are mostly equity funds, with the exposure to the United States, global or emerging markets equities; two BlackRock funds track the corporate bonds benchmarks. However, there are no ESG ETFs with exposure exclusively to the UK equities—they are also rather infrequent taking into account the entire UK market (the largest funds with such profile is ranked 14th in terms of assets). This apparent scarcity of the UK-focused ESG ETFs stems from a number

Table 4.6 The largest sustainable investing ETFs primarily listed in the United Kingdom (according to the assets under management). September 2021 data.

Name of the fund	Total net assets (bln USD)	Asset class of exposure (Lipper's classification)	Benchmark	Provider	Inception date	Total expense ratio (%)
iShares MSCI USA SRI UCITS ETF USD (Acc)	7.36	Equity US	MSCI USA SRI Select reduced Fossil Fuel Index	BlackRock Asset Management Ireland	July 11, 2016	0.20
iShares Global Clean Energy UCITS ETF USD (Dist)	5.47	Equity Global	S&P Global Clean Energy Index TR	BlackRock Asset Management Ireland	July 6, 2007	0.65
iShares MSCI USA ESG Screened UCITS ETF USD Acc	3.87	Equity US	MSCI USA ESG Screened Index	BlackRock Asset Management Ireland	October 19, 2018	0.07
iShares MSCI World SRI UCITS ETF EUR (Acc)	3.84	Equity Global	MSCI WORLD SRI Select reduced Fossil Fuel Index	BlackRock Asset Management Ireland	October 12, 2017	0.20
iShares Automation & Robotics UCITS ETF USD A	3.62	Equity Global	STOXX Global Automation & Robotics Index	BlackRock Asset Management Ireland	September 8, 2016	0.40

Continued

Table 4.6 The largest sustainable investing ETFs primarily listed in the United Kingdom (according to the assets under management). September 2021 data.—cont'd

Name of the fund	Total net assets (bln USD)	Asset class of exposure (Lipper's classification)	Benchmark	Provider	Inception date	Total expense ratio (%)
L&G Cyber Security UCITS ETF USD Acc	2.90	Equity Global	ISE Cyber Security UCITS Index	LGIM Managers	September 28, 2015	0.69
iShares € Corp Bond ESG UCITS ETF EUR Inc	2.81	Bond Global Corporates EUR	Bloomberg MSCI Euro Corporate Sustainable SRI Index	BlackRock Asset Management Ireland	June 28, 2018	0.15
iShares MSCI EM SRI UCITS ETF USD (Acc)	2.77	Equity Emerging Markets Global	MSCI EM SRI Select reduced Fossil Fuel Index	BlackRock Asset Management Ireland	July 11, 2016	0.25
iShares € Corp Bond 0-3y ESG UCITS ETF EUR Dist	2.67	Bond ETF	Bloomberg MSCI Euro Corp 0-3 Sustainable SRI Index	BlackRock Asset Management Ireland	January 7, 2016	0.15
iShares Healthcare Innovation UCITS ETF USD A	2.41	Equity Global	STOXX Global Breakthrough Healthcare Index	BlackRock Asset Management Ireland	September 8, 2016	0.40

Source: own elaboration based on Lipper's and justETF databases as well as websites of the funds' providers.

of reasons. For example, obtaining exposure to the UK assets consistent with the sustainability assumptions is hindered by the relatively low number of equities of companies with the high ESG scores and low carbon emission scores, thus complicating the construction of the associated benchmarks (Lesyk & Dougan, 2021, pp. 1–17). Another reason is the high number of fossil fuel companies with high capitalization listed on the UK stock exchange (Robins & Krosinsky, 2008). Nevertheless, some ETFs with the exposure to the UK assets are available—for example, in 2020 and 2021 BlackRock launched such funds; there are also some relatively new funds managed by the other providers (Cowie, 2021; Gordon, 2021; Lord, 2021b). The withdrawal from the assets problematic in the climate perspective applies also to the other types of assets potentially held by the UK ETFs. For instance, since 2021, the UK government substantially restricted the financing of the projects focused on fossil fuels abroad (Eurosif, 2021). An important issue determining the launch and development of the ESG funds is the motivations and beliefs of the funds' managers—the case of the UK managers was analyzed in-depth by Syed (2017) who generally provided evidence for their support of the key ESG aspects in the investment process.

There are also, though, certain factors that can affect positively the development of the United Kingdom sustainable investing at large (or be neutral), potentially influencing also the relevant segments of the ETFs market. Sustainability rules concerning the investment portfolios may be adopted by the pension funds (Biehl & Atkins, 2016; Woods & Urwin, 2010) or in the other types of retirement plans (Eurosif, 2018; Owadally et al., 2021). The development of sustainable investments in the United Kingdom (not only ESG ETFs) has also been spurred by the initiatives concerning the access to the ESG-linked information such as the financial services of the London Stock Exchange Group (Gordon, 2020). Another example is the activity of the community development financial institutions supported by various entities within the UK authorities (Camilleri, 2017).

The factor that still remains under study as the possible determinant of the sustainable investments development is their financial performance in relation to the conventional investments—for an overview of the selected country-level evidence, including the UK market, see, for example, Chakrabarty et al. (2017). In the pioneering study most consistent with the topic of the current case study, Rompotis (2022) evaluated the performance of the 49 UK ESG ETFs—the conclusions were mixed, with no strong evidence for their overperformance. Moreover, the higher ESG scores of the UK ETFs seemed unrelated to increased inflows of capital from investors—on the contrary, the funds with the lower scores managed relatively more assets. Performance and flows to the UK equity pension funds with the ESG focus were compared to the conventional counterparts by Alda (2020) indicating the relative benefits of the sustainable funds. Nevertheless, in the most recent perspective, the results of the study by Hoang et al. (2020) showed that the UK companies with the high ESG scores in some dimensions were less affected by the developments linked to the Covid-19 pandemic (still, the effects on their stocks' performance were negative). In a more general perspective, the financial performance of the UK companies was examined by Ahmad et al. (2021) who provided evidence for the superior financial performance of the companies with the high ESG ratings when compared to the ones with the low ESG scores.

4.7 Sustainable investing ETFs in the European countries: case study (IV)—France

In the fourth case study of sustainable investing ETFs in Europe, we discuss the French market—the country being among the leaders of the region in terms of both the size of the local ETFs market and the sustainable investing industry; moreover, French asset management industry is one of the largest in the world (Crifo & Mottis, 2016; Krupa, 2013). However, its case is slightly different with regard to the sustainable investing ETFs market than in the three previous countries, mostly due to the structure of the local stock exchange, comprising a part of the regional trading venue operating in a few European countries. In line with the previous case studies, we start our discussion with an overview of the history of sustainable investing in France, followed by the regulatory environment and a presentation of the French sustainable investing industry. The last part of the section focuses on the ESG ETFs primarily listed in France.

From a historical perspective, the beginnings of contemporary sustainable investing in France can be traced back to the second half of the 1990s and the influence of the religious movements (Giamporcaro, 2016). On the global level, France was one of the pioneers of the adoption of sustainable investing rules (Crifo, Durand et al., 2019). The development of the sector was boosted by the establishment of the French CSR rating agency (Arese, later after the merger transformed into Vigeo) as well as Novethic—think tank and media platform dedicated to the sustainability issues (Crifo, Escrig-Olmedo et al., 2019; Leite & Cortez, 2015; Petrillo et al., 2016).

Among the vital regulatory developments with regard to the sustainable investing, an important role can be assigned to the laws concerning employee savings plans adopted in the early 2000s, requiring the managing companies to disclose their approach toward ESG factors as well as the condition to include in their portfolios the funds managing, among others, community investments (Giamporcaro, 2016). Moreover, requirements regarding ESG issues in the pension funds and disclosures of the listed companies concerning ESG reporting were also introduced (Crifo, Escrig-Olmedo et al., 2019; Crifo & Mottis, 2016). In 2016, further acts were passed, imposing on the institutional investors the obligation to disclose their approach to accounting for the ESG issues in the investment decisions and the alignment of their policies with the national strategies of ecological and energy transition (Sládková et al., 2021).

The leading group of investors on the French sustainable investing market in the early 2010s were institutional investors, with over 70% market share, and retail investors accounted for about 30% (Giamporcaro, 2016). Important role was played by the pension funds, engaged in the ESG investments (Jemel-Fornetty et al., 2011). The commitment of the French pension funds is also proven by the fact that they are one of the biggest groups of the European signatories of this kind of Net Zero Alliance (Nikulina, 2021, pp. 1–20). Nonetheless, insurance companies contributed most strongly to the growth of the French sustainable investing sector (Crifo, Durand et al., 2019). Since the beginning of the PRI initiative, French financial institutions were among the largest group among the European signatories of the PRI, behind only the UK ones (Giamporcaro, 2016). According to data disclosed in Eurosif (2018), institutional investors remain in France the largest group, with a 75% share in the total sustainable investing market and more than 50% with regard to the ESG funds.

From the European perspective, the French sustainable investing market has been the regional leader of the best-in-class ESG investing strategies rather than negative screening or exclusions as in most other countries—the popularity of this investing theme can be traced back to the beginning when it had been adopted as the preferred approach by the pioneering providers of sustainable financial products (Camilleri, 2020; Crifo & Mottis, 2016; Giamporcaro, 2016). Nevertheless, more recent data show that also in France norms-based screening has gained popularity (Eurosif, 2018). Moreover, also more recently, due to the actions of the French government, themed sustainable investments devoted to the topics such as water management or renewable energy have been developing rapidly (Crifo, Durand et al., 2019).

In the 1990s, there were merely a few investment funds that could be classified as sustainable (or using the dominant terminology as ethical) and the sector remained underdeveloped (Crifo, Durand et al., 2019; Giamporcaro & Gond, 2016). However, already in the mid-2010s the assets of the French sustainable investing funds reached substantial levels—in broader scope (with at least minimal inclusion of ESG criteria) their value in 2015 was slightly below 750 billion EUR, out of which approximately 320 billion EUR was managed by the funds with the main focus on ESG. In terms of share in total assets in 2014 sustainable funds accounted for c. 20% (Crifo, Durand et al., 2019). Taking into account some aspects typical for sustainable investing has become common even for the majority of French conventional funds and the other types of asset managers (Crifo & Mottis, 2016).

As of the end of September 2021, the total net assets of the French sustainable investing ETFs were close to 41 billion USD; the highest value ever was reached in the preceding month when it was slightly higher, at about 41.3 billion USD. In terms of the share in the total assets of ETFs primary listed in France, September 2021 marked, though, the record-high level of over 25%. As explained in the previous section, the data on the French primary listed ETFs are based on the data for the ETFs primary listed on the Euronext Paris; the remaining segments of Euronext were considered separately. In terms of the structure by the management approach, all French ESG ETFs were passive funds when the information extracted from the Lipper's and justETF databases is taken into account, that is, there were no active funds in this category, in contrast with the markets discussed in the previous case studies. It shows that relatively more recent active funds have not yet become part of the French sustainable investing industry (at least with regard to ETFs). The vast majority of the French sustainable investing ETFs are domiciled in Luxembourg; there are, though, also some funds with France as their domicile country. The leading providers of the French ESG ETFs are local financial corporations, the asset management branches of BNP Paribas as well as Amundi and Lyxor. The position of non-French financial institutions is almost negligible.

Table 4.7 presents the biggest sustainable investing ETFs in France in terms of their assets under management. The largest fund in France (and the fourth largest in Europe—see Table 4.2), "Amundi Index MSCI USA SRI UCITS ETF DR C," is the only one on the list with the assets exceeding 4

Table 4.7 The largest sustainable investing ETFs primarily listed in France (according to the assets under management). September 2021 data.

Name of the fund	Total net assets (bln USD)	Asset class of exposure (Lipper's classification)	Benchmark	Provider	Inception date	Total expense ratio (%)
Amundi index MSCI USA SRI UCITS ETF DR C	4.34	Equity US	MSCI USA SRI Filtered ex Fossil Fuels Index	Amundi Luxembourg	September 25, 2018	0.18
Amundi MSCI Europe SRI UCITS ETF DR C	2.27	Equity Europe	MSCI Europe SRI Filtered ex Fossil Fuels Index	Amundi Luxembourg	September 25, 2018	0.18
Amundi Index MSCI EMU ESG Leaders Select ETF C	2.05	Equity EuroZone	MSCI EMU ESG Leaders Select 5% Issuer Capped Index	Amundi Luxembourg	April 20, 2017	0.25
Amundi Index Euro Corp SRI – UCITS ETF DR C	1.71	Bond ETF	Bloomberg MSCI Euro Corporate ESG Sustainability SRI	Amundi Luxembourg	June 29, 2016	0.14
Amundi Index MSCI World SRI UCITS ETF DR C	1.71	Equity Global	MSCI World SRI Filtered ex Fossil Fuels Index	Amundi Luxembourg	September 25, 2018	0.18
Lyxor MSCI Water ESG Filtered (DR) UCITS ETF – Dis	1.37	Equity Global	MSCI ACWI IMI Water ESG Filtered Net Total Return Index	Lyxor Intl AM	October 9, 2007	0.60

Continued

Table 4.7 The largest sustainable investing ETFs primarily listed in France (according to the assets under management). September 2021 data.—cont'd

Name of the fund	Total net assets (bln USD)	Asset class of exposure (Lipper's classification)	Benchmark	Provider	Inception date	Total expense ratio (%)
Lyxor New Energy (DR) UCITS ETF - Dist	1.36	Equity Sector Utilities	MSCI ACWI IMI New Energy ESG Filtered	Lyxor Intl AM	October 10, 2007	0.60
BNPP Easy Low Carbon 100 Europe PAB UCITS ETF C	1.09	Equity Europe	Low Carbon 100 Europe PAB (NTR)	BNP Paribas AM LU	June 2, 2017	0.30
Amundi Float Rate Euro Corporate ESG ETF DR EUR A	1.03	Bond ETF	iBoxx MSCI ESG EUR FRN Investment Grade Corporates	Amundi Luxembourg	April 5, 2018	0.18
Lyxor MSCI Europe ESG Leaders (DR) UCITS ETF A	1.02	Equity ETF	MSCI Europe ESG Leaders Net Total Return Index	Lyxor Intl AM	February 12, 2019	0.20

Source: own elaboration based on Lipper's and justETF databases as well as websites of the funds' providers.

billion USD. In the case of the three funds, their size was above 2 billion USD. What is worth noticing is the fact that 6 out of 10 ETFs in the ranking are managed by the leading country's provider of ETFs, that is, Amundi (to be more exact, its branch located in Luxembourg), followed by three Lyxor's funds and one offered by BNP Paribas, in line with the structure of the overall French ESG ETFs market. The composition of the list of the largest funds in the dimension of their exposure is similar to the one for the previously presented case studies—the key group are equity ETFs tracking the indexes of the major stock markets, with just two corporate bonds funds with ESG profile. Analysis of the inception dates shown in Table 4.7 clearly unveils that most funds were launched since 2016 onwards, that is, over the last few years, presumably due to the increasing interest in the sustainable investing financial products as well as developments in the ESG ETFs markets' environment. The only two funds with longer history are two thematic Lyxor ETFs, one focused on the water-related assets and the other devoted to, for example, equities in the renewable energy sector.

In the final part of the case study, we discuss the selected factors of the development of the French ESG ETFs. In contrast with most other European sustainable investing industries, the French sector since its beginnings has been dominated by the entities linked strongly to the state as well as mainstream financial institutions (unlike the mostly peripheral entities playing the key role at the earlier stages in the other countries) (Crifo, Durand et al., 2019; Giamporcaro & Gond, 2016; Krupa, 2013). Further fundamental state-related development determinant was the high level of unification of definitions and labels used with regard to sustainable investing in France, imposed by the direct and indirect state interventions, with the important role of the aforementioned French ESG rating agency (Crifo, Durand et al., 2019); these labels are also utilized by the providers of ETFs (Barclays, 2021; Eckett, 2019). Another possible factor affecting the development of the French ESG ETFs (as a part of the broader category of French sustainable investing funds) are the attitudes of the funds' managers toward the inclusion of the ESG principles in their investment decision making—according to the results of the study by Syed (2017) French managers view favorably the application of the ESG criteria, in particular the environmental and social aspects.

Financial performance (potentially one of the key development determinants) of the French sustainable investing funds was examined in a number of studies. In one of the first and earliest publications on the topic (updating their previous analysis, with similar conclusions), Amenc and Le Sourd (2010) concluded underperformance of French sustainable funds in the period covering the 2008 global financial crisis and the considerable volatility of the prices of their shares. Nevertheless, Leite and Cortez (2015) showed that during the crisis periods the performance of both French sustainable and conventional equity funds was comparable. Nevertheless, the differences could be noticed in the noncrisis periods, with the poorer performance of the ESG funds, in particular the ones following a negative screening approach. There are also some studies indirectly linked to the discussed issue, that is, focused on the influence of the ESG issues on the financial standing of French companies. For example, Hamrouni et al. (2019) examined their CSR disclosures and stated that the overall higher score in this dimension leads to a lower cost of debt, with the most important contribution of the environmental disclosures. Still, one of the fundamental barriers to the development of the French ESG ETFs seems the insufficient awareness among retail investors—according to 2021 data, almost 70% of the French adult population has no knowledge of these financial instruments (Zamfiroiu & Pînzaru, 2021). From the infrastructural perspective, the development of the French market for sustainable investing ETFs would be impossible without the actions of the Euronext stock exchange supporting the launch and expansion of these funds such as the introduction of the ESG-linked stock market indexes (e.g., launched in partnership with the French ESG rating agencies (Mooij, 2017)) or specialized markets for certain sustainable financial instruments (Siddy, 2009). The new or modified indexes include the ESG-compliant versions of the most popular indexes such as CAC 40 ESG Index (Lord, 2021a).

References

Ahmad, N., Mobarek, A., & Roni, N. N. (2021). Revisiting the impact of ESG on financial performance of FTSE350 UK firms: Static and dynamic panel data analysis. *Cogent Business & Management, 8*(1), 1—18.

Alda, M. (2020). ESG fund scores in UK SRI and conventional pension funds: Are the ESG concerns of the SRI niche affecting the conventional mainstream? *Finance Research Letters, 36.*

Amenc, N., & Le Sourd, V. (2010). *The performance of socially responsible investment and sustainable development in France: An update after the financial crisis.* Edhec-Risk Institute.

Barclays. (2021). *Ossiam ESG low carbon shiller Barclays CAPE US sector ETF celebrates its third anniversary with 2.8% annualized outperformance versus S&P500.* Retrieved 1st March 2022 https://home.barclays/news/press-releases/2021/04/ossiam-esg-low-carbon-shiller-barclays-cape-us-sector-etf-celebr/.

Bialkowski, J., & Starks, L. T. (2016). *SRI funds: Investor demand, exogenous shocks and ESG profiles.* Retrieved 3rd December 2021 https://ir.canterbury.ac.nz/handle/10092/12492.

Biehl, C., & Atkins, J. (2016). Responsible investment in the United Kingdom. In T. Hebb, J. P. Hawley, A. G. Hoepner, A. L. Neher, & D. Wood (Eds.), *The Routledge handbook of responsible investment* (pp. 355–363). Routledge.

Bioy, H., & Lamont, K. (2018). Passive sustainable funds: The global landscape. *The Journal of Index Investing, 9*(3), 4–17.

Bryan, A., Choy, J., Lamont, K., & Sanzgiri, Z. (2020). *Passive Sustainable Funds: The Global Landscape 2020: Choice expands as products and assets double in three years.* Morningstar.

Camilleri, M. A. (2017). *Corporate sustainability, social responsibility and environmental management: An introduction to theory and practice with case studies.* Springer.

Camilleri, M. A. (2020). The market for socially responsible investing: A review of the developments. *Social Responsibility Journal, 17*(3), 412–428.

CFA Institute & Principles for Responsible Investment. (2018). *ESG integration in the Americas: Markets, practices, and data.*

CFA Institute & Principles for Responsible Investment. (2019a). *ESG integration in Asia pacific: Markets, practices, and data.*

CFA Institute & Principles for Responsible Investment. (2019b). *ESG integration in Europe, the Middle East, and Africa: Markets, practices, and data.*

CFA Institute. (2020). *Climate change analysis in the investment process.*

Chakrabarty, B., Lee, S. B., & Singh, N. (2017). Doing good while making money: Individual investor participation in socially responsible corporations. *Management Decision, 55*(8), 1645–1659.

Cowie, D. (2021). *European asset managers ramp up provision of sustainable ETFs.* Retrieved 15th January 2022 https://www.ft.com/content/6e63d432-6e8c-4a4f-95b5-0a26e676cd95.

Crifo, P., Durand, R., & Gond, J. P. (2019). Encouraging investors to enable corporate sustainability transitions: The case of responsible investment in France. *Organization & Environment, 32*(2), 125–144.

Crifo, P., Escrig-Olmedo, E., & Mottis, N. (2019). Corporate governance as a key driver of corporate sustainability in France: The role of board members and investor relations. *Journal of Business Ethics, 159*(4), 1127–1146.

Crifo, P., & Mottis, N. (2016). Socially responsible investment in France. *Business & Society, 55*(4), 576–593.

Deloitte. (2018). *ETF's and sustainability: Link 'n' learn.*

Dowell-Jones, M. (2012). Investing in emerging markets: The ethical context. *Journal of Corporate Citizenship, 48*, 75–90.

Eckett, T. (2019). *Lyxor receives SRI label from French government for two ESG ETFs.* Retrieved 1st March 2022 https://www.etfstream.com/news/lyxor-receives-sri-label-from-french-government-for-two-esg-etfs/.

ETFGI. (2022). *ETFGI ETF/ETP growth charts.* Retrieved 3rd January 2022 https://etfgi.com/.

European Fund and Asset Management Association. (2021a). *Asset Management in Europe: An overview of the asset management industry.*

European Fund and Asset Management Association. (2021b). The European ESG market at end Q1 2021 – introducing the SFDR. *EFAMA Market Insights, 7*, 1–8.

Eurosif. (2016). *European SRI study 2016.*

Eurosif. (2018). *European SRI study 2018.*

Eurosif. (2021). *Eurosif report 2021.*

Gerber, M. S., Norman, G., & Toms, S. (2021). *ESG in 2021 so far: An update.* Harvard Law School Forum on Corporate Governance.

Giamporcaro, S. (2016). Responsible investment in France. In T. Hebb, J. P. Hawley, A. G. Hoepner, A. L. Neher, & D. Wood (Eds.), *The Routledge handbook of responsible investment* (pp. 262–275). Routledge.

Giamporcaro, S., & Gond, J. P. (2016). Calculability as politics in the construction of markets: The case of socially responsible investment in France. *Organization Studies, 37*(4), 465–495.

Global Sustainable Investment Alliance. (2013). *Global sustainable investment review 2012.*

Global Sustainable Investment Alliance. (2015). *Global sustainable investment review 2014.*

Global Sustainable Investment Alliance. (2017). *Global sustainable investment review 2016.*

Global Sustainable Investment Alliance. (2019). *Global sustainable investment review 2018.*

Global Sustainable Investment Alliance. (2021). *Global sustainable investment review 2020.*

Glow, J. (2022a). *European ETF industry review: 2021.* Refinitiv.

Glow, J. (2022b). *Monday morning memo: Will ESG funds continue to drive the growth of the European fund industry?.* Retrieved 11th May 2022 https://lipperalpha.refinitiv.com/2022/01/monday-morning-memo-will-esg-funds-continue-to-drive-the-growth-of-the-european-fund-industry/.

Gordon, M. (2020). The sustainable investment assessment: Data and methodologies. *Journal of Securities Operations & Custody, 13*(1), 72–81.

Gordon, J. (2021). *BlackRock unveils UK ESG leaders ETF.* Retrieved 13th January 2022 https://www.etfstream.com/news/blackrock-unveils-uk-esg-leaders-etf/.

Hale, J. (2018). *Sustainable funds U.S. Landscape report* (pp. 1–48). Morningstar.

Hale, J. (2021). *Sustainable Funds U.S. Landscape Report: More funds, more flows, and impressive returns in 2020.* Morningstar.

Halper, J., Busssiere, S., & Shriver, T. (2021). *Investors and regulators turning up the heat on climate-change disclosures.* Retrieved 15th January 2022 https://corpgov.law.harvard.edu/2021/10/04/investors-and-regulators-turning-up-the-heat-on-climate-change-disclosures/.

Hamrouni, A., Uyar, A., & Boussaada, R. (2019). Are corporate social responsibility disclosures relevant for lenders? Empirical evidence from France. *Management Decision, 58*(2), 267–279.

HM Government. (2021). *Greening finance: A roadmap to sustainable investing.*

Hoang, T. H. V., Segbotangni, E. A., & Lahiani, A. (2020). *Does ESG disclosure transparency help mitigate the Covid-19 pandemic shock? An empirical analysis of listed firms in the UK.* Retrieved 25th February 2022 https://papers.ssrn.com/sol3/papers.cfm?abstract_id=3738256.

Hummels, H. (2012). Coming out of the investors' cave?: Making sense of responsible investing in Europe in the new millennium. *Business and Professional Ethics Journal, 31*(2), 331–348.

Investment Association. (2021). *Investment management in the UK 2020-2021: The investment association annual survey.*

Jemel-Fornetty, H., Louche, C., & Bourghelle, D. (2011). Changing the dominant convention: The role of emerging initiatives in mainstreaming ESG. In C. Louche, R. Perez, & W. Sun (Eds.), *Finance and sustainability: Towards a new paradigm? A post-crisis agenda* (pp. 85–117). Emerald Group Publishing Limited.

John, D. (2021). *UK ESG funds dip toes into SFDR.* Retrieved 20th December 2021 https://www.refinitiv.com/perspectives/regulation-risk-compliance/how-are-fund-managers-responding-to-the-sfdr/.

Kinderman, D. (2012). 'Free us up so we can be responsible!'. The co-evolution of Corporate Social Responsibility and neo-liberalism in the UK, 1977–2010. *Socio-Economic Review, 10*(1), 29–57.

KPMG. (2019). *European responsible investing fund market 2019: A focus on "tagged" sustainable funds.*

Krupa, D. (2013). Fundusze SRI we Francji [SRI funds in France]. *Prace Naukowe Uniwersytetu Ekonomicznego We Wrocławiu, 311,* 125—133.

Le Sourd, V., & Safaee, S. (2021). The European ETF market: Growth, trends, and impact on underlying instruments. *The Journal of Portfolio Management, 47*(7), 95—111.

Lean, H. H., Ang, W. R., & Smyth, R. (2015). Performance and performance persistence of socially responsible investment funds in Europe and North America. *The North American Journal of Economics and Finance, 34,* 254—266.

Leite, P., & Cortez, M. C. (2015). Performance of European socially responsible funds during market crises: Evidence from France. *International Review of Financial Analysis, 40,* 132—141.

Lesyk, S., & Dougan, A. (2021). Sustainability in the UK. *Index Insights Sustainable Investment: Factor,* 1—17. July 2021.

Lord, J. (2021a). *Amundi set to launch CAC 40 ESG ETF.* Retrieved 1st March 2022 https://www.etfstrategy.com/amundi-set-to-launch-cac-40-esg-etf-euronext-paris-28384/.

Lord, J. (2021b). *BlackRock launches UK ESG leaders ETF on LSE.* Retrieved 13th January 2022 https://www.etfstrategy.com/blackrock-launches-uk-esg-leaders-etf-on-lse-98547/.

Mahmood, R. (2021). *Fund ESG transparency quarterly report 2021 Q1 spotlight: ETFs.* MSCI.

McCann, L., Solomon, A., & Solomon, J. F. (2003). Explaining the growth in UK socially responsible investment. *Journal of General Management, 28*(4), 15—36.

Méndez-Suárez, M., Monfort, A., & Gallardo, F. (2020). Sustainable banking: New forms of investing under the umbrella of the 2030 agenda. *Sustainability, 12*(5), 2096.

Mooij, S. (2017). The ESG rating and ranking industry; Vice or virtue in the adoption of responsible investment?. *Vice or Virtue in the Adoption of Responsible Investment.* https://papers.ssrn.com/sol3/papers.cfm?abstract_id=2960869. Retrieved 1st March 2022.

Moreira, M. (2021). *Refinitiv sustainable finance: Turning the art of ESG into science.* Refinitiv.

Nikulina, L. (2021). Global pensions and ESG: Is there a better way? *Wharton Pension Research Council Working Paper, 8,* 1—20.

Owadally, I., Mwizere, J. R., Kalidas, N., Murugesu, K., & Kashif, M. (2021). Long-term sustainable investment for retirement. *Sustainability, 13*(9).

Petrillo, A., De Felice, F., García-Melón, M., & Pérez-Gladish, B. (2016). Investing in socially responsible mutual funds: Proposal of non-financial ranking in Italian market. *Research in International Business and Finance, 37,* 541—555.

Principles for Responsible Investment. (2021). *PRI Signatory growth.*

Quak, S., Heilbron, J., & Meijer, J. (2014). The rise and spread of sustainable investing in The Netherlands. *Journal of Sustainable Finance & Investment, 4*(3), 249—265.

Refinitiv. (2019a). *Fund data for investment professionals: Lipper on Eikon.*

Refinitiv. (2019b). *Lipper global classification: Category definitions.*

Refinitiv. (2020a). *Refinitiv Lipper for marketing funds.*

Refinitiv. (2020b). *Refinitiv Lipper fund ESG scores: Pivotal data metrics partner for the transition to sustainable investing.*

Refinitiv. (2020c). *Refinitiv Lipper fund ESG scores — methodology.*

Reichenberg Gustafsson, A., & Stewart, B. (2021). *ESG matters: Global trends and transitions.* Retrieved 14th December 2021 https://blogs.cfainstitute.org/investor/2021/02/25/esg-matters-global-trends-and-transitions/.

Richardson, B. J. (2012). From fiduciary duties to fiduciary relationships for SRI: Responding to the will of beneficiaries. In T. Hebb (Ed.), *The next generation of responsible investing* (pp. 61—82). Dordrecht: Springer.

Robins, N., & Krosinsky, C. (2008). After the credit crunch: The future of sustainable investing. *Public Policy Research, 15*(4), 192—197.

Rompotis, G. G. (2022). The ESG ETFs in the UK. *Journal of Asset Management, 23,* 114—129.

Ruggie, J. G., & Middleton, E. K. (2019). Money, millennials and human rights: Sustaining 'sustainable investing. *Global Policy, 10*(1), 144–150.

Schueth, S. (2003). Socially responsible investing in the United States. *Journal of Business Ethics, 43*(3), 189–194.

Siddy, D. (2009). *Exchanges and sustainable investment.* World Federation of Exchanges.

Sládková, J., Kolomazníková, D., Formánková, S., Trenz, O., Kolomazník, J., & Faldík, O. (2021). Sustainable and responsible investment funds in Europe. *Measuring Business Excellence.* in print.

Swiss Sustainable Finance. (2021a). *Annual report 2021.*

Swiss Sustainable Finance. (2021b). *Swiss sustainable investment market study 2021.*

Syed, A. M. (2017). Environment, social, and governance (ESG) criteria and preference of managers. *Cogent Business & Management, 4*(1), 1–13.

US SIF Foundation. (2018). *Report on US sustainable, responsible and impact investing trends,* 2018.

US SIF Foundation. (2020). *Report on US sustainable and impact investing trends 2020.*

Woods, C., & Urwin, R. (2010). Putting sustainable investing into practice: A governance framework for pension funds. *Journal of Business Ethics, 92*(1), 1–19.

XPS Investment. (2021). *Investment fund ESG review 2021.*

Zamfiroiu, T. P., & Pînzaru, F. (2021). Advancing strategic management through sustainable finance. *Management Dynamics in the Knowledge Economy, 9*(2), 279–291.

Zeb & Morningstar. (2021). *European sustainable investment funds study: Catalysts for a greener Europe.*

CHAPTER 5

Consequences of the spread of the sustainable investing ETFs in Europe

5.1. Empirical evidence

The first section of the chapter is devoted to the presentation of the results of the multidimensional empirical analysis concerning the relationships between the development of the sustainable investing (ESG) exchange-traded funds (ETFs) markets in Europe and selected financial, socio-economic, and environmental variables; the discussion of the obtained results with reference to the other publications can be found in the subsequent section. This section starts with the discussion of the methodological issues of the ESG funds, with the focus on the ESG scoring methodology applied within the Refinitiv Lipper's database that served as our primary data source on the sustainable investing ETFs. Next, we concentrate on the sources of data, variables uses in the analysis, time period, and sample of the study. The second subsection of the chapter focuses on the examination of the ESG rankings of the European ETFs, in particular, the differences between the funds labeled as ESG and conventional ones—the aim of this subsection is to establish whether the analyzed ESG funds are in fact ranked higher in terms of their sustainability than the other ETFs in examined countries. In the main, third part of the chapter, we present both the graphical evidence and estimated models (together with the correlation analysis); we examine various aspects of sustainable development, thus our analysis is conducted on the macro level. It should be added that in this chapter we do not discuss the methodological issues concerning the econometric methods applied in our study as they are addressed in the Methodological annex.

Sustainable Investing
ISBN 978-0-12-823871-4
https://doi.org/10.1016/B978-0-12-823871-4.00007-6

5.1.1 Methodological remarks, sources of data, and list of variables

The first step of our empirical study is the assessment of the sustainability attributes of the ETFs covered within our sample. Our primary data source is the Refinitiv Lipper's database, and all funds labeled as 'ethical' are regarded as equivalent to ESG (sustainable investing) funds, with some additional cross-checks with supplementary databases. However, the labeling of the funds as ESG, even in the highly reliable database, seems insufficient evidence for their sustainability-focused profile. Consequently, to determine the sustainability of the funds included in our sample, we check their ESG scores supplied by Lipper's, concentrating on the differences between the scores of the aforementioned ETFs and conventional (non-ESG) ETFs; in addition to the Lipper's ESG scores, as supplementary and comparative evidence we consider the sustainability scores of MSCI (extracted from the FactSet database).[1] As the Lipper's ESG scores of the investment funds are based on the scores of the securities in their portfolios (depending in the vast majority of cases on the sustainability rankings of the issuing entities), we discuss not only the Lipper's methodology but also the fundamentals of the Refinitiv's ESG scores, awarded in particular to the companies. Finally, it should be added that there are multiple other sustainable investing methodologies that could be applied (see discussion in Chapter 3), including the classification of funds based on the SFDR that came into force in the EU in 2021 (Moreira, 2021). However, their usefulness in the context of our study is limited by the insufficient data (especially in the time dimension but also in terms of geographic coverage), various ambiguities, and lack of their reliability proven sufficiently through the earlier studies.

Lipper's ESG scores of the funds are created using data on approximately 200 most consistent, material and comparable out of over 600 company-level ESG measures, included in the following 10 categories (corresponding to 10 themes regarded as key by Refinitiv) and three pillars (Moreira, 2021; Refinitiv, 2021, 2022a,b):

---

[1] Methodology of the MSCI's ESG fund scores is provided in MSCI (2021). Similar to the Lipper's approach, company-level ESG scores are transformed into scores calculated for mutual funds and ETFs. Each fund is awarded both ESG rating (AAA to CCC) and ESG score (0—10; higher score indicates a higher level of ESG compliance in the fund's portfolio). The MSCI's ESG scores ("Fund ESG Quality Scores") are explained as assessing the resilience of the holdings in the fund's portfolio to key medium- and long-term ESG risks.

- resource use, emissions, innovation: aggregated into the environmental (E) pillar;
- workforce, human rights, community, product responsibility: aggregated into the social (S) pillar;
- management, shareholders, CSR: aggregated into the governance (G) pillar.

The abovementioned categories are aggregated into the three pillars using weighting schemes (with weights of E and S pillars differing by the sector whereas applied G pillar weights are the same in all industries (Refinitiv, 2022b)). The pillar scores are further summed up to obtain the overall ESG score.[2] Additionally, Lipper provides an ESG controversies score (indicating the impact of the negative events (Refinitiv, 2020)) that, together with the overall ESG score, is developed into the combined ESG score, that is, the base indicator of the fund's sustainability compliance that will be used in our analysis. The final scores are calculated with the application of the percentile rank scoring methodology, resulting in a score in the range between 0 and 100 as well as supplementary letter grades indicating the ranking, between A+ (ESG leaders) and D- (ESG laggards) (Refinitiv, 2021).

Lipper's ESG scores are provided on a monthly basis (on portfolio's reporting end date), through the bottom-up approach, using ESG data on the assets (securities) held in the funds' portfolios (more specifically, the data on their issuers as of the end of the last fiscal year). They are presented exclusively for the funds for which at least 70% of the assets held can be assessed and there are at least 10 separate components of the portfolio; exclusively equities and fixed debt securities are examined. The weights of the securities correspond to their share in the total net assets of the fund yet the weights are rebased to account for the elements with no ESG scores. The companies with zero transparency are excluded from the calculation of the percentile ranks (Moreira, 2021). The sources of data used in the calculation of the ESG scores consist of, among others, the reports of companies, their websites, news sources, and websites of the NGOs (Refinitiv, 2021).

The coverage of the Lipper's ESG fund scores as of mid-2020 was more than 19,000 funds' portfolios, representing almost 16 trillion USD of assets; ESG scores were provided for over 9000 companies amounting to more

---

[2] For detailed information on the Refinitiv's ESG scoring methodology, including the full list of variables and technical details, see Refinitiv (2021).

than 80% of the global equity market capitalization, mostly from North America and Europe (Refinitiv, 2020, 2021). The increasing coverage of Refinitiv's ESG scores in terms of companies has led to a broadened range of stock market indexes covered. This trend should be considered particularly important taking into account the passive attributes of most ETFs—by 2022 Refinitiv's database included data on the ESG scores of the companies within the vast majority of the major stock market indexes globally (Refinitiv, 2022b).

The second step of our empirical investigation consists of a few elements: correlation analysis, nonparametric graphical evidence, and panel models. The list of the variables used for the study of the relationships between ESG ETFs and financial and socio-economic systems is presented in Table 5.1.

The explanatory variable in our analysis is labeled as 'ETF'—the total values of the net assets managed by the sustainable investing ETFs primarily listed in certain countries are expressed as the percentage of the local GDP. We do not use the data on the share of ESG ETFs in the total ETFs markets as the preliminary analysis conducted using data on both absolute and relative dimensions of the sustainable investing ETFs markets' role indicated much more robust results for the values of assets rather than market shares. Moreover, the adopted approach is more consistent with the previous studies in the field.

The other variables in Table 5.1 are financial, socio-economic and environmental variables possibly affected by (with some stipulations[3]) the development of the European ESG ETFs markets (i.e., measured using the 'ETF' variable), selected in line with the literature review (see the discussion in Section 5.2) and sustainable development policies (see Section 5.4). The variables are additionally divided into three groups: financial (F), socio-economic (S), and environmental (E) to enable a separate analysis of the role of ESG ETFs in the most closely linked part of the socio-economic system, that is, financial sector, and distinguish the environmental aspects from the other topics. Moreover, taking into account the sustainable

---

[3] Due to the insufficient data and complexity of the issue, we do not conduct in-depth analysis of the factors affecting the explained variables, for example, in the form of the multiple variable panel models; we also do not utilize the cause-effect framework such as the VAR models. Instead, we focus exclusively on the role of sustainable investing ETFs. Consequently, we use the term 'explained' as an approximation of the actual research procedure.

Table 5.1 Variables summary.

Variable	Full name	Units	Sources of data	Additional remarks	Category of variables/SDG
ETF	Total net assets of sustainable investing ETFs primarily listed in certain countries in relation to the size of the local economy	% of GDP	Lipper	—	Explanatory
FD	Financial development index	Index	IMF Financial Development Index Database	Normalized between 0 and 1.	F/SDG 8
Econ_freedom	Economic freedom	Index	The heritage Foundation's database	Values between 0 and 100.	S/SDG 1
Prop_rights	Property rights	Index	The heritage Foundation's database	Values between 0 and 100.	S/SDG 1
SMC	Stock market capitalization	% of GDP	Global Financial Development Database	—	F/SDG 8
BD	Bank deposits	% of GDP	Global Financial Development Database	—	F/SDG 8

Continued

Table 5.1 Variables summary.—cont'd

Variable	Full name	Units	Sources of data	Additional remarks	Category of variables/SDG
HDI	Human Development Index	Index	United nations Development programme/Statista	Values between 0 and 1.	S/SDG 1
RQ	Regulatory quality	Index	World Governance Indicators	Composite measure with values −2.5 to 2.5.	S/SDG 16
Health_exp	Domestic general government health expenditure	% of GDP	World Development Indicators	—	S/SDG 1
ODA	Total net ODA provided	% of GNI	World Development Indicators	—	S/SDG 17
Researchers	Researchers in R&D	Number per million inhabitants	World Development Indicators	—	S/SDG 9
CO2_intensity	CO_2 intensity of GDP	Emissions per unit of GDP	World Development Indicators	—	E/SDG 9
Waste_gener	Municipal waste generated	kkg per capita	OECD Green Growth Indicators	—	E/SDG 11
Water_stress	Water stress, total freshwater abstraction	% of total available	OECD Green Growth Indicators	—	E/SDG 6

		renewable resources			
Temperature	Annual surface temperature	Change since 1951–80	OECD Green Growth Indicators	—	E/SDG 13
Environ_tech	Development of environment-related technologies	Inventions per capita	OECD Green Growth Indicators	—	E/SDG 7
CO2_emission	CO_2 emissions	Metric tons per capita	World Development Indicators	—	E/SDG 9
Nat_resour	Total natural resources rents	% of GDP	World Development Indicators	—	E/SDG 12
Women_manag	Proportion of women in senior and middle management positions	%	UN SDG Indicators Database	—	S/SDG 5
Multidim_pov	Proportion of population living in multidimensional poverty	%	UN SDG Indicators Database	—	S/SDG 1
PM25	PM2.5 air pollution, population exposed to levels exceeding WHO guideline value	% of total population	World Development Indicators	—	E/SDG 11

Continued

Table 5.1 Variables summary.—cont'd

Variable	Full name	Units	Sources of data	Additional remarks	Category of variables/SDG
Food_insecur	Prevalence of moderate or severe food insecurity in the population	% of total population	UN SDG Indicators Database	—	S/SDG 2
Renew_electr	Renewable electricity output	% of total electricity output	World Development Indicators	—	E/SDG 7
Below_med	Proportion of people living below 50% of median income	% of total population	UN SDG Indicators Database	—	S/SDG 10
Healthy_life	Healthy life years at birth	Years	Eurostat Sustainable Development Indicators	—	S/SDG 3
Digit_skills	Share of individuals having at least basic digital skills	% of total population	Eurostat Sustainable Development Indicators	—	S/SDG 4
Recyc_waste	Recycling rate of municipal waste	%	Eurostat Sustainable Development Indicators	—	E/SDG 11

Note: categories of variables: *E*, environmental; *F*, financial; *S*, socio-economic. For the list of the SDGs see Section 3.3.
Source: Own elaboration.

development goals (SDGs) and subsequent discussion in Section 5.4, we provide in case of each explained variable the most relevant associated SDG, identified using information from the documentation supporting the data sources and proprietary analysis. It should also be added that for comparative purposes all variables are expressed in units allowing for between-country analysis and creating a consistent dataset. Data were extracted from broadly recognized databases, used in similar studies of this kind, and all sources are listed in Table 5.1.

The selection of the variables presented in Table 5.1 was preceded not only by the aforementioned review of literature and sustainable development policies but also by the preliminary analysis of the much broader set of indicators (almost 300), from which the variables for which no impact of ESG ETFs could be reliably hypothesized or the ones with substantial data breaks were eliminated. Additionally, an initial correlation analysis was conducted. Finally, we chose almost 30 indicators, representing the vast majority of SDGs; in some cases, more than one variable was attributed to a particular SDG.

Time period of our analysis is 2006–20, to ensure consistency and due to data availability constraints; in some cases, the number of observations is limited due to missing data, in particular with regard to the most recent years. In all cases annual observations are used—no data of higher frequency could be acquired for almost all studied measures. Due to the limited number of observations, we concentrate exclusively on the joint (panel) evidence for the European sustainable investing ETFs markets examined in the previous chapter, that is, France, Germany, Italy, Switzerland, and the United Kingdom; Euronext_non_Paris is omitted as non-ETFs variables cannot be used due to their country-level attributes (whereas this market consists of ETFs primary listed in more than one country). The other reason why we do not disaggregate the evidence into country-level analysis is that we intend to formulate region-level conclusions rather than assess various interactions specific for certain economies.

5.1.2 Assessment of the sustainability of the European ETFs

Before the analysis of the financial, socio-economic, and environmental impact of the sustainable investing ETFs in Europe, it is necessary to provide some basic insights into their sustainability attributes. In particular, the key aim of this section is to compare the ESG rankings of various categories of ETFs (for methodological details concerning the ESG scores see Section 5.1.1). To extend our analysis, we discuss both region- and country-level evidence. Consequently, the conclusions from this section can be regarded in the context of the reliability of our selection criteria, that is, whether the ETFs that we included in our sample are in fact different than the remaining ones in this dimension. It should be emphasized, though, that the final conclusion concerning the consistency of the studied ETFs with their declared sustainability-related aims will be based on the subsequent analysis of their effects on various aspects of sustainable development—even high ESG scores do not necessarily mean noticeable impact on the sustainable development elements, in particular at macrolevel as in our analysis (Table 5.2).

In Tables 5.2 and 5.3, we present the average ESG scores of the European ETFs, according to the end-of-2021 data, first for all types of funds (in Table 5.2), followed by the scores of the specific categories of sustainable investing funds (in Table 5.3). As it can be concluded from the evidence provided in Table 5.2, in the case of all European ETFs (i.e., primarily listed

Table 5.2 Average ESG scores of ETFs in Europe, end of 2021.

		Mean ESG score		
Region/country	Provider of ESG scores	All ETFs	Conventional ETFs	Sustainable investing ETFs
Europe (all ETFs primary listed in the region)	Lipper	56.08	55.33	58.29
	MSCI	7.61	7.33	8.45
France	Lipper	57.08	56.42	58.72
	MSCI	8.04	7.83	8.76
Germany	Lipper	56.26	55.74	58.65
	MSCI	7.53	7.31	8.40
Italy	Lipper	55.90	55.32	56.73
	MSCI	7.27	6.97	7.84
Switzerland	Lipper	57.18	56.25	59.60
	MSCI	7.88	7.54	8.65
United Kingdom	Lipper	54.37	53.44	56.67
	MSCI	7.32	7.03	8.16

Note: arithmetic means used. Lipper's ESG scores (full name of the indicator: 'ESG Combined Score') extracted from the Refinitiv's database. MSCI's scores (full name of the indicator: 'Fund ESG Quality Score') are derived from the FactSet database. Lipper's scores range 0–100, MSCI's scores range 0–10 (in both cases higher score indicates higher assessed sustainability compliance). Number of funds assessed differs depending on the provider—in case of most countries, more funds were awarded MSCI's scores than Lipper's. For the methodology of the sustainability scores, see Section 5.1.1.
Source: Own elaboration.

Table 5.3 Average ESG scores of the selected categories of sustainable investing ETFs in Europe, end of 2021.

Category of sustainable investing ETFs	Region/country	Provider of ESG scores	Mean ESG score
Alternative energy	Europe (all ETFs primary listed in the region)	Lipper	58.85
		MSCI	9.25
	Germany	Lipper	58.85
		MSCI	9.25
	United Kingdom	Lipper	58.85
		MSCI	9.25
Green	Europe (all ETFs primary listed in the region)	Lipper	62.85
		MSCI	6.89
	France	Lipper	62.85
		MSCI	8.22
	Germany	Lipper	—
		MSCI	6.92
	Italy	Lipper	—
		MSCI	8.03
	Switzerland	Lipper	—
		MSCI	5.97
	United Kingdom	Lipper	—
		MSCI	3.91
Water	Europe (all ETFs primary listed in the region)	Lipper	55.92
		MSCI	9.35
	France	Lipper	60.97
		MSCI	9.60
	Germany	Lipper	53.40
		MSCI	—
	Switzerland	Lipper	—
		MSCI	9.29
	United Kingdom	Lipper	53.40
		MSCI	8.91

Note: arithmetic means used. Lack of data means no ETFs of this type in certain countries were awarded ESG scores.
Source: Own elaboration.

on the stock exchanges in the region), the ESG scores of the sustainable investing ETFs are noticeably higher than the scores of the conventional funds. The application of the Lipper's scores indicates an average result higher by about 5.4%; the difference is much more substantial for the MSCI's scores as it exceeds 15%. However, these two results are not fully comparable as some funds received the ESG scores exclusively from one provider. It can therefore be stated that, on a regional level, the adopted selection approach has led to the identification of the funds that are on average more sustainability-compliant than the remaining ETFs. Nevertheless, taking into consideration the most relevant Lipper's scores (with the aim of ensuring consistency of various steps of our analysis—earlier, we utilized the selection criteria applied in the Lipper's database to identify the ESG funds), the difference of approximately 5% is still rather small that could signal potential problems with either too mild approach to labeling of the funds as sustainable or too strict exclusion criteria from this category. Another possible reason, already signaled in preceding parts of the book, is related to the investment profile of the majority of the European sustainable investing ETFs, tracking the major stock market indexes albeit with some type of ESG filter imposed (the exact inclusion/exclusion and weighting criteria differ substantially and would require case-by-case discussion). As a result, despite various ESG labels used, they are rather similar to their non-ESG counterparts, even though there are some changes introduced to their benchmarks—this can be observed through the ESG scores that are, as already mentioned, different yet to a limited extent. Despite the raised stipulations, we believe we managed to create a correct sample of ETFs to be used in further study.[4]

Some additional insights into the ESG scores of the European ETFs can be gained through the analysis of the values within the three pillars calculated by Lipper as well as country-level results (for the latter, see Table 5.2).

Comparison of the levels of the three ESG pillars scores in the Lipper's database for all European ETFs (conventional and sustainable investing considered jointly) shows the highest results for the social pillar (mean of 73), followed by environmental and governance with similar average scores of about 66. In case of the ESG funds, the comparison to the values for the overall market proves their better performance in all three dimensions yet the difference is rather negligible for the social and governance pillars and slightly more pronounced for the environmental, in line with the focus of many European ESG ETFs on this issue.

---

[4] For another approach to the assessment of the funds' sustainability and comparison between various categories of funds, with much less optimistic conclusions, see Utz and Wimmer (2014). However, our results are similar to the ones presented in the report by the United Nations Conference on Trade and Development (United Nations Conference on Trade and Development [UNCTAD], 2020) that concluded that ESG ETFs are characterized by higher ESG scores than their non-ESG counterparts.

Country-level scores can be considered from two perspectives. First, they may be used in relation to the regional values, to assess the scores of the local ETFs in comparison to the ones in the other countries. Such analysis proves that France and Switzerland are the primary listing locations of ETFs with above-average sustainability scores; in both cases, the mean Lipper's ESG scores are at least by one point higher than the regional mean. For Germany, the evidence is mixed and depends on the source of scores used; overall, German ESG ETFs have scores comparable to the European mean level. Finally, taking into account the Lipper's scores, Italian ETFs at large (of total net assets much lower than in other countries considered) are slightly below the European average and the UK ones perform noticeably poorer (in case of MSCI's scores Italian lag behind UK ones); the same applies to the scores of the local ESG ETFs. It proves the clear sustainability focus of the French and Swiss ESG ETFs and the problematic utilization of the sustainability labels by many UK ETFs when considered in the context of the other European funds.

The abovementioned conclusions are also to some extent supported by the second perspective, that is, comparison of the ESG scores within a certain country's ETFs market. The difference between the mean Lipper's sustainability scores of conventional versus ESG funds is the highest for the Swiss market yet the second place can be noted for the UK market thus indicating a clear distinction between the two categories of ETFs on a local level (yet with stipulations raised above with regard to the application of the UK identifications in the regional context). The differences are also clear for the French and German ETFs. However, for the smallest market considered, in Italy, the ESG scores are rather similar (with a more visible difference for MSCI's rather than Lipper's scores); still, due to the small number of local sustainable investing ETFs and scarcity of Lipper's scores (awarded for only about 15 ES G ETFs) they should be interpreted with caution.

Table 5.3 provides supplementary evidence—ESG scores calculated for the three categories of sustainable investing ETFs available in the Lipper's database (i.e., second-level categories): alternative energy, green, and water. As these designations were awarded to a small number of ESG funds, the evidence is rather scarce and formulation of any reliable conclusions is hindered. This becomes clearly visible when the alternative energy ETFs are examined—for all markets the scores are identical as they represent in fact the same fund cross-listed in various countries as separate entities. Analysis of its ESG scores unveils substantial discrepancies between the data provided by Lipper and MSCI—according to the former, its sustainability performance is comparable to that of the average European ESG ETF yet the scores by the latter provider clearly indicate its above-average sustainability. Interestingly, in the case of the second category, the green ETFs, the relationship is reversed (for the water ETFs the relationship between the data from the two sources is similar to alternative energy ETFs). The between-country differences in the ESG performance of the green funds are extreme when MSCI's scores are considered yet again the key reason is the small number of funds in the sample. Another factor distorting the results is in some cases unclear reasons for the use of the second-level ESG categories in the Refinitiv's database.

5.1.3 Graphical evidence and panel regression estimates

In this subsection, we provide empirical evidence on the relationships between the selected variables representing various dimensions of sustainable development and the variable showing the development of the European sustainable investing ETFs markets. For the discussion of the obtained results, see Sections 5.2—5.4. To provide basic insights into the key attributes of our data, we present summary statistics in Table 5.4.

In the first step of our analysis, we calculated the pairwise correlation coefficients to study the basic attributes of the relationships (see Table 5.5). By convention, our analysis involves exclusively coefficients of each financial, socio-economic, and environmental variable calculated in relation to ETF.[5]

In the second step, we conducted an analysis involving graphical approximations and panel regression modeling. Fig. 5.1 presents the graphical nonparametric approximation using locally weighted scatterplot smoothing (hereafter: LOWESS), to unveil statistical relationships between selected pairs of variables. In Table 5.6, we include the estimates of panel regressions. Following the results of Hausman tests, we applied random-effects models.

Note: bandwidth set at default; nonparametric graphical approximation applied.

---

[5] Respective correlation matrices are available on request.

Table 5.4 Summary statistics of the selected financial, socio-economic, and environmental variables and the total net assets of sustainable investing ETFs. Period 2006—20 (annual data).

Variable	No. of obs.	Mean	Std. dev.	Min.	Max.
ETF	73	0.22	0.35	0.0002	1.77
FD	70	0.82	0.08	0.69	1.00
Econ_freedom	75	71.12	7.64	58.80	82.00
Prop_rights	75	80.38	13.73	50.00	93.80
SMC	62	104.67	73.07	18.82	273.21
BD	55	90.99	28.05	58.05	167.38
HDI	70	0.91	0.03	0.86	0.96
RQ	75	1.40	0.37	0.51	1.91
Health_exp	65	6.83	1.84	2.95	8.87
ODA	55	0.41	0.14	0.13	0.71
Researchers	56	3677.8	1085.7	1510.5	5450.4
CO2_intensity	75	0.14	0.04	0.06	0.23
Waste_gener	70	573.68	84.11	454.7	741.58
Water_stress	18	13.66	2.81	3.82	17.57
Temperature	75	1.43	0.58	−0.63	2.52
Environ_tech	65	27.56	16.05	7.55	62.67
CO2_emission	65	0.16	0.05	0.06	0.28
Nat_resour	70	0.22	0.31	0.009	1.31
Women_manag	65	29.63	5.27	21.16	39.19
Multidim_pov	27	22.1	4.61	17.00	30.00
PM25	40	87.71	13.16	49.30	99.69
Food_insecur	20	5.46	1.68	2.70	8.60
Renew_electr	50	25.81	17.73	4.61	62.19
Below_med	61	11.49	1.98	8.50	16.10
Healthy_life	67	62.97	2.87	56.50	68.30
Digit_skills	17	62.53	11.38	42.00	77.00
Recyc_waste	72	46.88	11.88	19.20	67.20

Source: Own calculations.

5.2. Discussion: impact of the sustainable investing ETFs on the investment industry, financial sector, and socio-economic systems

In Section 5.1, we presented the empirical evidence concerning the relationships between the development of the sustainable investing ETFs markets in Europe and chosen financial, socio-economic, and environmental aspects. This section is devoted to the discussion of these results, placed in the context of the earlier publications related to the topic considered. It needs to be added that in our literature review accompanying

Table 5.5 Correlation of the selected financial, socio-economic and environmental variables with the total net assets of sustainable investing ETFs. Period 2006–20 (annual data).

Variable	Correlation coefficient versus ETF
FD	0.5186
Econ_freedom	0.4253
Prop_rights	0.3053
SMC	0.6558
BD	0.6217
HDI	0.5858
RQ	0.2541
Health_exp	−0.6719
ODA	0.2504
Researchers	0.5104
CO2_intensity	−0.5573
Waste_gener	0.5105
Water_stress	−0.5082
Temperature	0.3980
Environ_tech	0.2274
CO2_emission	−0.7148
Nat_resour	−0.2392
Women_manag	0.2374
Multidim_pov	−0.4754
PM25	−0.5929
Food_insecur	−0.5964
Renew_electr	0.8557
Below_med	−0.2673
Healthy_life	−0.0898
Digit_skills	0.5377
Recyc_waste	0.2114

Source: Own elaboration.

the examination of the empirical results we do not refer to the general consequences of the development of the ETFs markets—for the discussion on this topic, see Section 2.3. Discussion of the empirical results continues in more detail in Section 5.4.

The evaluation of the sustainability profile of the ETFs included in our sample, outlined in Section 5.1.2, indicated clearly that the funds selected perform better in terms of their ESG scores than the other (conventional) ETFs. It can thus be hypothesized that the funds identified as sustainable investing may affect certain aspects of sustainable development, in line with their declared aims, more strongly than the remaining ETFs. Consequently, they are used in our analysis and represented by the "ETF" variable.

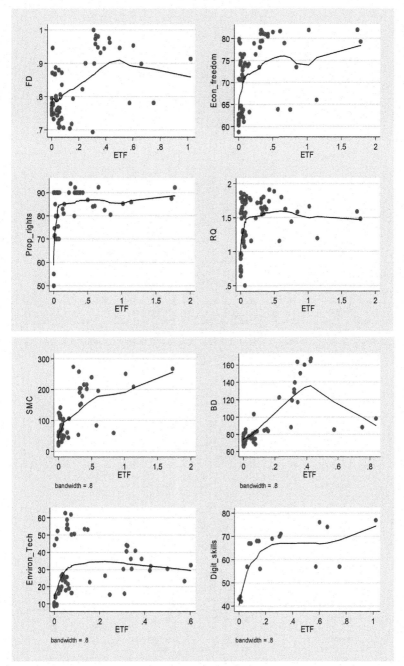

Figure 5.1 Total net assets of sustainable investing ETFs versus selected variables: local polynomial regressions. Period 2006—20 (annual data).

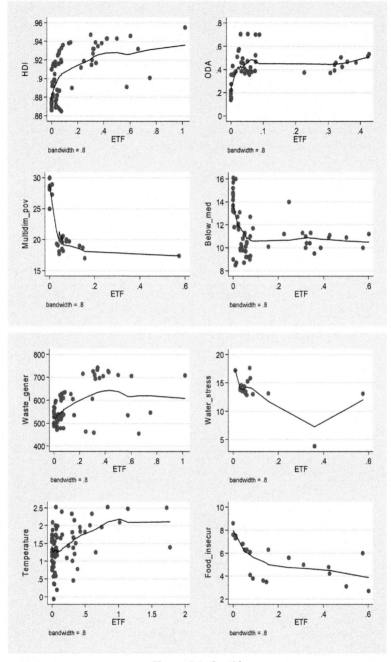

Figure 5.1 Cont'd

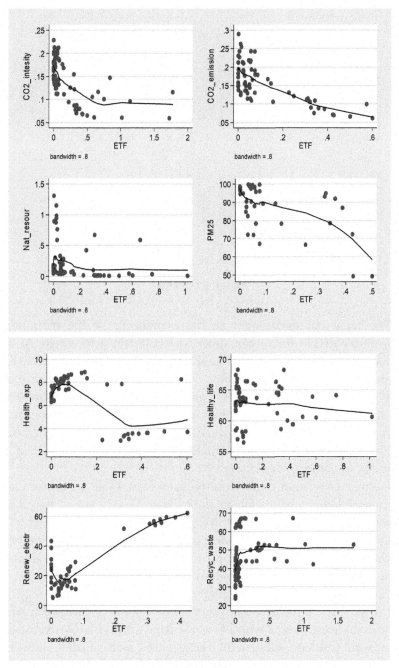

Figure 5.1 Cont'd

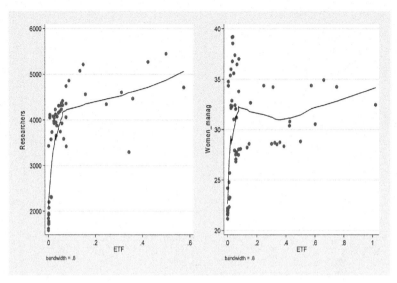

Figure 5.1 Cont'd

We begin our discussion with the examination of the relationships between ESG ETFs and certain dimensions of the financial system. As they are multiple possible interactions to be verified, we selected three variables representing varying aspects of the financial system, based on their materiality in the context of the ETFs markets and their coverage in the SDGs' indicators: general financial development index (FD), capitalization of the stock markets (SMC)—showing the development of the financial markets, and bank deposits (BD)—representing development of the financial institutions, in particular banks.

Pairwise correlation coefficients summarized in Table 5.5 unveil a clear and unambiguous picture for all three financial variables as they range between c. 0.52 (FD) and 0.66 (SMC), thus indicating positive and statistically significant association between these variables and the ETF indicator. However, the estimates of the panel models (Table 5.6) and graphical representations of the local polynomial regressions (Fig. 5.1) show that the relationship is slightly more complicated in the case of FD and, to a lesser extent, also BD. Estimated coefficient of the ESG ETFs market development in the panel model with FD as the dependent variable is statistically insignificant (the value close to 0). The graphical approximation shows that even though for the majority of the ETF levels the relationship is positive, it becomes negative for the highest values of the assets of the sustainable

Table 5.6 Total net assets of sustainable investing ETFs versus selected variables: models with single explanatory variable. Period 2006–20 (annual data).

	$FD_{y,c}$	$Econ\_freedom_{y,c}$	$Prop\_rights_{y,c}$	$SMC_{y,c}$	$BD_{y,c}$	$HDI_{y,c}$
$ETF_{y,c}$	-0.004	0.006	0.03	0.11	0.05	0.007
	[0.00]	[0.00]	[0.00]	[0.03]	[0.00]	[0.00]
R^2 [overall]	0.19	0.38	0.58	0.54	0.39	0.48
F stat	1.4	14.	25.9	13.4	56.3	73.0
(prob > F)	[0.2368]	[0.00]	[0.00]	[0.00]	[0.00]	[0.00]
# of obs.	68	73	73	60	54	68

	$RQ_{y,c}$	$Health\_exp_{y,c}$	$ODA_{y,c}$	$Researchers_{y,c}$	$CO2\_intensity_{y,c}$	$Waste\_gener_{y,c}$
$ETF_{y,c}$	-0.009	0.01	0.12	0.07	-0.08	-0.009
	[0.00]	[0.00]	[0.02]	[0.01]	[0.00]	[0.00]
R^2 [overall]	0.36	0.14	0.57	0.77	0.38	0.24
F stat	1.08	6.36	19.7	46.8	114.9	5.16
(prob > F)	[0.29]	[0.01]	[0.00]	[0.00]	[0.00]	[0.02]
# of obs.	73	63	53	54	73	68

	Water_stress	$Temperature_{y,c}$	$Environ\_tech_{y,c}$	$CO2\_emission_{y,c}$	$Nat\_resour_{y,c}$	$Women\_manag_{y,c}$
$ETF_{y,c}$	-0.12	0.07	0.01	-0.13	-0.17	0.01
	[0.06]	[0.03]	[0.01]	[0.01]	[0.03]	[0.00]
R^2 [overall]	0.31	0.03	0.41	0.37	0.19	0.39
F stat	4.23	1.94	0.75	61.1	30.1	5.44
(prob > F)	[0.04]	[0.02]	[0.38]	[0.00]	[0.00]	[0.02]
# of obs.	18	72	63	63	68	63

	Multidim_pov$_{y,c}$	PM25$_{y,c}$	Food_insecur$_{y,c}$	Renew_electr$_{y,c}$	Below_med$_{y,c}$	Healthy_life$_{y,c}$
ETF$_{y,c}$	−0.03	−0.05	−0.08	0.24	0.02	0.004
	[0.00]	[0.02]	[0.03]	[0.04]	[0.00]	[0.00]
R^2 [overall]	0.81	0.23	0.49	0.08	0.31	0.0007
F stat	9.69	6.73	6.61	23.6	4.96	1.70
(prob > F)	[0.00]	[0.00]	[0.01]	[0.00]	[0.02]	[0.19]
# of obs.	27	40	20	48	59	65

	Digit_skills$_{y,c}$	Recyc_waste$_{y,c}$
ETF$_{y,c}$	0.02	0.06
	[0.00]	[0.01]
R^2 [overall]	0.63	0.24
F stat	4.26	34.5
(prob > F)	[0.03]	[0.00]
# of obs.	17	70

Note: Random effects applied; all values are logged; SE below coefficients; panel—strongly balanced; in bold—results statistically significant at 5% level of statistical significance; Hausman tests results available on request.
Source: Own elaboration.

investing ETFs. This could be interpreted as showing that the positive effects of the ESG ETFs on general financial development are noticeable up to certain threshold after which the relationship becomes negative. Nevertheless, the scarcity of data on the higher values of ETF and very low R^2 of the panel model means that the part with the negative relationship can be ignored and the overall impact can overall be hypothesized to be positive. For the banking variable, BD, the estimates of the panel model are consistent with the positive association identified using the correlation coefficient; for LOWESS, similar stipulations as in the case of FD apply. The relationship between ETF and SMC is positive in all three perspectives considered in our analysis. Consequently, it may be concluded that our evidence provides some ground for stating that the development of the European sustainable investing ETFs markets can be associated with development of the financial sector in all three dimensions considered. The linkages seem the strongest with the stock markets which can be perceived as the closest part due to the fundamental attributes of most ESG ETFs (i.e., passive equity funds). Still, identically as in the subsequent parts of the analysis, the possible conclusions concerning the direction of the impact or the causal relationship must be formulated with caution due to the limitations of the adopted approach and on average very low values of ESG ETFs' assets in relation to the sizes of the local economies.

The possible role of the ESG ETFs for the development of the financial system may be explained by referring to the general influence of sustainable investing on this part of the economy. The impact of sustainable investing on the financial sector is multidimensional and the relationships are in many cases far from clear-cut. Pouget (2016) discussed how sustainable investments can address the problem of short-termism in the financial markets and linked negative macroeconomic effects, including the occurrence of financial crises. More specific channels of transmission can consist of the microlevel mechanisms implemented in the ESG-compliant financial products (Pouget, 2016): improved incentives along the entire investment chain (from the asset managers to the boards of directors of the companies), motivations aimed at extending the length of the investing horizon, and improved design of the products with the purpose of the enhanced quality of the decision making of investors. Moreover, as shown by Chen and Diaz (2012), some specific types of the sustainable investing ETFs (such as certain faith-based funds) can affect the behavior of the related stock market indexes in terms of returns and risks due to the spillover and leverage effects. Additionally, Chen (2011) demonstrated that ethical ETFs affect the current returns on the tracked indexes. Finally, one of the crucial (if not the most fundamental) elements of impact is the effects on the individual companies related in some way to sustainable investing financial products—for in-depth discussion, see the final part of this section.

It should be added that in this study we focus exclusively on the sustainable investing ETFs yet the impact on the financial system was also confirmed for the other types of ETFs, in particular with regard to the stock markets, bond markets, financial development, and mutual funds; for more detailed analysis of various types of relationships between the development of the overall ETFs markets and the financial system at large as well as its segments (supplemented by the examination of the other macroeconomic variables), see our previous studies, among others, Marszk and Lechman (2019a, 2019b, 2021) and Marszk et al. (2019).

The largest group of variables considered in our analysis are multidimensional indicators of the socio-economic development. We begin our discussion with the studied aspects of the institutional environment of the social and economic systems: economic freedom index (Econ_freedom), property rights protection index (Prop_rights), and regulatory quality index (RQ). Correlation coefficients in all three cases are positive yet their values are noticeably lower than in case of the previously mentioned financial measures. The estimated panel models confirm the possible positive role of ESG ETFs in Europe with regard to Econ_freedom and Prop_rights (the R^2 of the two models are among the highest covered in Table 5.6 thus indicating their explanatory contribution) but for RQ the returned parameter of the ETF variable is insignificant. The picture unveiled by the graphical approximation suggests strong positive relationship between the institutional indicators and the development of the European ESG ETFs markets in case of the lower values of the assets of these funds, and much weaker or even neutral relationship for the higher ones (starting from as low as 0.1% of GDP; still, most observations are clustered for the low or very low levels). Consequently, it may be claimed that the development of the sustainable investing ETFs in Europe has been related to the improvements in the institutional features of the European countries including the level of economic freedom, protection of property rights, and the quality of imposed regulations; stipulations similar to the analysis of the linkages with the financial variables apply. However, the explanation of these relationships, in particular in terms of channels of transmission between ETFs markets and institutional environment, requires further studies. One of the potential effects can be through the selection of the funds' holdings and inclusion of the securities of companies taking actions aimed at improving the local institutions as well as general promotion of sustainable investing fundamental ideas in a particular country. As most such changes are elements of the public policies rather than the actions of the private sector, the linkages remain highly vague.

The second type of socio-economic variables used throughout our study are indicators representing various dimensions of the quality of life in certain countries. HDI and proportion of population living in multidimensional poverty (Multidim_pov) are the two most general measures utilized in our analysis. The former is strongly positively correlated with the development of the sustainable investing ETFs markets whereas the latter reversely has correlation coefficient close to -0.5. Graphical representations of the nonparametric regressions and estimates of panel models confirm unequivocally the positive relationship for HDI and negative for Multidim_pov respectively; it is worth noticing that R^2 of the model with the latter as the explained variable is the highest among all reported in Table 5.6. Therefore, it may be stated that development of the ESG ETFs markets and improvements in the quality of life (at least measured using the two selected indicators) are the two processes taking place concurrently in the European countries. Assessment of the exact contribution of ESG ETFs to the socio-economic development or the distinction between cause and effect is in this case particularly difficult yet the possible influence of the analyzed funds should not be disregarded due to the long-term and broadranging effects being the purpose of sustainable investing (see discussion in Chapter 3). We explore this topic in more detail in Section 5.4. Finally, we also verified the linkages between the ETF variable and the proportion of people living below 50% of median income (Below_med) albeit in case of this variable the evidence is mixed, hindering any clear-cut conclusions.

The health dimension of the quality of life is represented by the domestic general government health expenditure (Health_exp), prevalence of moderate or severe food insecurity in the population (Food_insecur), and healthy life years at birth (Healthy_life). Consistently with the general indicators of socio-economic development, the relationship between the development of the sustainable investing ETFs markets and Food_insecur is clearly negative using all three research approaches (correlation coefficients, graphical approximations, and panel models). Nevertheless, as basic parameters of this dataset in Table 5.4 show, the prevalence of this problem in the countries in our sample is rather negligible, with a small percentage of population affected, thus studying the impact of the ESG funds is difficult.

In the case of the two remaining health-dimension indicators, the results of our analysis implicate that their overall association with the ETF variable is almost neutral. The high negative correlation coefficient calculated for Health_exp should be interpreted as distortion linked to the composition of our sample, consisting of countries with substantially different levels of this indicator rather than the effect of ESG ETFs (it is clearly visible on the relevant graph in Fig. 5.1).

The remaining four socio-economic variables are highly heterogeneous as they represent various dimensions of sustainable development. The official development assistance (ODA) variable indicates the country's engagement in supporting the development of the other countries—its relationship with the development of the ESG ETFs markets appears to be clearly positive, with the exception of the highest levels of the assets of these funds. It can be therefore hypothesized that the increasing involvement of the ESG funds in the local economy contributes to some extent to the growth also in the nonlocal aspects of sustainable development. However, the trends in the ODA development are highly dependent on governmental decisions thus the role of ETFs is potentially highly limited.

In the case of the three other socio-economic variables, researchers in R&D (Researchers), proportion of women in senior and middle management positions (Women_manag), and share of individuals having at least basic digital skills (Digit_skills), the results of our analysis provide almost unambiguous support for the conclusion of their positive association with the development of the European sustainable investing ETFs markets. Among these three indicators possibly the most identifiable and explainable (in line with the investment strategies of the ESG ETFs) impact of sustainable investing funds can be hypothesized for Women_manag—as ETFs, in particular the most frequent passive funds tracking major stock market indexes, held securities of multiple companies and to an increasing extent act as active shareholders, they can contribute to the increased diversity of the management boards, at least with regard to the public companies. Furthermore, they can also influence the decisions of the companies through the exclusion of the securities with the low ESG scores such as the ones performing poorly with regard to the governance pillar which covers, among others, various policies of the companies concerning employment guidelines and their execution. The positive role of the ESG funds for the increased number of researchers or digital skills of the population is more difficult to establish yet it can be associated with the focus of these funds on the securities of companies that invest considerable amounts of funds in the

R&D activities (such as alternative energy corporations with substantial expenses concerning, e.g., clean energy sources or energy use efficiency) and the ones operating in the information and communication technologies (ICT) sector (usually with high ESG scores (Grishunin et al., 2022)), contributing to the higher digital skills prevalence in given societies.

Again, as discussed earlier with regard to the financial variables, the core channel of the impact of ESG ETFs on the socio-economic systems is through the effects on the companies whose securities are held in the funds' portfolios—see the outline at the end of this section.

The final group of the examined variables potentially affected by the development of the European sustainable investing ETFs are the ones representing various environmental issues—we selected exclusively the ones for which at least some effects of the ESG funds can be reasonably explained; the other criteria were their links to the SDGs. We discuss the results of our analysis for all variables in this category jointly as disaggregation of the evidence would lead to substantial interpretational difficulties. Estimates of the panel models show that for almost all environmental variables the coefficients of the variable representing the development of the sustainable investing ETFs in Europe are statistically significant and imply a type of connection that should be assessed positively from the perspective of the sustainable development. For instance, the growth of the assets of ESG ETFs appears to be a factor leading to decreases in the water stress explained as a total freshwater abstraction (Water_stress), CO_2 emissions (CO2_emission), PM2.5 air pollution (PM25), or amount of municipal waste generated (Waste_gener); conversely, our results imply the positive effect on the share of the renewable electricity output (Renew_-electr) and the recycling rate of municipal waste (Recyc_waste). With some exceptions, the estimated nonparametric regressions provide a similar picture, as uncovered by the LOWESS graphs. These effects can be explained by the focus on environmentally related securities, one of the most frequent investment themes of the European ESG ETFs, and the long-term consequences of the inflow of capital to the companies engaged in, for instance, green energy industry, as well as withdrawal from the companies performing poorly in terms of their environmental ESG scores. However, due to the rather short history of the European ESG ETFs market, the contribution of these funds to any already noticeable changes can be assessed as very minor. Finally, it can be added that there is one environmental variable for which the relationship indicates potential negative effects of sustainable investing ETFs—annual surface temperature

(Temperature); nonetheless, it would be an extreme exaggeration to claim that ESG ETFs could have significantly affected this parameter in either positive or negative way. The effects of ESG investing on the environmental variables were infrequently examined in the empirical studies. For example, Naaraayanan et al. (2021, pp. 1–69) studied the impact of the environmental activist investing on individual firms in terms of the climate risks, providing evidence that companies selected by such investors tend to act through the reduction of the toxic releases, cancer-causing pollution, and greenhouse gasses emissions, thus leading to the improved air quality in the vicinity of their production plants.

Any conclusions concerning possible linkages between ESG ETFs and environmental issues should, though, be regarded with substantial caution as the examined environmental variables are potentially affected by a large number of determinants, including the ones related to the nonhuman inflicted changes. It is thus impossible to explicitly identify the role of the analyzed funds in relation to the other factors or even state definitely whether there is in fact any impact or if the relationship is spurious and both variables are affected by some other set of factors. It should be addressed in the subsequent analyses.

To enrich our analysis, we provide an overview of yet another, particularly important aspect, linked to all relationships covered in the preceding paragraphs. As we adopt mostly the macroeconomic perspective in our analysis, we did not examine closely the effects of ESG ETFs for the linked companies (above all the entities whose securities or other types of assets are components of the portfolios of the sustainable investing ETFs; the other affected entities may be the competitors of the aforementioned companies, cooperating companies, companies whose securities are potentially to be included in the ETFs' portfolios or simply other companies operating on certain markets in certain countries). Still, it can be claimed that the influence of the sustainable investing ETFs on the related companies is among the most fundamental channels of transmission between the development of these funds and the abovementioned financial, socio-economic and, to some degree, environmental dimensions (one of the key channels is the shareholders engagement as discussed in Eurosif (2021)).[6] In other words, the firm- and fund-level microeffects transpose to

---

[6] Kölbel et al. (2020) listed three fundamental mechanisms of the sustainable investing impact on sustainable development: capital allocation, shareholder engagement, and indirect impacts.

the macro-level interactions. To address this issue, we provide below a discussion of the consequences of the development of the sustainable investing ETFs on the companies linked in some way, based on the wide-ranging review of the literature.

In the first perspective, recognized already before the rapid development of the sustainable investing ETFs and other similar funds, it is argued that all types of ETFs can potentially affect the corporate governance practices of certain companies whose securities are kept in the funds' portfolios, with the impact being negative or positive (Ben-David et al., 2017). In the former case, the negative impact applies mostly to the companies that consider IPO of their equities thus they are not the elements of the current but rather potential ETFs' holdings. In particular, the small companies can decide against the public listing of their equities to avoid becoming a negligible part of the large index funds' portfolios and thus being affected by the noncompany specific factors (Bradley & Litan, 2011, pp. 1–31). In the perspective of corporate governance, this could mean not adhering to the standards required from public companies. In case of the latter effects, that is, positive, increasing number of the world's largest ETF providers has over the last few years adopted active shareholders position in the companies, with a particular focus on the issues such as corporate governance (Appel et al., 2016). The impact of the entities such as investment funds on corporate governance was examined by Matos (2020) who analyzed, among others, the role of passive funds, listing both negative (e.g., insufficient monitoring and stewardship expenses, predominant promanagement voting, encouraging the corporations whose securities they hold to engage in anticompetitive behavior to generate monopolistic rents) and positive effects (similar to the already mentioned ones). Corum et al. (2022, pp. 1–60) stated that the effects of passive funds in the discussed dimension depend on their impact on the position of the active funds in the shareholders' structure of certain—the crowding out of active funds may lead to worsened corporate governance.

The second perspective (adopted in the remainder of the section) focuses exclusively on the impact of the ESG funds.[7]

Sustainable investing ETFs (as well as the other ESG investment funds) can influence the actions of the companies whose securities they hold in their portfolios through a number of channels. One of the major elements is

---

[7] For the discussion concerning the impact of various types of institutional investors on the company-level ESG compliance, see Matos (2020).

active ownership, understood primarily as exercising formal power during the general meetings of shareholders, both annual and extraordinary (Silvola & Landau, 2021). Shareholders may influence the selection of the issues to be discussed during these meetings or present the proposals related to sustainability (such as the introduction of the code of ethics (Cowton, 2021)). However, the possibility to exercise substantial impact on the corporate actions through these engagements is limited by the necessity to gather sufficient backing from the other shareholders (another limitation may be the impracticality of the proposals). Another possibility yet limited mostly to the largest shareholders is affecting the nominations for the board of directors, potentially having own representative. Further elements of the active ownership include (Silvola & Landau, 2021): stewardship codes (referring to institutional investors, covering issues such as encouraging engagement and cooperation of these investors with their investees or integration of the ESG principles in the investment decisions), informal dialogues with the companies or alliances with other investors (Principles for Responsible Investment (PRI) is one of the most prominent examples); moreover, activist investors constitute a separate category with the strict focus on certain ESG issues. The impact of the ESG funds on the companies may also be considered in the value creation framework, stressing the contribution of sustainable investors to the establishment and preservation of intangible assets (Prall, 2021).

The discussion of the role of sustainable investing for the related companies may also focus on one important element, that is, various forms of the company's boycott. Still, it should not be limited to the actions of customers but must also take into account the decisions of investors, consisting above all of the divestments. In this perspective, as noted by Waygood (2008), the actions of investors withdrawing from certain sectors or companies can establish substantial barriers for their activities. Nevertheless, Davies and Van Wesep (2018) demonstrated that divestments campaigns are of higher importance for the managers of the affected companies interested in the short-run stock prices rather than long-term profits—such actions may thus be counterproductive with regard to their declared aims.

Another problematic issue associated with the sustainability effects of the funds with such investment profile is the persistence of their ESG profiles—Wimmer (2013) demonstrated that ESG mutual funds tend to undergo substantial changes in their ESG scores, in particular in the time perspective exceeding 3 years which hinders both their usefulness for the value-driven investors and their potential role for the socio-economic systems. Another problem mentioned in this study is the issue of the lower attention given by the funds' managers to the ESG issues in relation of the financial performance. Further stipulation concerning the role of, among others, active ownership, is the question whether the shareholders (including the investment funds, also passive ones) are actually able to assess the sustainability profile of the company better than its managers, due to, for example, differences in the access to information—this issue remains a topic of intensive studies (Gutiérrez & Saez Lacave, 2018; Kahan & Rock, 2020; McNulty & Nordberg, 2016; Min & You, 2019; Schoenfeld, 2020).

There are also some firm-level effects that are specific to certain types of impact investments such as impact investing—the lower financial returns that can be accepted by their investors, as shown by Barber et al. (2021), may result in lower costs of capital for the companies whose assets are held within such sustainable investment portfolios.

The relationship between the ESG-induced behavior (e.g., related to the actions and expectations of the sustainable investing entities) and the multidimensional performance of the companies was the topic of numerous empirical studies, some of them aggregated into comprehensive literature reviews.

Li et al. (2021) provided evidence for the substantial impact of the ESG-focused mutual funds on the ESG ratings of companies whose securities comprise the funds' portfolios, in particular through improvements in the strong sides of particular company's ESG standing rather than diminishing of their ESG weaknesses; again, the main field of impact is the corporate governance pillar. In one of the most recent studies of the topic, Goldstein et al. (2022) demonstrated that sustainable investing had an impact on the cost of capital of companies and their asset prices, mostly through the improved ESG disclosures and activity of green investors. The other related important element is market signals and incentives (Eurosif, 2021). Moreover, Schneeweiß (2019), based on the conducted empirical study, concluded that sustainable investing can to some extent contribute to the improvement of companies in the following dimensions: generation of higher profits and attracting more substantial inflows from investors. However, the impact of both sustainability-oriented investors and ESG ratings, agencies on companies are immaterial in comparison to the other entities such as clients, authorities, or regulatory bodies. According to the cited study, the ESG issues become material to investors only in case of actions undertaken by the aforementioned actors such as customers' boycott. Furthermore, as concluded by Basdekidou and Styliadou (2017) the long- and short-term performance of the companies with high social performance should be distinguished, with the higher returns on their equities in the longer perspective yet lower in the shorter one; the issue of the corporate sustainability performance and stock returns in various time perspectives is examined in detail by Serafeim (2020). Based on the analysis of the high yield bonds held by ETFs, Kanamura (2021) stated that higher ESG compliance reduces the risks (and thus to some extent boosts demand for) such securities issued by companies. There is also country-level evidence. For example, Hamrouni et al. (2019) studied the CSR disclosures of the French companies, concluding that a higher CSR score results in a lower cost of debt, most strongly due to the impact of the environmental disclosures.

In a wide-ranging discussion of over 2000 publications on the topic of ESG compliance and company's financial results, Friede et al. (2015) stated that the vast majority of the examined publications implied positive association. According to the recent review of the studies concerning the relationship between sustainability (that may be affected by the actions of ESG-focused shareholders such as sustainable investing ETFs) and financial performance of companies presented in Silvola and Landau (2021), the association of these two dimensions is generally found to be statistically significant and positive. More specifically, the relationship comprises the following elements: linkages between ESG ratings and financial profitability, positive impact of sustainability on the market value of company, decreased volatility of market value[8] and higher return on capital of the companies with high ESG ratings in comparison to the ones with low ratings, better performance during the periods of recession (also, more recently, during the Covid-19 pandemic (Sun & Small, 2022)). Additionally, Silvola and Landau (2021) claimed, based on the analysis of the studies in this area, that companies adhering to the ESG-compliance requirements can gain access to cheaper financing to a higher degree in comparison to the other companies, have more loyal customers in the periods of recessions, and reach higher levels of valuation during the public listings of their securities. The positive link between ESG and financial performance was also proven by the in-depth literature review of the analyses on the relationships between corporate financial performance and corporate social performance

---

[8] The volatility may also decrease in terms of the returns on the company's equities (Sahut & Pasquini-Descomps, 2015) and financial profitability (Djoutsa Wamba et al., 2018).

(extended to the overall ESG compliance) by Schiereck et al. (2019). For a more recent review of research on the relationships between ESG compliance and company's corporate finance features, see Gillan et al. (2021). In the recent study of both sustainable investing ETFs and PRI-compliant asset management companies, Weston and Nnadi (2021) concluded lack of outperformance in the financial terms of the ESG ETFs in relation to the conventional funds yet indicated that their activity leads potentially to a number of other benefits such as higher access to equity and debt financing, increased credit ratings, and general environmental effects.

5.3. Consequences for the managing financial institutions

The perspective adopted in our empirical study, whose results are discussed in the other sections of this chapter, is mostly macro level as we focus on the interactions observed in the dimension of the entire financial and socio-economic systems or their parts (such as the relationships between the development of the ESG ETFs markets and various aspects of the economic development). In this section, we provide a different perspective—we discuss the possible effects of the introduction and development of the sustainable investing ETFs (or, more broadly, the rising popularity of sustainable investing) on the financial companies acting as their providers, using the insights from the review of literature in the field. The formulated conclusions will serve as the starting point for the planned future empirical study to be conducted by merging data on the European sustainable investing ETFs with data on the key attributes (such as financial indicators) of their providers. We discuss literature covering all types of investment funds, not limited to ETFs.

One of the core elements of the abovementioned relationship is the influence exercised on the ETFs' providers through the investors, that is, the investors holding (actually or potentially) the units of these funds, in particular the investors interested in sustainable investing. In the literature the impact of investors has been discussed mostly in relation to the units of mutual funds rather than ETFs due to their higher prevalence in the global investment funds industry. Ceccarelli et al. (2019) discussed this issue by focusing on the eco-label of mutual funds launched in 2018 by Morningstar, called 'Low Carbon —the introduction of this designation' has resulted in substantial growth of the assets of funds with the label through the inflow of capital from investors in relation to the noncompliant funds. From the perspective of the managers of the mutual funds (in particular the ones close to fulfilling the label's requirements), the observed demand for the funds with the eco-label was a motivation to adjust the holdings with the aim of lower carbon risk and fossil fuel exposure. In a broader perspective, of the entire mutual funds industry, the cited study provided evidence for the active role of the managers in response to the demand for the sustainability-related investment products, aimed at attracting flows from investors (importantly, the effects appear to be stronger for the European funds rather than the United States ones).

The effects are not limited to the eco-labels—the discussion can be extended to the element of particular importance for the sustainable investing ETFs, i.e., sustainable stock market indexes, as shown by Fowler and Hope (2007). They demonstrated how such indexes shape, among others, the behaviors of the providers of investment funds. Another highly recognizable example in recent years is the growing popularity of the ETFs with the exposure to the green energy assets among investors, resulting to a certain degree in the withdrawal from the funds holding assets linked to nongreen energy sources (e.g., based on fossil fuels), affecting certain dimensions of the investment funds industry (Rizvi et al., 2022). However, the adherence to sustainable investing strategies, including the ones based on the ESG-focused indexes, can become less attractive for investors and, consequently, also for the providers of funds, in periods of underperformance and high volatility such as the outbreak of the Covid-19 pandemic (Albuquerque et al., 2020; Capelle-Blancard et al., 2021; Pavlova & de Boyrie, 2022).

Another possible area of impact can be noticed with regard to the limitations imposed on the investment funds by the investment mandates and regulatory authorities (as well as self-regulation); similar restrictions apply to, among others, pension funds (Woods & Urwin, 2010). As noted by Xiao et al. (2013), the inclusion of sustainable investing strategies by the institutional investors should not be perceived as possible breach of the fund's fiduciary duties—the reason is the lack of sufficient evidence for the inferior performance associated with ESG investment strategies in relation to the conventional ones (for more in-depth discussion on the studies of the performance of ESG investing see the vast literature on the topic). Similar conclusions were formulated by Hayat (2015) who provided arguments for regarding sustainability as an integral element of the fiduciary duty obligations. Increasing compliance with the ESG investing strategies can also lead to the development and adoption of internal rules by the investment companies. For example, Couvert (2020) analyzed the voting policies of the largest mutual funds in the United States and demonstrated the significance of the active voting guidelines adopted by the funds in line with the fundamental elements of sustainable investing. Furthermore, providing sustainable investing financial products requires the establishment of the proper research procedures focused on the assessment of the sustainability of assets to be included as the holdings of the funds. Nonetheless, the empirical studies of such procedures show some problematic aspects. For instance, Benijts (2008) examined the sustainability-related aspects of the research procedures of the Belgian asset management companies applied in the management of portfolios of sustainable investment funds, with the focus on their assessment of corporate sustainability, concluding the inconsistency of these procedures not only with the policies of the other companies but also with the generally accepted concepts of sustainable development. Moreover, as noticed by Botsari and Lang (2020) in their study devoted to a different type of financial investments, that is, venture capital and business angel investments, explicit formal ESG policies and metrics are adopted and implemented usually by the larger companies, with the smaller ones lagging behind.

With reference to the global ETFs market, the most prominent (due to the size of the company) and, at the same time, most publicized example of the adoption of some of the procedures presented in the preceding paragraphs is the 2018 declaration by the BlackRock asset management firm's CEO Larry Fink's, concerning active engagement with the companies whose securities are held in the BlackRock's funds' portfolios to generate positive sustainability contributions (Christianson et al., 2019). As a result, BlackRock introduced a number of measures such as development of ESG data and analytical tools for investors, formation of ESG-focused investment departments, establishment of modified proxy voting guidelines, and activity during shareholders meeting with regard to the climate risk. Still, some stipulations concerning the actual impact of these actions on the possible contribution to sustainable development were formulated such as their scope limited to selected funds. Further actions by BlackRock were announced in 2020 and over the next years (Christianson & Pinchot, 2020). For the other, industry-wide initiatives concerning sustainable investing in the asset management companies, see the discussion in Chapter 3.

There is also another perspective than can be studied, considerably different from the previously discussed. The increased attention devoted by the general investing audience as well as other stakeholders of the financial companies to the issues of sustainability and other, to lesser or higher extent overlapping, elements of ethical investing, can lead to substantial changes in, among others, the behaviors of the providers' management. McCann and Sweet (2014) studied the ethical and sustainability attributes of the leaders of financial corporations, using the example of the mortgage loan originators. They concluded the substantial improvement post the 2007–2009 global financial crisis, observed by various groups of stakeholders, for example, employees. For a detailed discussion concerning the noticed and recommended changes to the management of the asset management companies, also linked to the sustainability, see Ware et al. (2017).

5.4. Can ETFs contribute to the implementation of the sustainable development policies?

After the discussion of various micro- and macrolevel interactions between the development of the sustainable investing ETFs markets in Europe and selected aspects of the financial sectors and other elements of the socioeconomic systems presented in Sections 5.2 and 5.3, in the current part of the chapter, we concentrate on their significance in the context of the sustainable development policies, in particular the fulfillment of the SDGs. We also refer briefly to some European policy initiatives yet the SDG approach is used as the core one. In order to facilitate such overview, while providing the empirical evidence in Section 5.1 we assigned each variable potentially affected by the ESG ETFs to one of the SDGs (see Table 5.1). Similarly to the previous sections, the formulation of the conclusions of our study is accompanied by the literature review, aimed at indication of the possible explanations of the identified mechanisms.

Before the discussion of the specific empirical results, it should be emphasized that the possible role of ETFs as the key financial instruments contributing to sustainable development has already been identified in the reports of some international organizations. For example, the UNCTAD's report on the ESG ETFs concluded that they are crucial tools for supporting sustainable development due to three groups of reasons (UNCTAD, 2020):

1. due to their predominantly passive investing attributes ETFs are low-cost financial instruments and their high availability linked to the fact that their shares are listed and traded comparably to equities of the public companies gives the investors the opportunity to obtain exposure to various sectors as well as countries or groups of countries;

2. the number and diversity of ETFs with the sustainability-linked focus have been increasing in the last decade, with many funds following

the broadly accepted ESG benchmarks consistent with the international standards of, for example, PRI;

3. institutional investors (including pension funds and sovereign wealth funds) are the biggest group of investors holding the shares of ESG ETFs—these entities manage substantial funds and such investments can significantly contribute to the goals of sustainable development.

In a broad perspective, the possible effects of the ESG ETFs with regard to sustainable development can be explained through the externalities generated for the society through investments in the ESG-compliant companies.

In the aforementioned report (UNCTAD, 2020) also some limitations of the sustainable investing ETFs as the instruments supporting sustainable development were listed. They included higher costs than in their conventional counterparts, insufficient consistency of the methodologies applied (in terms of data provided, ESG scores used, and sustainability-related quality of the tracked indexes), almost complete absence of sustainable investing ETFs in the underdeveloped or emerging economies (potentially having most requirements and expectations with regard to the development opportunities supported by the ESG financial instruments), and narrow scope of the SDGs' coverage (there are some SDGs almost absent from the investing aims of the ESG ETFs, mostly due to the lack of related indexes—this can change in line with the launch of such indexes, conceivable for most SDGs as they are investable).

Within the empirical study, we considered the possible effects of sustainable investing ETFs on a number of variables (see Section 5.1). Below, we discuss the results of the analysis in line with the adopted division between the SDGs, mostly in line with their order (see Table 5.1), drawing also from the conclusions reached in the previous sections.

To assess the importance of the ESG ETFs in Europe for the completion of the SDG 1 (ending all forms of poverty), we focused on the following five variables: Econ_freedom, Prop_rights, HDI, Health_exp, and Multidim_pov (it was the SDG with the largest number of variable considered among all aims analyzed). Consequently, we considered both the institutional variables and the ones representing selected aspects of the quality of life (level of socio-economic development) with regard to this goal. The results of our analysis confirmed clearly the identifiable positive association of the development of the European ESG ETFs markets with all variables mentioned (in case of the institutional indicators the relationship is the strongest for the lower values of the assets of sustainable investing ETFs in relation to GDP), with the exception of Health_exp (for the possible explanation see Section 5.2). As shown in the report by UNCTAD (2020).[9] SDG 1 remains one of the goals neglected by the ESG ETFs in terms of the declared exposure yet our results imply that it is still affected by the growth of these funds. SDG 16 (associated mostly with the institutions, similar to some degree to SDG 1) represented by the RQ variable was also found to be positively influenced by the development of the European ESG ETFs, in line with the already noted contribution to the improvements in the institutional environment.

In case of SDGs 2 (zero hunger), 3 (health), 4 (education), 5 (equality), and 6 (water and sanitation), only one variable was used in the analysis for each goal, subsequent to the preliminary examination and elimination of the other possible indicators (see Section 5.1). Consequently, the assessment of the possible role of the sustainable investing ETFs in Europe concerning these goals was much more limited than in the case of the ones related to SDG 1.

Linkages with SDG 2 were analyzed using the Food_insecur variable—we concluded the possible contribution of the ESG ETFs to the reduction of the problem of food insecurity in the countries in our sample yet with the important stipulation concerning the highly limited scope of this problem in these economies (in relation to many other regions of the world). As a result, we do not discuss further SDG 2 due to limited empirical evidence.

In the case of the SDG 3 indicator, that is, Healthy_life, no statistically significant relationship with the sustainable investing ETFs was identified thus showing that the health dimension of sustainable development has remained unaffected by the development of these funds (it can be hypothesized that it has been shaped by a large number of different factors).

SDG 4 covers the educational attributes of sustainable development. As the countries studied are among the global leaders in terms of the scope and quality of the basic educational services as well as, for example, tertiary education, we did not consider the variables representing these aspects but rather a more specific element of SDG 4, that is, digital skills, measured using the Digit_skills variable. We confirmed the possible positive role of

[9] Data on the SDG coverage provided in the report should be interpreted with caution as it applies exclusively to the ETFs with thematic strategies linked to a specific goal(s) thus omitting the vast majority of funds with the other ESG investment approaches. Major SDG-focused ETFs are discussed in Kuang (2021), Miralles-Quirós et al. (2019), and Naffa and Fain (2020).

the ESG ETFs for this aspect of sustainable development, explained through the investments of these funds in the equities of the highly ESG-compliant ICT companies. Another mechanism of transmission between ESG funds and sustainable development in the ICT aspect is linked to the significance of the FinTech services for the ETFs markets (see Chapter 2 for the presentation of this issue) and their multidimensional relationship (e.g., some FinTech companies utilize the shares of ETFs while some ETFs provide directly or indirectly financing of the FinTech projects). FinTech services can also be regarded as the catalyst of the economic and societal changes consistent with the assumption of sustainable development, for instance, in the fields of pension systems, supply chains, and clean energy (see the report of University of Cambridge Institute for Sustainability Leadership (CISL) with detailed analysis (University of Cambridge Institute for Sustainability Leadership [CISL], 2017)).

SDG 5 was represented in our analysis by the Women_manag variable—we demonstrated that sustainable investing ETFs can influence positively the equality dimension of sustainable development (at least in terms of the women's position in the companies) through, among others, the actions linked to the corporate governance. Moreover, as outlined in UNCTAD (2020), SDG 5 is the second-most popular goal covered by sustainable investing ETFs which further indicates the importance of the discussed relationship.

SDG 6 is covered in the further part of the section, together with the other environmental aspects (this applies also to the variables linked to SDG 7 (clean energy).

Apart from SDG 1 discussed earlier, most variables potentially related to the development of the European ESG ETFs markets were analyzed with regard to SDGs 8 (work and economic growth) and 9 (industry, innovation, and infrastructure). For almost all variables within these two aims (for the full list, see Table 5.1), we identified the possible effects of the development of the European markets for the sustainable investing ETFs that were consistent with the sustainability framework. It can thus be stated that the growing assets of the ESG ETFs in Europe are accompanied by improvements in the areas such as some aspects of financial development (included in SDG 8), number of researchers (SDG 9) or CO_2 emissions and intensity (SDG 9; these variables can also be examined in the context of the environmental impact of the ESG funds). While the possible contribution of ETFs to the fulfillment of the goals linked to the financial sector could be expected (also based on the previous studies), their impact on innovation-related issues is to some extent surprising yet it also shows that the role of the ESG funds can extend indirectly to many fields, through a number of channels of transmission such as the focus on the R&D intensive companies in the construction of the portfolios. Similar conclusions (i.e., of positive impact) can be formulated with regard to the links between ETFs and SDG 17 (global partnerships) measured using the ODA indicator yet with substantial stipulation concerning the possibly more important role of the other determinants.

In Section 5.2, we discussed the possible impact of the European sustainable investing ETFs on the variables representing the environmental issues, stating the prevalent possible positive effects of the development of these funds—in terms of specific aspects of sustainable development, the variables covered following SDGs: 6, 7 (the third most popular in the SDG-oriented SDGs (UNCTAD, 2020)), and 11−13 (sustainable municipalities, responsible consumption and production, and climate action, respectively). SDG 13 is the goal most frequently addressed by the SDG-focused ESG ETFs according to the 2019 data (UNCTAD, 2020). No variables were utilized for the analysis of SDGs 14 and 15 (due to highly improbable and weak possible links to the ETFs markets; the other reason was weak evidence on their correlation with the ETFs variable obtained in the preliminary analysis). As a consequence, it can be concluded that ESG ETFs in Europe exert some positive impact on the environments of the European countries in which they are listed. Moreover, these effect can be seen as a contribution not only to the SDGs but also to the EU-level policies entailing this dimension of sustainable development, including the EU Action Plan, European Green Deal, or the EU Sustainable Finance Disclosure Regulation (for more details see Chapter 3), in particular their elements focused on the financial markets and sustainable investing.

The relationships between the ETFs markets and environmental aspects of the development should be regarded, though, as highly complex and indirect, with many possible transmission steps thus hindering the exact assessment of their presence or strength. There are some important issues that can be identified. Environmental factors constitute an important element of the ESG investing strategies yet various aspects of the climate risks are increasingly more frequently included in the investment analysis of all types of financial companies, with the application of tools such as prices of carbon (current and expected), climate metrics or relevant accounting standards (CFA Institute, 2020; Orsagh et al., 2018). The utilization of those and similar methods can result in the fulfillment of the environmental aims of, for example, ESG investment funds, as indicated in our analysis.

Another important aspect is the utilization of the financial instruments aimed at low-carbon economy financing in the portfolios of ETFs—the group of such instruments has become substantially diversified in the last years, with both equities and fixed income securities as well as other asset classes available (Swiss Sustainable Finance, 2020). Still, not all attempts to link the ETFs markets with the environmental impact undertook in the last years have been successful—the most striking example is the UN-backed climate-focused ETF (aimed at providing exposure to the index covering companies pledged substantially to support the transition to a low-carbon economy) launched in the late 2021 that failed to gather even the seed funds necessary to initiate its full operations and was approaching closure as of February 2022; it is the first ESG ETF developed in cooperation between UN agencies, NGOs, and major asset management company (Singh, 2022). Another problem is frequent narrow definition of the environmental problems, with the focus on, e.g., reduction of the greenhouse gases emissions while neglecting the negative effects of the companies held in the portfolios of funds on the other aspects such as loss of biodiversity, or further elements of the ESG framework, for example, damage caused to the indigenous peoples in the areas in which these companies operate (Etchart, 2022).

To sum up, our analysis has provided empirical ground for the conclusion of the possible (yet limited due to a large number of other potential determinants) contribution of the European sustainable investing ETFs to the fulfillment of the goals of sustainable development including in particular the aims focused on the financial and economic issues.[10] In addition, we uncovered some evidence for their social and, through some indirect mechanisms, also environmental impact that can be regarded as a contribution to the relevant SDGs as well as the aims of the European policies concerning the environment. Nevertheless, as far as the contribution to these areas of SDGs and other sustainable development policies is concerned, the evidence is much more limited which hinders the

---

[10] The impact of the ESG funds in terms of the contribution to the fulfillment of the SDGs or similar aims of sustainable development was rarely analyzed in the previous empirical studies, thus it is difficult to compare our conclusions to those of the other analyses. One of the rare exceptions is the study of CISL (2019), addressing the effects of investment funds in the context of selected SDGs, yet due to substantially different research methods any reliable comparisons of the results are impossible; furthermore, it focused predominantly on the methodological aspects.

formulation of robust conclusions. With regard to all assessed dimensions of the sustainable development process, in particular, we identified the potential role of ESG ETFs for the elements covered by SDGs 1, 8, 9, 16, and 17 which should not be regarded as unexpected due to the position of these funds in the economic system. A more detailed discussion of some relationships between ETFs and sustainable development follows in the next paragraphs.

Busch et al. (2016) considered a broad perspective of the relationships discussed in this chapter as they examined the contribution of the financial markets at large to sustainable development stating that, as of the time of their presentation (i.e., 2015), it was rather limited. One of the main limitations was (and it can be hypothesized that the problem continues to be substantial) the incremental improvements of sustainable investing in terms of supporting sustainable development rather than their fully focused nature—the main reasons were the flaws in the adopted ESG investment strategies and problems with the ESG data utilization. Overcoming the aforementioned problematic issues of sustainable investing, in a long time perspective and broad scale, may lead to a higher level of social and environmental sustainability of the business practices and development of self-sustainable ecological, human and social systems. The key channel of transmission between ESG investing and sustainable development would be the allocation of capital in line with the sustainable development goals.

One of the key elements of the relationship between the ESG ETFs and sustainable development is linked to the impact of sustainable investing on the companies whose assets are held in the portfolios of funds (see the discussion in Section 5.2). In the perspective of sustainable development, one of the most important elements is the impact on the corporate investment choices, motivating the companies to invest in the areas consistent with the sustainable development principles and dissuading from the noncompliant choices (Eurosif, 2021; Matos, 2020). These actions can have many long-term consequences, not only financial and economic ones but also with regard to the social systems and environment. The other, already discussed, key element is active shareholders engagement; nevertheless, the actions of the ESG investors tend to be more efficient in terms of their impact on sustainable development if they are coordinated with the public policymakers (Eurosif, 2021).

The possible contribution of the sustainable investing ETFs to sustainable development can also be identified in another area—through the support of microfinance services (Arandia & Hepp, 2021). Through the development of the microfinance sector (including various credit, savings, transfer, and insurance services), a number of aims linked to sustainable development can be reached such as increased financial inclusion or empowerment of women (Hansen et al., 2021). Financial means can be allocated by the investors in the microfinance investment funds— microfinance investment vehicles (MIVs), often domiciled in the most developed economies and operating on a global scale; MIVs provide funding to the microfinance institutions that deal directly with the final clients such as entrepreneurs in the least developed or emerging countries (Stüttgen, 2019). Similar linkages can be noted also for the funds aimed toward impact and community investing (Signori, 2021).

It needs to be emphasized, though, that the exact channels of transmission between development of the ESG ETFs markets and sustainable development depend on a number of factors boosting or hindering the possible positive role of the sustainable funds. As noted by Narula (2012) with regard to another type of investments, that is, foreign direct investments, their impact on sustainability of the country's economic growth depends on the public policy and regulatory framework. Another important element is eco-labeling initiatives, including the ones introduced by the providers of the ESG scores and ratings—the launch of such labels triggers responses from both investors and providers of funds (Ceccarelli et al., 2019). As the units of mutual funds and ETFs are frequently used as part of the retirement savings holdings, their potential to contribute to sustainable development depends also on the retirement policies and their attitudes toward ESG investing (Falk, 2016).

It must also be added that not in all cases the declared sustainability targets of the investment funds lead to the expected effects in terms of the ESG compliance of their holdings as shown by the empirical studies. For example, Kim and Yoon (2020) demonstrated that funds provided by the companies signatories of the PRI initiative in some cases exhibit lower ESG scores in their portfolios than the other funds, start voting less on environmental issues, and the held companies are more frequently subject to environmental controversies; overall, they concluded that only minority of funds improves their ESG performance subsequent to the PRI signing and for the remainder such decision serves mostly for the marketing purposes to attract increased inflows of funds from investors. Similar conclusions were formulated with regard to the US PRI signatories in the study by Gibson et al. (2020). The other limitations are the lack of active shareholders engagement in some passive ESG ETFs thus hindering the achievement of the declared sustainability targets (Singh, 2022) as well as the construction of the tracked indexes, with a prevalent focus on the financial indicators in the weighting mechanisms rather than the possible contribution of the companies to the ESG goals thus leading to portfolio greenwashing (Amenc et al., 2021).

The future analysis of the effects of the sustainable investing ETFs can cover the role of the thematic ESG ETFs, that is, funds focused on one of the SDGs, in the fulfillment of the related goal (as of 2019 most funds focused on the goals associated with the climate change, equality, and energy issues (UNCTAD, 2020)) yet currently, such study is impossible to the still negligible size of these ETFs, even in relation to the other ETFs. The same applies to the ETFs tracking nonequity indexes, for example, of green bonds.

Even though our analysis was strictly focused on the European ESG ETFs markets and their impact, the conclusions presented in this section may also be examined with regard to the other regions—the European region is the global leader in terms of the assets of these funds and has reached the highest level of their development on the global scale. Therefore, it can be predicted that if the other regions reach similar levels then comparable interactions with the presented dimensions of sustainable development may be reached. This statement would apply, first, to the second-largest ESG ETFs market globally, that is, the United States— despite some differences in, for instance, the structure of the ETFs markets and, even more importantly, their socio-economic environment, the growth of the assets of the US sustainable investing ETFs can lead to some positive contributions to the local sustainable development as well as interactions in international scale (through, e.g., development assistance or, more substantially, international holdings in the portfolios of the US ETFs selected based on the ESG criteria). Their exact assessment requires further studies. Similar conclusions apply to the other, much smaller ESG ETFs markets such as the Asia—Pacific ones. Finally, it can be concluded that launch and expansion of the ESG ETFs markets would be important in particular for the regions at low levels of economic development as it may be perceived as one of the verified tools for advancements in their sustainable development (Eurosif, 2021; UNCTAD, 2020). If the ESG funds corresponded to a similar share in the aggregate ETFs markets in countries with ETFs already present in the local financial systems such as China, India, Indonesia, Philippines, or South Africa, it could imply the availability of the funds worth billions of USD to be used for supporting the companies contributing to the sustainable development. The barriers to the development of the emerging ESG ETFs markets include, among others, insufficient institutional capabilities and know-how, substantial data availability problems, and overall low levels of financial development, together with capital markets (UNCTAD, 2020).

5.5. Sustainable investing ETFs in the European countries: case study (V)—Sweden

The fifth case study of the European sustainable investing ETFs market is to some extent different in comparison to the preceding ones, above all due to its coverage. The previous case studies were devoted to the discussion of a single selected European market for the ESG ETFs. In this study, we outline not only one market, that is, in Sweden, but we also present the broader context of the Scandinavian sustainable investing sector—the reason for such approach is the relatively high homogeneity of the Scandinavian countries with regard to the legal and macroeconomic conditions of both sustainable investing and other related issues such as CSR (Jensen, 2016a). Moreover, another reason for the analysis at the regional level is the integration of the majority of the local stock exchanges (see the discussion of the sample of our study in Chapter 4)—the stock exchanges in both Sweden and Denmark are parts of the Nasdaq Nordic consortium of exchanges (the other members are, for instance, stock exchanges in the two Nordic countries, i.e., Iceland and Finland). Stock exchange in Oslo for many years remained the only exception yet it has also become a part of the larger group of trading venues—Euronext. Consequently, in our examination, including this case study, we use data on all ETFs listed on the Nasdaq Nordic stock exchanges group (labeled simply 'Nordic'), identifying why these funds are related most strongly to the Swedish financial markets rather than in the other Nordic countries. We also briefly analyze the sustainable investing ETFs market in Norway.

The further explanation for the adopted approach is that, in the historical dimension, Scandinavian countries can be regarded jointly as being among the pioneers concerning the introduction of regulations promoting the consideration of the ESG aspects by the financial companies. Another important issue is the substantial involvement of the local governments in the actions leading to the development of sustainable investing (Jensen, 2016a). In our case study, we devote most attention to Sweden as the largest economy in the Scandinavian (or, more broadly, Nordic region).

Nevertheless, in terms of assets of sustainable investments the structure of the region is more complicated—Sweden is undeniable regional leader in terms of, for instance, number of financial companies being PRI signatories. Still, with regard to assets, it is surpassed by, for example, Norway, due to the significant assets of the Norwegian sovereign wealth fund, established in 1990 with the aim of managing the Norwegian revenues from the sale of gas and oil as well as, in the longer perspective, mitigating the potential macroeconomic issues with the aging of the local population; the fund holds foreign securities in its portfolio (Jensen, 2016a, 2016b). The afore-mentioned fund, more formally the Government Pension Fund Norway, is among the leading financial institutions engaged globally in the promotion of sustainability issues, in particular concerning the climate risks of in-vestments (linked to the adoption of the Task Force on Climate-related Financial Disclosures—see Chapter 3)—its policies enforce the re-sponsibility to identify and address the sustainability risks by the fund's management; one of the important aspects is active ownership (Silvola & Landau, 2021). Also, according to data presented in Jensen (2016a), the assets managed by the Danish PRI signatories were larger than their Swedish counterparts. One of the important factors that boosted the development of the Danish sustainable investing sector was the introduc-tion of the CSR reporting requirements concerning certain entities by the Danish authorities. Another factor was the activity of the Danish organi-zation of sustainable investors, that is, Dansif (Buhmann, 2016). In 2018, Danish government published guidelines on the responsible investment (Eurosif, 2018). Drawing the division line between Swedish and overall Nordic sustainable investing is also hindered by the cross-Nordic product offerings of the majority of the Swedish financial corporations (Du Rietz, 2016).

Sweden was one of the first countries on a global scale with an ethical investment fund that could be accessed by the general community of investors—such fund, Aktie-Ansvar Aktienfond, focused on exclusions of certain industries, and it was launched in the mid-1960s by the organization linked to religion-motivated movement (Du Rietz, 2016; Jensen, 2016a). Furthermore, the next ethical investment funds were initiated by the Church of Sweden. However, starting from the late 1980s and early 1990s the scope of the institutions developing sustainable funds in Sweden has broadened; changes could also be noticed with regard to the offered in-vestment themes. One of the important factors that contributed to the development of the Swedish sustainable investing sector was the establishment of various nongovernmental organizations concentrating on the CSR issues, including the aspects covered by the international conventions. Similar pressure, leading to more broad-spread usage of negative screening investment strategies, resulted from the actions of, for example, churches and trade unions. Moreover, participants of the Swedish compulsory pension system receive sustainability profile reports of the investment funds, consistent with the PRI requirements (Du Rietz, 2016; Eurosif, 2018). In contrast with, for example, Finland where the inclusion of the sustainable investing criteria in the pension funds was related mostly to the actions of the funds' insiders, in Sweden the crucial role was played by the legislators (the other difference between the approach toward sustainability in these two pension systems is the focus on the competition in the former and on cooperation in the latter (Väänänen, 2021)). Swedish sustainable investing industry (as well as in the other Scandinavian countries) is dominated by the institutional investors (Jensen, 2016a,b; Nachemson-Ekwall, 2017; Schoenmaker, 2018). Swesif is the organization of the Swedish financial institutions utilizing responsible investing and majority of the largest asset management companies are its members (Du Rietz, 2016; Eurosif, 2018).

Swedish approach to sustainable investing should be considered in the context of the common attributes of the Scandinavian model of ethical investing, with the focus on the norms-based screening and exclusion strategies accompanied by active participation in the asset management (e.g., through shareholders actions (Bengtsson, 2008; Serafeim, 2018)), managed in highly diversified portfolios (rather than focused on thematic investments). Another distinctive attribute is the high formalization of the screening mechanism, with strong legal and regulatory framework as well as an emphasis on transparency. The dominant asset class in the Scandinavian sustainable investing[11] are fixed income securities (Du Rietz, 2016; Jensen, 2016a) and both Norway and Sweden are among the pioneers of the green bonds markets, with the latter country having a more developed market for these financial instruments (Liaw, 2020; Maltais & Nykvist, 2021; Torvanger et al., 2021). The domination of the three types of ESG investing strategies in Sweden is confirmed by the data on assets allocated to each one—according to the newest data available, published in 2018 (Eurosif, 2018), most sustainable investing assets were managed within the

---

[11] For a detailed discussion of ESG investing in the context of fixed income securities, see Inderst and Stewart (2018).

shareholders engagement strategies (c. 875 billion EUR) (used, among others, by the Swedish pension funds (Hamilton & Eriksson, 2011)), followed by exclusions (c. 720 billion EUR) and norms-based screening (c. 306 billion EUR).

Norwegian sustainable investing sector has long history albeit slightly shorter in comparison to its Swedish counterpart, with the first environmental investment funds launched in the late 1980s (Jensen, 2016b). Nonetheless, the development of the sector was boosted above all by the adoption of the ethical principles by the Government Pension Fund Norway due to the legal requirements imposed by the 2005 pension act—over time the investment strategy of this fund has become a benchmark for the other financial institutions engaged in the sustainable investing in Europe (Jensen, 2016b). The unique feature of the Norwegian ESG investing in relation to the other Scandinavian markets is the prevalence of equities in sustainable investing portfolios rather than fixed debt securities. Due to the approach adopted by the sovereign wealth fund, the dominant ESG investment strategy is exclusion and norms-based screening. Apart from the sovereign wealth fund, other important participants of the Norwegian sustainable investing sector are entities controlled by pension funds, insurance companies, and savings banks (Jensen, 2016b). The growth of the Norwegian sustainable investing sector has been shaped by the regulatory developments concerning, for example, corporate governance procedures (Webber et al., 2020).

Still, it should be emphasized that despite various important contributions of the Scandinavian region to the European sustainable investing industry (in terms of, e.g., pioneering instruments) according to the data as of 2018 the position of the region in the perspective of the total size of the European sustainable investing funds sector was rather minor, with the aggregated share of Denmark, Norway, and Sweden in terms of the number of domiciled funds below that of, for example, Switzerland or France (Sládková et al., 2021).

The total net assets of the sustainable investing ETFs listed on the Nasdaq Nordic stock exchange reached approximately 5.31 billion USD at the end of September 2021, indicating a slight decline after the record-high level of 5.55 billion USD in the preceding month; nevertheless, this ESG ETFs market has remained much smaller than its counterparts in countries such as Switzerland (yet larger than in, for example, Italy) indicating its low development level in the European perspective. These assets were managed by 11 ES G ETFs, all of them were provided by Handelsbanken Fonder under the 'XACT' brand and domiciled in Sweden. In our further discussion, we treat these sustainable investing ETFs as constituting the Swedish ETFs market not only due to their domicile but also because of their other attributes—most ESG ETFs primary listed on Nasdaq Nordic are registered for sale exclusively in Sweden, their base currency is in most cases Swedish krona; in terms of exposure this group of ETFs is more diversified as they track various stock market indexes, either of the multiple Nordic countries (still most companies covered are Swedish) or single markets (e.g., Denmark), there is also one bond fund. All Swedish sustainable investing ETFs are passive funds and most of them apply physical replication method. What is worth noticing, is the possible distortion of data on the sustainability of the examined funds in the Lipper's database (our main source of data)—according to the Lipper's classification, 11 funds out of 15 in total primary listed on Nasdaq Nordic are labeled as ethical, thus being regarded as ESG in our study (accounting for almost 90% of the total assets of the local ETFs). Assessment of the benchmarks of the funds, as well as their holdings, shows, though, that in some cases such a label is an overstatement—not all Swedish ESG ETFs were even awarded Lipper's or MSCI ESG scores; moreover, according to the justETF database, only one ETF was classified as ESG fund (the only fund with clearly ESG-complaint benchmark for the majority of its operations—some other funds switched to such indexes quite recently). Therefore, our results presented in this case study should be regarded with caution. Nevertheless, a comparison of the ESG scores of the Swedish sustainable investing ETFs included in our sample (for which the values could be obtained) to the mean values for Europe (see Table 5.3) implies their above-average sustainability levels, in particular in the case of the largest funds.

The analysis of the largest Swedish sustainable investing ETFs (i.e., listed on the Nasdaq Nordic exchange) shows that the assets of only three funds exceeded 1 billion USD (see Table 5.7.). The largest ESG ETF on this market, 'XACT Norden' (also known as 'XACT Norden (UCITS ETF)'), managed total net assets of about 1.71 billion USD; its investment aim is offering exposure to the 30 companies with the most actively traded equities listed on Nasdaq Nordic (interestingly, its base currency is euro—it is the only such ESG fund on this market). Similarly to the other ESG ETFs markets presented in the previous case studies, the majority of the biggest ETFs are passive equity funds, with one bond fund on the list, tracking the bonds denominated in the Swedish krona such as the bonds issued by the Swedish government; it is, though, much smaller in terms of assets than

Table 5.7 The largest Swedish sustainable investing ETFs (primary listed on Nasdaq Nordic, according to the assets under management). September 2021 data.

Name of the fund	Total net assets (bln USD)	Asset class of exposure (Lipper's classification)	Benchmark	Provider	Inception date	Total expense ratio (%)
XACT norden	1.71	Equity nordic	Handelsbanken nordic ESG Index	Handelsbanken fonder	May 4, 2006	0.15
XACT nordic High dividend Low Volatility ETF	1.37	Equity nordic	Handelsbanken nordic High dividend Low Volatility Criteria	Handelsbanken fonder	March 31, 2017	0.30
XACT OMXS30 ESG UCITS ETF	1.04	Equity Sweden	OMX stockholm 30 ESG Responsible Index	Handelsbanken fonder	October 30, 2000	0.10
XACT Obligation	0.35	Bond Swedish krone	Handelsbanken Sweden All Bond tradable Index	Handelsbanken fonder	February 9, 2016	0.10
XACT OMXC25	0.23	Equity Denmark	OMX copenhagen 25 Index GI	Handelsbanken fonder	January 29, 2019	0.20

Source: own elaboration based on Lipper's and just ETF databases as well as websites of the funds' provider.

the three biggest Swedish ESG ETFs. Five largest ETFs are diversified with regard to their history—while three funds were launched in 2016 or later, 'XACT OMXS30 ESG UCITS ETF' was incepted in 2000, thus being among the oldest ETFs in the entire region (it must be stressed that for many years it had not tracked the ESG-compliant index (change was introduced in 2019 (Lord, 2019))—this applies to the first ETF on the list as well). Recently, the provider of the funds labeled them in line with the SFDR classification (see Chapter 3)—the first three were awarded SFDR 8 category, whereas the fifth one (the only one with non-Swedish exposure, i.e., to the Danish equities, with the Danish krone as the base currency) SFDR 6 with the statement of integration of the ESG factors in the investment process, and the bond fund was also given the SFDR 6 status yet without the inclusion of the ESG aspects.

The second sustainable investing ETFs market is the one in Norway and it consists of three equity funds primarily listed on the Oslo Stock Exchange, tracking the same blue-chip index of this exchange—the biggest fund aims to mirror its performance, the other two are leveraged and leveraged-inverse ETF. Their total net assets as of the end of September 2021 were at merely c. 140 million USD, corresponding to approximately 40% of the aggregated assets of the Norwegian ETFs. The Norwegian ESG ETFs are also strongly linked to the Swedish financial sector—all three are domiciled in Sweden and managed by Handelsbanken Fonder. Their base currency is, though, the Norwegian krone. According to the Lipper's database, all three funds were launched in 2017.

Some of the key factors affecting the Swedish ESG ETFs market and, in a broader perspective, the aggregate market for the sustainable investing funds were already mentioned in the previous paragraphs—they include, among others, the activities of Swesif or sustainability disclosure requirements for the funds offered within the pensions system. The development of the Swedish sustainable investing funds markets has also been boosted by the establishment of the industry-broad ESG disclosure standards by The Swedish Investment Fund Association in 2015, obligatory for all its members, increasing transparency for the clients and enabling analysis of the ESG issues over time and between funds (Eurosif, 2018). Other important initiatives, with a potential positive influence on the sustainable investing funds in Sweden, are governmental support for the Nordic ecolabelling scheme (Nordic Swan Ecolabel for funds, with 25 criteria to be fulfilled such as the exclusion of the fossil fuels investments) or climate-related initiatives of the financial supervision authorities (Eurosif, 2018;

Wiklund, 2021). However, some studies (e.g., Arvidsson & Durnay, 2022) showed that the contribution of the ESG investments in Sweden is most recently (as of 2021) hindered not by the reporting limitations but rather the ESG performance of the Swedish companies (whose securities constitute one of the elements of the portfolios of the Swedish ESG funds). The strong preference of the Swedish private users of investment funds toward sustainable funds was confirmed in, among others, Lagerkvist et al. (2020) who concluded that sustainability attributes of the equity funds are the key factor of the fund's selection among the Swedish retail investors.

Another factor that should not be disregarded is the financial performance of the ESG funds. Dopierała et al. (2020) analyzed the climate-friendly mutual funds (classified as such using the relative carbon footprint indicator) in the Scandinavian economies, concluding that there was no evidence for their abnormal returns in relation to the other types of funds. In the upcoming years, the development of the Swedish ESG ETFs markets can also be boosted by the launch of the new sustainable investing funds, offering more diversified exposure; nevertheless, it remains to be seen if they are primarily listed on the Nordic exchange or rather some larger trading venues, with more potential clients available (for example, in 2019 gold mining ESG ETF was launched by the Swedish asset management company yet on the London Stock Exchange (Garzic, 2021)). The other problematic issue is the controversies surrounding the actual ESG compliance of the investment portfolios of some Swedish financial institutions, for instance, the state pension funds (Lindeberg, 2021).

References

Albuquerque, R., Koskinen, Y., Yang, S., & Zhang, C. (2020). Resiliency of environmental and social stocks: An analysis of the exogenous COVID-19 market crash. *The Review of Corporate Finance Studies, 9*(3), 593−621.

Amenc, N., Goltz, F., & Liu, V. (2021). *Doing good or feeling good? Detecting greenwashing in climate investing.* EDHEC Business School.

Appel, I. R., Gormley, T. A., & Keim, D. B. (2016). Passive investors, not passive owners. *Journal of Financial Economics, 121*(1), 111−141.

Arandia, O., & Hepp, S. (2021). Poverty alleviation through financial practices: The importance of microfinance: The importance of microfonance. In L. San-Jose, J. Retolaza, & L. Van Liedekerke (Eds.), *Handbook on ethics in finance* (pp. 397−421). Springer.

Arvidsson, S., & Dumay, J. (2022). Corporate ESG reporting quantity, quality and performance: Where to now for environmental policy and practice? *Business Strategy and the Environment, 31*(3), 1091−1110.

Barber, B. M., Morse, A., & Yasuda, A. (2021). Impact investing. *Journal of Financial Economics, 139*(1), 162–185.

Basdekidou, V. A., & Styliadou, A. A. (2017). Corporate social responsibility & market volatility: Relationship and trading opportunities. *International Business Research, 10*(5), 1–12.

Ben-David, I., Franzoni, F. A., & Moussawi, R. (2017). Exchange traded funds. *Annual Review of Financial Economics, 9*, 169–189.

Bengtsson, E. (2008). Socially responsible investing in Scandinavia—a comparative analysis. *Sustainable Development, 16*(3), 155–168.

Benijts, T. (2008). Measuring corporate sustainability: An analysis of the research practices used by two Belgian asset management firms in the field of socially responsible investing. *Journal of Corporate Citizenship, 32*, 29–42.

Botsari, A., & Lang, F. (2020). ESG considerations in venture capital and business angel investment decisions: Evidence from two pan-European surveys. *EIF Research & Market Analysis Working Paper, 63*, 1–56.

Bradley, H. S., & Litan, R. E. (2011). *ETFs and the present danger to capital formation.* Ewing Marion Kauffman Foundation Research Paper.

Buhmann, K. (2016). Responsible investment in Denmark: Practices among institutional investors in a context of statutory CSR reporting requirements. In T. Hebb, J. P. Hawley, A. G. Hoepner, A. L. Neher, & D. Wood (Eds.), *The Routledge handbook of responsible investment* (pp. 317–326). Routledge.

Busch, T., Bauer, R., & Orlitzky, M. (2016). Sustainable development and financial markets: Old paths and new avenues. *Business & Society, 55*(3), 303–329.

Capelle-Blancard, G., Desroziers, A., & Zerbib, O. D. (2021). Socially responsible investing strategies under pressure: Evidence from the COVID-19 crisis. *The Journal of Portfolio Management, 47*(9), 178–197.

Ceccarelli, M., Ramelli, S., & Wagner, A. F. (2019). When investors call for climate responsibility, how do mutual funds respond? *CEPR Discussion Papers, 13599*, 1–55.

CFA Institute. (2020). *Climate change analysis in the investment process.*

Chen, J. H. (2011). The spillover and leverage effects of ethical exchange traded fund. *Applied Economics Letters, 18*(10), 983–987.

Chen, J. H., & Diaz, J. F. (2012). Spillover and leverage effects of faith-based exchange-traded funds. *Journal of Business and Policy Research, 7*(2), 1–12.

Christianson, G., McClamrock, J., & Pinchot, A. (2019). *Serious about sustainability? Some progress, but not yet persuaded by BlackRock's efforts.* https://www.eco-business.com/opinion/serious-about-sustainability-some-progress-but-not-yet-persuaded-by-black-rocks-efforts/, 14th April 2022.

Christianson, G., & Pinchot, A. (2020). *BlackRock is getting serious about climate change. Is This a Turning Point for Investors?.* https://www.wri.org/insights/blackrock-getting-serious-about-climate-change-turning-point-investors, 14 April 2022.

Corum, A. A., Malenko, A., & Malenko, N. (2022). *Corporate governance in the presence of active and passive delegated investment.* European Corporate Governance Institute—Finance Working Paper, 695.

Couvert, M. (2020). What is the impact of mutual funds' ESG preferences on portfolio firms? *Swiss Finance Institute Research Paper, 21*(42), 1–57.

Cowton, C. J. (2021). Financial institutions and codes of ethics. In L. San-Jose, J. Retolaza, & L. Van Liedekerke (Eds.), *Handbook on ethics in finance* (pp. 3–15). Springer.

Davies, S. W., & Van Wesep, E. D. (2018). The unintended consequences of divestment. *Journal of Financial Economics, 128*(3), 558–575.

Dopierała, Ł., Mosionek-Schweda, M., & Ilczuk, D. (2020). Does the asset allocation policy affect the performance of climate-themed funds? Empirical evidence from the scandinavian mutual funds market. *Sustainability, 12*(2).

Du Rietz, S. (2016). Responsible investment in Sweden. In T. Hebb, J. P. Hawley, A. G. Hoepner, A. L. Neher, & D. Wood (Eds.), *The Routledge handbook of responsible investment* (pp. 336–344). Routledge.

Etchart, L. (2022). *Global governance of the environment, indigenous peoples and the rights of nature extractive industries in the Ecuadorian amazon*. Palgrave Macmillan.

Eurosif. (2018). *European SRI study 2018*.

Eurosif. (2021). *Eurosif report 2021: Fostering investor impact. Placing it at the heart of sustainable finance*.

Falk, M. S. (2016). *Let's all learn how to fish… to sustain long-term economic growth*. CFA Institute Research Foundation.

Fowler, S. J., & Hope, C. (2007). A critical review of sustainable business indices and their impact. *Journal of Business Ethics, 76*(3), 243–252.

Friede, G., Busch, T., & Bassen, A. (2015). ESG and financial performance: Aggregated evidence from more than 2000 empirical studies. *Journal of Sustainable Finance & Investment, 5*(4), 210–233.

Garzic, M. (2021). *Swedish commodity manager launches ESG-based gold ETF*. https://amwatch.com/article13097193.ece, 26 April 2022.

Gibson, R., Glossner, S., Krueger, P., Matos, P., & Steffen, T. (2020). Responsible institutional investing around the world. *European Corporate Governance Institute—Finance Working Paper, 712*, 1–61.

Gillan, S. L., Koch, A., & Starks, L. T. (2021). Firms and social responsibility: A review of ESG and CSR research in corporate finance. *Journal of Corporate Finance, 66*.

Goldstein, I., Kopytov, A., Shen, L., & Xiang, H. (2022). On ESG investing: Heterogeneous preferences, information, and asset prices. *NBER Working Paper, 29839*, 1–79.

Grishunin, S., Suloeva, S., Nekrasova, T., & Erorova, A. (2022). Study of relationship between the corporate governance factors and ESG ratings of ICT companies from the developed markets. In *International conference on next generation wired/wireless networking, conference on internet of things and smart spaces* (pp. 158–169). Springer.

Gutiérrez, M., & Saez Lacave, M. (2018). Strong shareholders, weak outside investors. *Journal of Corporate Law Studies, 18*(2), 277–309.

Hamilton, I., & Eriksson, J. (2011). Influence strategies in shareholder engagement: A case study of all Swedish national pension funds. *Journal of Sustainable Finance and Investment, 1*(1), 44–61.

Hamrouni, A., Uyar, A., & Boussaada, R. (2019). Are corporate social responsibility disclosures relevant for lenders? Empirical evidence from France. *Management Decision, 58*(2), 267–279.

Hansen, N., Huis, M. A., & Lensink, R. (2021). Microfinance services and women's empowerment. In L. San-Jose, J. Retolaza, & L. Van Liedekerke (Eds.), *Handbook on ethics in finance* (pp. 161–182). Springer.

Hayat, U. (2015). *Sustainable investing and fiduciary responsibility: Conflict or confluence?*. https://blogs.cfainstitute.org/investor/2015/09/21/sustainable-investing-and-fiduciary-responsibility-conflict-or-confluence/, 14 April 2022.

Inderst, G., & Stewart, F. (2018). *Incorporating environmental, social and governance (ESG) factors into fixed income investment*. World Bank Group.

Jensen, A. (2016a). Introduction to scandinavia. In T. Hebb, J. P. Hawley, A. G. Hoepner, A. L. Neher, & D. Wood (Eds.), *The Routledge handbook of responsible investment* (pp. 313–316). Routledge.

Jensen, A. (2016b). Responsible investment in Norway. In T. Hebb, J. P. Hawley, A. G. Hoepner, A. L. Neher, & D. Wood (Eds.), *The Routledge handbook of responsible investment* (pp. 345–354). Routledge.

Kahan, M., & Rock, E. B. (2020). Index funds and corporate governance: Let shareholders be shareholders. *Boston University Law Review, 100*(5), 1771–1815.

Kanamura, T. (2021). Risk mitigation and return resilience for high yield bond ETFs with ESG components. *Finance Research Letters, 41.*

Kim, S., & Yoon, A. (2020). *Analyzing active managers' commitment to ESG: Evidence from united Nations principles for responsible investment.* forthcoming: Management Science.

Kölbel, J. F., Heeb, F., Paetzold, F., & Busch, T. (2020). Can sustainable investing save the world? Reviewing the mechanisms of investor impact. *Organization & Environment, 33*(4), 554–574.

Kuang, W. (2021). The heterogeneity of the diversification effect of sustainable development goals related exchange-traded funds. *Journal of Sustainable Finance & Investment.* (In press).

Lagerkvist, C. J., Edenbrandt, A. K., Tibbelin, I., & Wahlstedt, Y. (2020). Preferences for sustainable and responsible equity funds-A choice experiment with Swedish private investors. *Journal of Behavioral and Experimental Finance, 28.*

Liaw, K. T. (2020). Survey of green bond pricing and investment performance. *Journal of Risk and Financial Management, 13*(9).

Lindeberg, R. (2021). *Swedish funds managing $250 billion get slammed for ESG record.* https://www. bloomberg.com/news/articles/2021-03-05/swedish-pension-funds-slammed-for-failed-fossil-fuel-agenda, 26 April 2022.

Li, Z. F., Patel, S., & Ramani, S. (2021). The role of mutual funds in corporate social responsibility. *Journal of Business Ethics, 174*(3), 715–737.

Lord, J. (2019). *Xact boosts ESG profile of nordic ETF.* https://www.etfstrategy.com/xact-boosts-esg-profile-of-nordic-etf-94578/, 26 April 2022.

Maltais, A., & Nykvist, B. (2021). Understanding the role of green bonds in advancing sustainability. *Journal of Sustainable Finance & Investment, 11*(3), 233–252.

Marszk, A., & Lechman, E. (2019a). *Exchange-traded funds in Europe.* Academic Press.

Marszk, A., & Lechman, E. (2019b). New technologies and diffusion of innovative financial products: Evidence on exchange-traded funds in selected emerging and developed economies. *Journal of Macroeconomics, 62.*

Marszk, A., & Lechman, E. (2021). Reshaping financial systems: The role of ICT in the diffusion of financial innovations–Recent evidence from European countries. *Technological Forecasting and Social Change, 167.*

Marszk, A., Lechman, E., & Kato, Y. (2019). *The emergence of ETFs in asia-pacific.* Springer International Publishing.

Matos, P. (2020). *ESG and responsible institutional investing around the world: A critical review.* CFA Institute Research Foundation.

McCann, J., & Sweet, M. (2014). The perceptions of ethical and sustainable leadership. *Journal of Business Ethics, 121*(3), 373–383.

McNulty, T., & Nordberg, D. (2016). Ownership, activism and engagement: Institutional investors as active owners. *Corporate Governance: An International Review, 24*(3), 346–358.

Min, G., & You, H. Y. (2019). Active firms and active shareholders: Corporate political activity and shareholder proposals. *The Journal of Legal Studies, 48*(1), 81–116.

Miralles-Quirós, J. L., Miralles-Quirós, M. M., & Nogueira, J. M. (2019). Diversification benefits of using exchange-traded funds in compliance to the sustainable development goals. *Business Strategy and the Environment, 28*(1), 244–255.

Moreira, M. (2021). *Refinitiv sustainable finance: Turning the art of ESG into science.* Refinitiv.

MSCI. (2021). *MSCI ESG fund ratings summary.* MSCI ESG Research LLC.

Naaraayanan, S. L., Sachdeva, K., & Sharma, V. (2021). The real effects of environmental activist investing. *European Corporate Governance Institute—Finance Working Paper, 743,* 1–69.

Nachemson-Ekwall, S. (2017). Leveraging on home bias: Large stakes and long-termism by Swedish institutional investors. *Nordic Journal of Business, 66*(3), 128–157.

Naffa, H., & Fain, M. (2020). Performance measurement of ESG-themed megatrend investments in global equity markets using pure factor portfolios methodology. *PloS One, 15*(12).

Narula, K. (2012). 'Sustainable Investing' via the FDI route for sustainable development. *Procedia-Social and Behavioral Sciences, 37,* 15−30.

Orsagh, M., Allen, J., Sloggett, J., Georgieva, A., Bartholdy, S., & Douma, K. (2018). *Guidance and case studies for ESG integration: Equities and fixed income.* CFA Institute.

Pavlova, I., & de Boyrie, M. E. (2022). ESG ETFs and the COVID-19 stock market crash of 2020: Did clean funds fare better? *Finance Research Letters, 44.*

Pouget, S. (2016). Financial markets' inefficiencies and long-term investments. In T. Hebb, J. P. Hawley, A. G. Hoepner, A. L. Neher, & D. Wood (Eds.), *The Routledge handbook of responsible investment* (pp. 689−704). Routledge.

Prall, K. (2021). *A framework to drive ESG financial Discipline.* https://blogs.cfainstitute.org/investor/2021/06/11/a-framework-to-drive-esg-financial-discipline/, 24 April 2022.

Refinitiv. (2020). *Refinitiv debuts Fund ESG Scores to facilitate industry transition to sustainable investing.*

Refinitiv. (2021). *Environmental, social and governance scores from Refinitiv.*

Refinitiv. (2022a). *Lipper ESG fund scores methodology.*

Refinitiv. (2022b). Refinitiv ESG company scores.

Rizvi, S. K. A., Naqvi, B., & Mirza, N. (2022). Is green investment different from grey? Return and volatility spillovers between green and grey energy ETFs. *Annals of Operations Research, 313,* 495−524.

Sahut, J. M., & Pasquini-Descomps, H. (2015). ESG impact on market performance of firms: International Evidence. *Management International/International Management/Gestiòn Internacional, 19*(2), 40−63.

Schiereck, D., Friede, G., & Bassen, A. (2019). Financial performances of green securities. In M. Migliorelli, & P. Dessertine (Eds.), *The rise of green finance in Europe* (pp. 95−117). Palgrave Macmillan.

Schneeweiß, A. (2019). Der Einfluss nachhaltiger Investoren auf Unternehmen. Eine explorative Recherche. In M. Stüttgen (Ed.), *Ethik von Banken und Finanzen* (pp. 165−190). Nomos Verlag.

Schoenfeld, J. (2020). Contracts between firms and shareholders. *Journal of Accounting Research, 58*(2), 383−427.

Schoenmaker, D. (2018). Sustainable investing: How to do it. *Bruegel Policy Contribution, 23,* 1−12.

Serafeim, G. (2018). Investors as stewards of the commons? *Journal of Applied Corporate Finance, 30*(2), 8−17.

Serafeim, G. (2020). Public sentiment and the price of corporate sustainability. *Financial Analysts Journal, 76*(2), 26−46.

Signori, S. (2021). Socially responsible investors: Exploring motivations and ethical intensity. In L. San-Jose, J. Retolaza, & L. Van Liedekerke (Eds.), *Handbook on ethics in finance* (pp. 183−205). Springer.

Silvola, H., & Landau, T. (2021). *Sustainable investing: Beating the market with ESG.* Palgrave Macmillan.

Singh, K. (2022). *On the Brink of collapse: Decoding a UN-backed climate fund.* https://thewire.in/political-economy/ntzo-brink-of-collapse-un-backed-climate-etf, 24 April 2022.

Sládková, J., Kolomazníková, D., Formánková, S., Trenz, O., Kolomazník, J., & Faldík, O. (2021). Sustainable and responsible investment funds in Europe. *Measuring Business Excellence.*

Stüttgen, M. (2019). Mikrokredite. Nachhaltige Geldanlage im Spannungsfeld von Marketing und Moral. In M. Stüttgen (Ed.), *Ethik von Banken und Finanzen* (pp. 117−139). Nomos Verlag.

Sun, L., & Small, G. (2022). Has sustainable investing made an impact in the period of COVID-19?: Evidence from Australian exchange traded funds. *Journal of Sustainable Finance & Investment, 12*(1), 251–273.

Sustainable Finance, Swiss (2020). *Financing the low-carbon economy. Instruments, barriers and recommendations. A compendium of innovative finance instruments prepared by Swiss Sustainable Finance in cooperation with its network.*

Torvanger, A., Maltais, A., & Marginean, I. (2021). Green bonds in Sweden and Norway: What are the success factors? *Journal of Cleaner Production, 324.*

United Nations Conference on Trade and Development. (2020). Leveraging the Potential of ESG ETFs for Sustainable Development.

University of Cambridge Institute for Sustainability Leadership. (2017). *Catalysing fintech for sustainability: Lessons from multi-sector innovation.*

University of Cambridge Institute for Sustainability Leadership. In *search of impact: Measuring the full value of capital. Update: Sustainable Investment Framework.*

Utz, S., & Wimmer, M. (2014). Are they any good at all? A financial and ethical analysis of socially responsible mutual funds. *Journal of Asset Management, 15*(1), 72–82.

Väänänen, N. (2021). Two different paths to sustainability? A comparison of a Finnish and a Swedish public pension reserve fund. *European Journal of Social Security, 23*(3), 298–317.

Wamba, L. D., Braune, E., & Hikkerova, L. (2018). Does shareholder-oriented corporate governance reduce firm risk? Evidence from listed European companies. *Journal of Applied Accounting Research, 19*(2), 295–311.

Ware, J., Robinson, K., & Falk, M. (2017). *Money, meaning, and Mindsets: Radical reform for the investment industry.* Focus Consulting Group.

Waygood, S. (2008). Civil society and capital markets. In C. Krosinsky, & N. Robins (Eds.), *Sustainable investing: The art of long-term performance* (pp. 177–188). Earthscan.

Webber, D., Barzuza, M., & Curtis, Q. (2020). Shareholder value (s): Index fund ESG activism and the new millennial corporate governance. *Southern California Law Review, 93*(6), 1243–1322.

Weston, P., & Nnadi, M. (2021). Evaluation of strategic and financial variables of corporate sustainability and ESG policies on corporate finance performance. *Journal of Sustainable Finance & Investment.* (In press).

Wiklund, S. (2021). Evaluating physical climate risk for equity funds with quantitative modelling—how exposed are sustainable funds? *Journal of Sustainable Finance & Investment.* (In press).

Wimmer, M. (2013). ESG-Persistence in socially responsible mutual funds. *Journal of Management and Sustainability, 3*(1), 9–15.

Woods, C., & Urwin, R. (2010). Putting sustainable investing into practice: A governance framework for pension funds. *Journal of Business Ethics, 92*(1), 1–19.

Xiao, Y., Faff, R., Gharghori, P., & Lee, D. (2013). An empirical study of the world price of sustainability. *Journal of Business Ethics, 114*(2), 297–310.

CHAPTER 6

Conclusions and recommendations

6.1 General comments

The rising popularity of various types of sustainable investing and the increasing position of exchange-traded funds (ETFs) are among the key processes influencing the contemporary financial markets in the most developed economies. The former process can be linked to a broad range of factors such as the actions undertaken at the international or regional level (focused on initiating and supporting sustainable development) and the shifts in the attitudes of the financial corporations and investors. The latter is driven by, among others, the advantages offered by ETFs for their users in relation to the conventional investment funds as well as the rise of passive investing, leading to the increased utilization of the predominantly passive shares of ETFs in the investment portfolios.

Our book addresses various dimensions of sustainable investing (ESG) ETFs, thus merging the two aforementioned perspectives. It is the first publication in which a detailed analysis of this type of ETFs was conducted. Despite the rapidly growing number of studies focused on varying dimensions of ESG in the context of financial investments, the topics related to ESG ETFs seem to attract the limited interest of the academic community, one of the possible reasons being the short presence of these funds in most major financial markets and associated data availability barriers. In our book, we attempted to mitigate this apparent and significant gap by presenting theoretical, methodological, and empirical issues concerning the sustainable investing ETFs, with a particular focus on the European markets.

In the empirical part of the book, we presented the results of our analysis of the sustainable investing ETFs markets. The sample of our study consisted of the ETFs primarily listed in Europe. Graphical analysis, together with the diffusion and panel models, covered predominantly the following

Sustainable Investing
ISBN 978-0-12-823871-4
https://doi.org/10.1016/B978-0-12-823871-4.00006-4
225

countries: France, Germany, Italy, Switzerland, and the United Kingdom. The time period of the analysis was in most cases since 2006 up to the most recent time point available in the utilized dataset.

6.2 ETFs and sustainable investing: background

Before the presentation of the results of the empirical study, in Chapters 2 and 3 we discussed certain most relevant concepts concerning ETFs and sustainable investing, thus providing the necessary background for the empirical study and describing many among the most recent developments in both fields.

The basic attributes of ETFs were presented as the first issue, explaining the differences between these funds and mutual funds. Even though there are various types of ETFs and this category of investment funds has become increasingly diversified, passive equity ETFs, tracking the major stock market indexes, remain the most frequent category. They can be compared to the mutual funds with similar exposure—one of the key relative benefits of ETFs is the higher liquidity of their shares resulting from the fact that the shares of ETFs are listed and traded on stock exchanges or other similar trading venues. Another important aspect of ETFs is the duality of their markets and the possibility to conduct arbitrage operations by certain entities, thus leading to a favorable performance in terms of benchmark tracking. The relationships between the markets for ETFs and their environment, in particular financial markets, were also covered in Chapter 2, with the focus on the identification of the effects of ETFs, based on an extensive literature review, addressed in particular with regard to the financial systems. In case of the consequences of the spread of ETFs, we outlined not only, as most common in the literature, their linkages with the tracked financial assets (or the ones held in their portfolios) but also their role for the entire investment industries and financial systems, also in the international perspective. Finally, we showed how the new technologies affect the development of the ETFs markets, providing various examples of the utilization of the shares of ETFs in the FinTech sector. Moreover, the impact of ETFs on the growth of the FinTech entities was considered, with the most recent example being ETFs tracking the performance of cryptocurrencies.

In the next chapter, we presented the issue of sustainable investing. First, we discussed the definitions of this and related concepts such as socially responsible or ethical investing as well as the broader concept of sustainable finance, indicating above all their common elements and examining them in the context of our empirical study. We explained that the most controversial point in various approaches to the clarification of the ESG or sustainable investing concept is their actual contribution to sustainable development or related processes. Additionally, we provided a brief insight into the history of sustainable investing, presenting different historical stages of its development, from the faith-linked organizations, through the focus on governance elements, to the most recent trends such as the integration of the ESG aspects in the mainstream investment industry. Growth of the global sustainable investing industry is linked, among others, to the substantial diversity of this part of the financial system in terms of, for example, investing approaches applied, with the integration and screening strategies among the most frequent. The next issue covered in the chapter was sustainable development policies—we discussed the most important initiatives in this area, especially the establishment of the 17 Sustainable Development Goals (SDGs), climate-related agreements, sustainability reporting standards, and the EU-level actions such as the European Green Deal. We explained their significance not limiting it to the public sector but that in many cases was adopted or even developed by the private entities, including the financial corporations. Subsequently, we provided various examples of the practical adoption of sustainable investing, in particular the ESG investment funds. In the next part of the chapter, we addressed the highly complicated yet also very significant issue of the methodological challenges with regard to defining and classifying sustainable investing. The key examples covered were Principles for Responsible Investment, EU Sustainable Finance Disclosure Regulation (SFDR), EU Taxonomy, and some other national (or regional) guidelines. We also showed the commercial approaches, discussing the key attributes of some ESG rating methodologies. Our presentation concluded with an overview of the ambiguities and controversies surrounding the methodologies of sustainable investing; as the last issue, we explained our approach to be used in the empirical study.

6.3 European sustainable investing ETFs markets—key insights into the heterogeneous development of ESG ETFs in Europe

In the first entirely empirical chapter (i.e., Chapter 4), we examined the development of the sustainable investing ETFs markets in Europe, preceded by the presentation of the global and European sustainable investing sectors as the background. The most striking conclusion of our analysis is the substantial heterogeneity of the European sustainable investing markets, including their ESG ETFs segments.

In the first part of the chapter, we examined the basic attributes of the global sustainable investing industry, using above all the reports published by the Global Sustainable Investment Alliance. The most recent data from late 2019 and early 2020 showed that the assets of the sustainable investments reached globally the record-high level of more than 35 trillion USD, after a rapid increase in the preceding several years, from approximately 13 trillion USD in 2012. In terms of the geographical structure, the majority of assets (about 55%) were managed by the North American financial institutions and most of the remaining belonged to the European financial companies (among the other markets, the largest single sustainable investing industry was the Japanese one). Taking into account the share of sustainable investing assets in the total assets of the certain investment industry, their relative popularity was, though, higher than in the United States (yet in both cases sustainable investing accounted for the minority of the total assets). Therefore, it could be clearly seen that these regions constitute the most substantial sustainable investing industries at a global level.

The second part of the chapter focused on sustainable investments in Europe. In 2020, their assets amounted to 12 trillion USD, following a decline in comparison to 2018, caused by the changes in the EU-level sustainability legislation. Sustainable investments accounted in 2020 for about 42% of the total assets managed in Europe, marking a decline from almost 60% in 2014, again explained by the legally binding changes in the identification and classification of these investments. In terms of the ESG investment strategies, the most frequently utilized by the European financial institutions was negative screening, followed by various types of active engagement and shareholders actions thus showing the significant diversity of the applied approaches, with both simple and more advanced among the most frequent. The United Kingdom was identified as the region's largest sustainable investing market in terms of assets. The important trend with regard to the structure of the European market was the increasing position of the retail investors in relation to the institutional, reaching the highest levels in the world, boosted by, among others, the regulatory changes. More generally, among the key development factors of the European sector, we listed the growing number and diversity of sustainable financial products available, collaboration between the financial institutions with regard to the sustainable finance credentials, and the EU-level regulatory and policy developments.

The next section addressed the topic of sustainable investment funds in Europe. Due to the significant differences in the data sources available, it is difficult to clearly determine the size of the sector—the estimates of the most recent value of assets range between 0.5 and close to 4 trillion EUR (the latter value in line with the SFDR classification). These problems hinder the cross-region comparisons as well.

In the fourth part of the chapter, we provided an overview of the European ETFs markets—according to our estimates, as of September 2021 the total net assets of the ETFs primary listed in Europe exceeded 1.4 trillion USD, thus reaching the highest level in history, with most assets managed by the funds listed in the United Kingdom, Germany, and France. In relation to the other regions, the European aggregate ETFs market was much smaller than its US counterpart yet significantly larger than in any other part of the world.

The fifth section consisted of the results of the main analysis undertaken with the aim of the region- and country-level assessment of the European sustainable investing ETFs markets, considered using two measures: assets of sustainable investing ETFs and share of sustainable investing ETFs in total ETFs market.

After the discussion of the methodological issues, we presented the regional evidence (i.e., for all ESG ETFs markets in Europe considered jointly). In terms of value, the assets of the European sustainable investing ETFs have increased rapidly over 2006—2021, to the levels exceeding 220 billion USD, with 2017—2021 recognized unequivocally as the take-off period. However, the picture unveiled through the analysis using the data on the share of sustainable investing ETF is more complicated as the decline in the initial years was identified. Still, since 2017 the trend was similar to the already mentioned for the former indicator and the maximum (also end-of-the period) share was over 15%. Consequently, we stated that our analysis confirmed the development of the European ESG ETFs market; additionally, the estimates of the diffusion models provided support for predicting continued growth in the future. We also examined the structure of the European market, concluding that the United Kingdom, Germany, and France accounted for about 80% of the total assets (the share of Switzerland was at c. 9%), thus implying a high concentration level, with significant differences between the major and remaining markets. Most

European ESG ETFs were equity funds managed by the major global or regional financial corporations (including BlackRock, UBS, or Amundi).

In the further part of the chapter, we outlined the country-level evidence. Analysis of the timelines led to the conclusion that the general trend of the values of the assets of sustainable investing ETFs was similar in all countries examined and the rapid development of local ESG ETFs began in approximately 2017. In the case of the share of the sustainable investing ETFs in the total assets of ETFs, the trend has generally been similar. However, for the early years in the analyzed time period, there were some differences between the trends of the two indicators, linked to the distortions related to the overall small size of the ETFs markets. The brief examination of the key attributes of the European ETFs markets unveiled the significant dissimilarities in their development levels in both dimensions studied (values of assets and their shares); the divergences were further confirmed by the estimated parameters of the diffusion models.

6.4 Sustainable investing ETFs and sustainable development: tracking possible contributions of the ESG funds

The second empirical chapter (i.e., Chapter 5) focused on the key topic of the book—the socio-economic and environmental impacts of the sustainable investing ETFs, considered in the perspective of the sustainable development policies, in particular the issues covered within the SDGs. The study was conducted predominantly at the macroeconomic level.

In the first section, the methodology, data sources, and variables used in the analysis were explained, including also a brief discussion of the selected issues concerning the ESG scores in the main databases from which data on ETFs were retrieved. These scores were used to conduct the assessment of the sustainability of the ETFs included in our sample. Based on the comparison of the ESG scores of various groups of ETFs we concluded, with some stipulations (such as small relative differences), that our selection approach allowed for the correct identification of the more sustainability-compliant funds than typical ones primary listed in the region; similar findings were noted concerning the country-level evidence. In terms of the three ESG pillars, the most convincing differences between the conventional and sustainable investing ETFs were identified for the environmental dimension, consistently with the investment focus of many European funds.

In the subsequent section, we discussed the results of our empirical analysis of the impact of the ESG ETFs in Europe, focusing on the three perspectives; wherever possible, we provided the explanations of the identified relationships formulated based on the extensive literature review.

The first perspective was their impact on the financial systems. Results of our analysis indicated that the expansion of the European sustainable investing ETFs affected at least three aspects of the financial sector: general financial development, capitalization of the stock markets, and bank deposits. The strongest linkages were noted for the stock markets as the segment closest to ETFs.

The second perspective focused on the indicators of socio-economic development. The results of our empirical analysis indicated that the development of the sustainable investing ETFs in Europe was linked to the improvements in the institutional attributes of the European economies (e.g., the level of economic freedom or protection of the property rights). Moreover, we compiled evidence for the conclusion that the growing assets of the ESG ETFs in relation to gross domestic product (GDP) were associated with the improvements in the quality of life (measured in terms of human development index (HDI) and proportion of the population living in multidimensional poverty). Finally, we confirmed the positive linkages between ESG funds and some other socio-economic indicators, representing the aspects such as health, number of researchers in R&D, proportion of women in senior and middle management positions, and basic digital skills of the population.

In the third and final perspective, we studied the effects of the sustainable investing ETFs for the environments of the European countries, concluding that there was sufficient evidence for hypothesizing, in case of almost all environmental variables utilized, that they were related to the development of the funds, implying a relationship assessed positively in the context of the sustainable development. However, we emphasized that this conclusion should be regarded with considerable caution as the environmental variables were potentially influenced by a large set of determinants.

In the brief interlude before the next section (also macro-level focused), we covered the issue of the impact of the sustainable investing ETFs (and more general effects of the sustainable investing) on the corporations being their providers, presenting key conclusions from the literature review.

The fourth section was devoted to the evaluation of the effects of the development of the European ESG ETFs markets for the sustainable development process, considered in various dimensions. To allow for a well-structured discussion, we presented our conclusions following the classification of the SDGs, assigning various indicators considered to selected goals. Nevertheless, in some cases, the assessment of the impact of the sustainable investing ETFs was impossible due to lack of data or highly improbable association with the ETFs markets.

Our study has led to the conclusion of the possible contribution of the European sustainable investing ETFs to the fulfillment of the goals of sustainable development concerning the financial and economic issues. In particular, we provided substantial evidence for the positive relationship with regard to SDGs 1 (ending all forms of poverty), 8 (work and economic growth), and 9 (industry, innovation, and infrastructure). We stated that the increasing assets of the ESG ETFs in Europe are accompanied by improvements in the areas such as some aspects of the financial development, number of researchers, or CO_2 emissions and intensity. The impact of ESG ETFs on the innovation-related issues was to some extent surprising and could be related to a number of channels of transmission such as the focus on the R&D intensive companies in the construction of the portfolios.

What is more, we unveiled important evidence for the social and, through some indirect mechanisms, also environmental impacts of the sustainable investing ETFs in Europe. Therefore, they can be considered as a contribution to the relevant SDGs as well as the aims of the European policies concerning the environment (including the EU Action Plan, European Green Deal, or the EU Sustainable Finance Disclosure Regulation). However, the evidence in these fields was much more limited than in the case of economic and financial aspects, thus hindering the formulation of robust conclusions. Variables adopted referred to the following SDGs: 6, 7, and 11-13 (with the last one mentioned being among the most frequently addressed by the ESG ETFs).

6.5 Case studies of the European sustainable investing ETFs markets: main findings

Throughout the book, we presented five case studies of the European sustainable investing ETFs markets; for each market, we provided also the background including the issues such as the local sustainable investing industry and its history. Our analysis comprised too the factors affecting the development of sustainable investing ETFs and the sustainable finance sector at large. The first country covered was Switzerland, a rather unique example of quite small economy yet being one of the global leaders in terms of sustainable investing. In a detailed examination, we outlined the highly developed ecosystem supporting sustainable investing (with many examples of both state-enacted and self-regulation), contributing also to the substantial growth of the local ESG ETFs. The second case study encompassed the German ESG ETFs, describing them in the context of the EU's largest economy. The role of the EU-level and local regulations, as well as the domestic financial entities for the ESG ETFs, was discussed. The other important covered topic was the substantial diversity of the German sustainable investing ETFs market, for instance, in terms of the participants or geographical exposure of the funds. In the third case study, we analyzed the ESG ETFs in one of the largest financial systems in Europe, of global significance, in the United Kingdom. We emphasized some controversies concerning the UK ESG ETFs and sustainable investing at large, such as greenwashing of the funds. Furthermore, we presented the aspects unique to this market. In the fourth case study, we discussed the next leading EU economy, that is, France. French sustainable investing industry was assessed as influenced strongly by the financial institutions linked to the state, and also as the regional leader of the best-in-class investments. The final case study was to some extent different in relation to the previous ones as it covered not only Sweden but also the entire Scandinavian region. As a result, it facilitated showing that in some instances ESG ETFs markets are influenced by the international factors linked to the cultural or historical similarities.

6.6 Recommendations and directions for the future studies

The results of our analysis can be used to formulate some recommendations for certain entities linked or potentially linked to sustainable investing. First, with regard to the financial companies, our study explicitly confirmed the increasing role of sustainable investing in the European financial systems, evidenced by, among others, the growing share of ESG ETFs in the total assets of these funds. It seems thus necessary for the asset management companies (albeit also for the other types of financial institutions) to adopt to these changing conditions, for instance through the inclusion of ESG ETFs in their product offer to withstand the competition. Second, our conclusions can also be of importance for investors, in particular retail ones. This category is still underrepresented in many markets for sustainable investing ETFs. Our presentation of the European sustainable investing

ETFs may serve for this group as a guide to the still relatively recent category of financial investments and facilitate the selection of the correct instruments with regard to investors' financial and nonfinancial motivations. Third, financial supervision authorities (as well as, e.g., central banks) need to integrate to an increasing degree the sustainable investing ETFs in their policies and consider them in relevant actions due to their growing assets and impact on the financial systems. Finally, ESG ETFs should be considered by the group of particular importance taking into account the topic of our book, that is, governments and international organizations engaged in the establishment and execution of the sustainable development policies. In line with the citation opening our book, we showed how the adoption of the sustainable investing ETFs has the potential to contribute to sustainable development—we uncovered some interactions even at the still relatively minor levels of the development of the markets for these funds. Consequently, ESG ETFs should become an integral element of plans aimed at achieving the goals of sustainable development.

In spite of the contribution of our study to uncovering some of the crucial uncertainties concerning sustainable investing ETFs, there are still many issues that will be addressed in future works, including the continuation of our research projects focused on sustainable investing. Future studies can be extended in two basic perspectives: categories of investment funds and geographical scope.

As far as the types of investment funds are considered, the future research will cover not only ETFs but also mutual funds with sustainability-focused investment aims. It will thus allow for, among others, the comparison of the contributions of both categories to sustainable development aims, with important conclusions concerning, for instance, the possible state-backed actions supporting the selected funds.

In geographical terms, the future studies can include an in-depth analysis of the issues presented in this book yet with the focus on the other regions, in particular the North American or Asia—Pacific sustainable investing sectors (the other parts of the world remain substantially underdeveloped in this dimension and it cannot be reliably predicted to change over the next few years).

Last but not least, the analysis of the impact of the ESG ETFs should be evaluated also in the microperspective; however, this topic requires further empirical studies in the areas including the influences on the companies (e.g., through investments, divestments, or lack of investments in their securities), dynamic analysis concerning important changes affecting ESG

ETFs (such as regulatory developments), comparisons of the effects of various categories of ESG ETFs, examination of microlevel channels of transmission between ETFs and, for instance, environmental changes. Yet another extension of the analysis is possible through the utilization of broader scope of the ESG rankings (concerning not only corporations but also, e.g., sovereign data), retrieved from various sources. Finally, the analysis of the determinants of the development of the sustainable investing ETFs markets would also be needed in our future research perspectives.

Methodological annex

Logistic growth model specification

Logistic growth function originates from the exponential growth model, which in ordinary differential form follows:

$$\frac{dY_x(t)}{dt} = \alpha\, Y_x(t). \tag{1}$$

In Eq. (1) $Y(t)$ denotes the level of variable x, (t) is time, and α is a constant growth rate, then Eq. (1) explains the time path of $Y(t)$. If we introduce e to Eq. (1), it can be reformulated as:

$$Y_x(t) = \beta e^{\alpha t}, \tag{2}$$

with notation analogous to Eq. (1) and β representing the initial value of x at $t = 0$.

The original growth model is predefined as exponential, thus the 'resistance' parameter needs to be added to Eq. (1), to return reliable estimates. If the latter modification is applied, the upper 'limit' to the exponential growth model is inserted, which modifies the original exponential growth curve to a sigmoid shape. The adjusted version of Eq. (1) is defined hence as:

$$\frac{dY(t)}{dt} = \alpha Y(t)\left(1 - \frac{Y(t)}{\kappa}\right), \tag{3}$$

where the parameter κ is the imposed upper asymptote that limits the growth of Y. We define $\left(1 - \frac{Y(t)}{\kappa}\right)$ as a 'slowing term' ('negative feedback'), which is close to 1 as $Y(t) \ll \kappa$, but if $Y(t) \to \kappa$, then $\left(1 - \frac{Y(t)}{\kappa}\right) \to 0$. By adding the slowing-down parameter to exponential growth generates an S-shaped trajectory.

The 3-parameter logistic differential equation — see Eq. (3), can be rewritten as a logistic growth function, taking nonnegative values throughout its path:

$$N_x(t) = \frac{\kappa}{1 + e^{-\alpha t - \beta}}, \tag{4}$$

where $N_x(t)$ stands for the value of variable x in time period t.

The parameters in Eq. (4) are:

- κ — upper asymptote — shows the limit of growth ($N(t) \rightarrow \kappa$), also labelled 'carrying capacity' or 'saturation';
- α — growth rate — shows the speed of diffusion;
- β — midpoint — shows the exact time (T_m) when the logistic pattern reaches 0.5κ.

To ease the economic interpretation, we replace α with a 'specific duration' parameter, defined as $\Delta t = \dfrac{\ln(81)}{\alpha}$, that allows approximating the time needed for x to grow from 10%κ to 90%κ. The logistic growth model defined in Eq. (4) generates logistic growth patterns, which resembles an S-shaped trajectory. The S-shaped trajectory may be divided into three characteristic phases: Phase 1 during which growth is spasmodic and no radical changes are observed; Phase 2 during which examined variable grows exponentially; and Phase 3 during which the system heads toward full saturation and maturity.

Locally weighted polynomial smoother

Locally weighted polynomial smoother is a nonparametric method used to graphically fit the curve displaying relationship between two variables. This method of analysis is useful and widely adopted as it allows relaxing rigid assumptions of conventional parametric analysis and regressions, and thus no assumption regarding the form of the relations is made. A huge advantage of using the LOWESS method is that it is outlier resistant and thus no disturbances in results are introduced.

We approximate

$$f(\cdot), \tag{5}$$

under assumption that all errors e_i generated by the model are identically zero. Having defined x_i as one of the covariates we can estimate the

$f(\cdot)$ by using the multivariate polynomial form where respective x_i is chosen to extrapolate:

$$y_i = f\left(x_i^*\right), \tag{6}$$

if $i = 1, \ldots\ldots k$, in the k-nearest neighborhood of x^*, with underlying assumption that f is the locally a smooth function.

Panel regression models

Random effects regression, which captured unobserved cross-country heterogeneity, follow the general specification as:

$$\Psi_{y,c} = \alpha + \beta\left(x_{y,\,c}^i\right) + u_{y,c} + \varepsilon_{y,c}, \tag{7}$$

where α is unknown intercept for each entity (country), $\Psi_{y,c}$ denotes dependent variable; β is the $L \times 1$ and $x_{y,c}^i$ stands for the yc in the observation on L explanatory variables. The subscripts $c = \{1, \ldots\ldots N\}$ stand for entity (country) and $y = \{1, \ldots\ldots T\}$ for the time period. In Eq. (1), $u_{i,y}$ explains between–entity error, and $\varepsilon_{y,c}$ the within-entity error.

In our approach we use single-explanatory variable approach, explaining the impact of ETFs, hence the empirical model applied follows the general form as:

$$ETF_{y,c} = \alpha + \beta\left(x_{y,c}\right) + u_{y,c} + \varepsilon_{y,c} \tag{8}$$

With notations as in Eq. (7).

Further reading

1. Baltagi, B. H. (1995). *Econometric analysis of panel data, 2.* Wiley.
2. Diggle, P., Diggle, P. J., Heagerty, P., Heagerty, P. J., Liang, K. Y., & Zeger, S. (2002). *Analysis of longitudinal data.* Oxford University Press.
3. Fan, J. (2018). *Local polynomial modelling and its applications: monographs on statistics and applied probability 66.* Routledge.
4. Geroski, P. A. (2000). Models of technology diffusion. *Research Policy, 29*(4), 603−625.
5. Green, W. H. (2003). *Econometric analysis.* Pearson Education India.
6. Karshenas, M., & Stoneman, P. (1995). Technological diffusion. *Handbook of the economics of innovation and technological change* (pp. 265−297).
7. Kucharavy, D., & De Guio, R. (2007). Application of S-shaped curves. In *7th ETRIA TRIZ Future Conference* (pp. 81−88).

8. Kwasnicki, W. (2013). Logistic growth of the global economy and competitiveness of nations. *Technological Forecasting and Social Change, 80*(1), 50–76.
9. Maddala, G. S., & Lahiri, K. (1992). *Introduction to econometrics, 2.* Macmillan.
10. Metcalfe, J. S. (2004). Mansfield and the diffusion of innovation: an evolutionary connection. *The Journal of Technology Transfer, 30*(1–2), 171–181.
11. Meyer, P. S., Yung, J. W., & Ausubel, J. H. (1999). A primer on logistic growth and substitution: the mathematics of the Loglet Lab software. *Technological Forecasting and Social Change, 61*(3), 247–271.
12. Royston, P. (1992). Lowess smoothing. *Stata Technical Bulletin, 1*(3).
13. Shumway, R. H., & Stoffer, D. S. (2011). Time series regression and exploratory data analysis. In *Time series analysis and its applications* (pp. 47–82). New York: Springer.

Index

Note: 'Page numbers followed by "*f*" indicate figures and "*t*" indicate tables'.